Education
beyond the
Mesas

Indigenous Education
Series editors

Margaret Connell Szasz
University of New Mexico

Brenda J. Child
University of Minnesota

Karen Gayton Swisher
Haskell Indian Nations University

John W. Tippeconnic III
The Pennsylvania State University

Education beyond the Mesas

HOPI STUDENTS AT SHERMAN INSTITUTE, 1902–1929

Matthew Sakiestewa Gilbert

University of Nebraska Press
Lincoln and London

Portions of chapter 3 previously appeared in "Dark Days: Native Sovereignty and American Presidents, 1880–1930," in American Indians/American
Presidents: A History, ed. Clifford E. Trafzer (New York: Harper and Smithsonian Institution, 2009). Chapter 4 previously appeared in a different
form as "'The Hopi Followers': Chief Tawaquaptewa and Hopi Student
Advancement at Sherman Institute, 1906–1909," in Journal of American
Indian Education 44, no. 2 (Fall 2005). Chapter 6 previously appeared in
a different form as "'I Learned to Preach Pretty Well, and to Cuss, Too':
Hopi Acceptance and Rejection of Christianity at Sherman Institute,
1906–1928," in Eating Fire, Tasting Blood: An Anthology of the American Indian
Holocaust, ed. MariJo Moore (New York: Thunder's Mouth Press, 2006).

Library of Congress Cataloging-in-Publication Data

Sakiestewa Gilbert, Matthew.
Education beyond the mesas: Hopi students at Sherman Institute,
1902–1929 / Matthew Sakiestewa Gilbert.
    p. cm. — (Indigenous education)
Includes bibliographical references and index.
ISBN 978-0-8032-1626-6 (cloth : alk. paper)
1. Hopi Indians—Education—History—20th century. 2. Hopi Indians—
Ethnic identity—History—20th century. 3. Hopi Indians—Cultural
assimilation—History—20th century. 4. Hopi Indians—Government
relations—History—20th century. 5. Government, Resistance to—
Southwest, New—History—20th century. 6. Sherman Institute (Riverside, Calif.)—History—20th century. 7. Indian students—
California—Riverside—History—20th century. 8. School children—
California—Riverside—History—20th century. 9. Off-reservation boarding schools—Social aspects—California—Riverside—History—20th
century. I. Title.
E99.H7S26 2010   371.8297'458079497—dc22   2010005710

Set in Quadraat by Bob Reitz. Designed by Mikah Tacha.

For my wife, Kylene, and our daughters,
Hannah, Meaghan, and Noelle

Contents

Preface

This book is first and foremost a historical account of the Hopi people of northeastern Arizona and their experiences at Sherman Institute, an off-reservation Indian boarding school in Riverside, California. The Hopi Tribe possesses no greater historical source than its people. Therefore, a book on the Hopi people should also rely on the involvement and cooperation of the Hopi Tribe. The protection of intellectual property has long been a concern for American Indians, and in response to years of misrepresentations of Hopi culture by Hopis and non-Hopis, the Hopi Tribe established the Hopi Culture Preservation Office (HCPO) in Kykotsmovi, Arizona. Since its founding in the 1980s, the HCPO has acted as a protector of Hopi intellectual property and determined rules and regulations for those who wish to perform research on the Hopi Reservation. Although in the past some researchers have bypassed community involvement and permission when they conducted research on the reservation, I made certain that the Hopi Tribe had a central role in a book that involved the Hopi people.

To accomplish this, I sought the assistance of Leigh J. Kuwanwisiwma from the village of Bacavi, director of the HCPO, and Stewart B. Koyiyumptewa from the village of Hotevilla, archivist for the Hopi Tribe. Both of these officials made helpful comments and suggestions on various aspects of my research, interpretations, and conclusions. Moreover, although an enrolled member of the Hopi Tribe from the village of Upper Moencopi, I did not assume that I had the right to conduct research on the Hopi Reservation without the written permission of the HCPO. In compliance with a series of protocols set forth by the Hopi Tribe, I submitted a research proposal to the HCPO in October 2003. After meeting with officials from the Hopi Tribe in February 2004 to discuss my research topic, the HCPO approved my proposal and issued me Research Permit 01-004, which granted me permission to conduct research, including oral interviews, on the Hopi Reservation.

A major component of my research methodology involved providing the Hopi people with copies of my research. Since 2004, I have provided the HCPO with primary documents for the Hopi Tribe's archival collection. These documents include letters written by Hopis and government officials; copies of the Sherman Institute's student-written newspaper, the *Sherman Bulletin*; pictures; and other materials. My desire to give back to the Hopi community rests on the understanding that the Hopi materials that I uncovered belong to the Hopi people. On several occasions I made copies of Hopi student case files and mailed them to the students' relatives on the Hopi Reservation. On occasion, I had the privilege of delivering the files in person. In March 2007, I traveled to the University of Arizona in Tucson and talked with Hopi scholar and elder Emory Sekaquaptewa. We spoke about collaborating together on a Hopi history textbook that teachers on the reservation could use in the Hopi schools. As our conversation came to an end, I told Emory that I had something important to give to him: "I have your father's student file from when he attended Sherman Institute." Emory seemed very interested in what I had uncovered. I handed Emory a manila folder with his father's records, which included letters that his father wrote, his school application, and his report card. While carefully examining documents that pertained to his father's academic achievements, Emory said, "Why look at here, my father was a good student!"

Providing people with copies of student case files and other materials was one of many ways that I gave back to my community. As a Hopi professor at a research university, I have a responsibility to the academy and to the Hopi people. When I published "'The Hopi Followers'" in the *Journal of American Indian Education* and "'I Learned to Preach Pretty Well, and to Cuss, Too'" in Cherokee writer MariJo Moore's book *Eating Fire, Tasting Blood*, I knew that many people on the Hopi Reservation would not have access to this journal or book. In response, I published a series of articles in the *Hopi Tutuveni*, the Hopi Tribe's official newspaper, which allowed people on the reservation to have access to their intellectual property. Finally, it is my hope that the following narrative will not only add to the scholarship on the history of Indian education, but also provide the Hopi people with a written history from one of many Hopi perspectives.

Champaign, Illinois
January 2010

Acknowledgments

The completion of this manuscript is credited to my wife, Kylene, and my daughters, Hannah, Meaghan, and Noelle, who sacrificed more than I could have asked or imagined as I completed this project. In addition to my wife and children, I am grateful for the support of my parents, Willard and Christine Gilbert, my siblings, Christopher and Angela and their spouses, Chrissy and Mitch, my grandparents, Ethel Sakiestewa Gilbert and Lloyd Gilbert of Upper Moencopi, Tio Tachias and Liz Fajardo, and other extended family members, including the Warner, Gmur, Hopewell, and Carl families. I also remain indebted to the Hopi Tribe, the Hopi Tribe Grants and Scholarship Program (HTGSP), and the Hopi Education Endowment Fund (HEEF). Without the patience, inspiration, encouragement, and financial assistance of the Hopi Tribe, I would not have been able to pursue or complete my education beyond the Hopi mesas. Furthermore, I am greatly appreciative of the cooperation and involvement of the Hopi Cultural Preservation Office in Kykotsmovi, Arizona. The Hopi Tribe had a critical role in my research, and its guidance in this project provided meaning and depth to my work that would not have existed otherwise. I extend my sincere appreciation to Leigh J. Kuwanwisiwma, director of the Hopi Cultural Preservation Office, Stewart B. Koyiyumptewa, author and archivist for the Hopi

Tribe, Terry Morgart, Marvin Lalo, Lee Wayne Lomayestewa, and Dawa Taylor.

I am also grateful for the help and assistance of Lorene Sisquoc, curator of the Sherman Indian Museum in Riverside, California, Paul Wormser and Gwen Granados of the National Archives Pacific Branch in Laguna Niguel, California, and Karen Underhill of Northern Arizona University's Cline Library Special Collections. The many Hopi-related documents that they provided for my research allowed the "Hopi voice" in this project to be heard to an even greater extent. Furthermore, incredible support for this manuscript came from my colleagues at the University of Illinois at Urbana-Champaign, including Robert Warrior, Antoinette Burton, Frederick E. Hoxie, LeAnne Howe, Debbie Reese, Jodi Byrd, David Anthony Clark, Robert Dale Parker, Brenda Farnell, Teresa Barnes, Augusto Espiritu, Adrian Burgos, Kenneth M. Cuno, John Randolph, David R. Roediger, Diane P. Koenker, James Brennan, James R. Barrett, Kathryn J. Oberdeck, Dana Rabin, R. Jovita Baber, Clarence Lang, Kristin Hoganson, Bruce Levine, Karen Carney, Ruth Watkins, Anna Gonzales, Durango Mendoza, John McKinn, and Wanda Pillow. In my first year at the University of Illinois, I served as a postdoctoral research associate of American Indian studies, which provided me with much needed time to work on my book. Additional gratitude is extended to Simon J. Ortiz, Rebecca (Monte) Kugel, Michelle Rahejah, Victoria Bomberry, Kristina Ackley, Gerald Vizenor, Joseph Bauerkemper, Jill Doerfler, Tol Foster, Dustin Tamahkerah, Keith Camacho, Louellyn White, John W. Troutman, Laurie Arnold, David Delgado Shorter, John Low, MariJo Moore, Jennifer Nez Denetdale, Lloyd Lee, Frances A. Washburn, Myla Vicenti Carpio, Evelina Zuni Lucero, Melissa K. Nelson, Lisa S. Pacheco, Ned Blackhawk, Alyssa Mt. Pleasant,

Shelly Lowe, Brian Klopotek, Devon A. Mihesuah, José Medina, Barbara Landis, William Medina, Jean A. Keller, Robert Oberhardt, Larry Burgess, Daniel Palm, John Hughes, Paul T. Plew, J. Gregory Behle, James D. Owen, Clyde P. Greer Jr., and John Stead. I am especially grateful for my friend and former graduate advisor, Clifford E. Trafzer, who provided me with mentoring and encouragement, and instilled in me a desire to "publish, publish, publish."

Furthermore, I remain indebted and thankful for the support of Thomas Biolsi, David Wallace Adams, Brenda J. Child, Jacqueline Fear-Segal, Margaret D. Jacobs, Margaret Connell-Szasz, Jon Reyhner, Denis F. Viri, Bruce J. Dinges, Tom Holm, Wesley Bernardini, Justin B. Richland, and Peter M. Whiteley, whose scholarship on the Orayvi Split has great meaning for the Hopi people. Critical support and assistance came from Hopi scholars and educators Lomayumtewa C. Ishii, Angela A. Gonzales, Sheilah E. Nicholas, the late Emory Sekaquaptewa, LeRoy Shingoitewa, Noreen Sakiestewa, the late Hartman Lomawaima, Patricia Sekaquaptewa, LuAnn Leonard, Barbara Poley, Theresa Lomakema, Loris Taylor, and the late Ferrell Sekacucu. I extend further gratitude to Samuel Shingoitewa of Upper Moencopi and Bessie Humetewa of Bacavi, who so generously shared with me about their "Sherman days" before their passing.

Additional appreciation goes to Stewart Nicholas of the Hopi Tutuveni, Marsah Balenquah, Bradley Balenquah, Leslie Robledo and Eileen Randolph of Bacavi, and Nick Brokeshoulder of Hotevilla. A special thanks is extended to film director and producer Allan Holzman of 716 Productions, and Gerald Eichner. In January 2006, Holzman and Eichner asked me to join them and the Hopi Cultural Preservation Office to produce a documentary film on the Hopi boarding school experience that

I titled "Beyond the Mesas." The film corresponds with this book. I am also appreciative for the help and support of the editorial staff at the University of Nebraska Press, especially Matthew F. Bokovoy, Elisabeth Chretien, and Kathryn L. Neubauer, and copyeditor Linda Wessels. Furthermore, as a professor of American Indian Studies and history, I am indebted to my undergraduate and graduate students whose insights and perspectives helped to deepen my understanding of the Hopi boarding school experience. Some of these students include Ashley A. Tsosie-Mahieu, Charlotte Davidson, Angelia Louise Naquayouma, Laura Guzman, Lara Mann, Jamie Singson, Judith Estrada, Jamie Ishcomer, Joe Feria-Galicia, Suzanne Reilly, Josh Rubin, Daniel Puglisi, Jon Treshansky, John Gerstner, James Carlson, Lance Sherry, Rachel Kittle, Krista DeMeuse, Anthony Garcia, Caitlin Romani, and Samantha Paige. Finally, I credit this project to my grandfather and former student of Sherman Institute, Victor Sakiestewa Sr. from Orayvi and Upper Moencopi. Victor often encouraged his family to receive an education "beyond the mesas," and I thank him for providing me with the reason and inspiration to write on Hopi involvement at his alma mater, "dear ole Sherman."

Introduction

Hopi oral history recalls that long ago, the Hopi people came into this "fourth way of life" from a series of three underworlds.[1] Following a time of unhappiness and discontent, the people emerged through an opening in their sky that brought them to present-day northeastern Arizona. When they arrived in this land the people made their way to three mesas where they met Ma'saw, creator and ruler of the "fourth way of life." Ma'saw told the people that they could live on the mesas, but they first needed to migrate to distant lands to learn ways to be useful to Hopi society. Following Ma'saw's instructions, the men, women, and children divided themselves into clans and each migrated in one of the four cardinal directions.[2] According to Hopi belief, the clans traveled to the Pacific Ocean, Central America, and occupied lands in present-day New Mexico and Colorado. During their migrations, the Hopi people experienced different climates and terrain and learned to survive by hunting, gathering, and planting. Life for the clans included great hardships, but they believed that their pain and suffering strengthened and preserved their culture for future generations of Hopi people.

The clans were not alone when they migrated to distant lands. Butterflies, other insects, birds, and many animals existed in the "fourth way of life." During their migrations, Hopi clans came across bears, badgers, eagles, and even parrots, and identified themselves with the animals they met on their journeys. In addition to seeing animals and insects, the clans encountered indigenous peoples from various cultures, which expanded their understanding of the world. These people spoke many languages, and they introduced the clans to new practices, skills, ways of thinking, and religious customs. Although the clans learned many things during their migrations, they also shared their Hopi knowledge with the people they met and welcomed the opportunity to teach others about their culture and philosophies of life. When the Hopi clans traveled back to their ancestral lands in northeastern Arizona, they brought new ideas and traditions with them to the Hopi mesas. Each clan experienced a different way of living and was required to contribute something useful to Hopi society.[3] The Sun Forehead clan returned to the Hopi mesas as warriors and protectors, while the Katsina clan hosted the katsina dances and prayed for rain.[4] The clans held vital roles in Hopi society and formed the foundation of Hopi identity.

But Hopi migration did not cease when the clans returned to their original lands. Many years after the clans established their roles in Hopi society, a second wave of migration developed when government officials sent Hopis to attend off-reservation Indian boarding schools in the late nineteenth and early twentieth century. Although Hopis were required to attend these schools, the movement of Hopi pupils to U.S. government institutions once again brought Hopis to new environments where they interacted with people from unique cultures, and shared their knowledge and abilities with those they encountered. Similar to the way the ancient Hopi clans migrated in the four cardinal directions, Hopi pupils attended Indian boarding schools throughout the U.S and furthered the tradition of migration among the Hopi people. Beginning in the 1890s, as more railroads were built and used to transport Indian people to off-reservation Indian schools, government officials sent Hopis to the Carlisle Indian Industrial School in Pennsylvania, the Phoenix Indian School in Arizona, and schools in Oklahoma, Oregon, Nevada, Utah, New Mexico, and California.[5]

In the 1890s, the Hopi people did not consider the U.S. government's insistence that Hopis adopt Western ways and values as a new requirement. Many years before, Europeans arrived uninvited on Hopi lands and attempted to civilize and educate the Hopis with Christianity and European ideals and practices. In 1540, Spanish explorer Don Pedro de Tovar led a small expeditionary force on Hopi lands. They were the first group of nonindigenous people the Hopi encountered. De Tovar had expected to uncover cities of gold on the Hopi mesas, but instead he found rock homes, small cornfields, and a people entirely committed to their spiritual ways and customs. By drawing on the ground with sticks and using different objects to convey their message, the Hopi people told de Tovar and his men about a nearby river that flowed through a very large canyon. Upon hearing about this majestic and grand canyon, the Spanish expedition continued their journey west in search of gold and other riches.

The early Spanish encounters paved the way for Catholic priests to conduct missionary work among the Hopi people. Between 1629 and 1680, Catholic priests forced Hopis to abolish their sacred ceremonies and punished others for not converting to Christianity. The cruel treatment Hopis received from the priests influenced the way Hopis responded to missionaries in the years to come. After the Hopis forced the priests off their lands in 1680, Catholic missionaries only occasionally intruded on the Hopi mesas to convert the people to Christianity. The Hopis practiced their religion without a major presence of Christian missionaries during this period, but this trend changed in the nineteenth century when Mormons arrived on Hopi land and taught the children the English alphabet and encouraged Hopi parents to send their children to Christian mission schools. Whereas Christian missionaries educated some Hopis in Christian and American ways and values, government officials drafted plans to educate Indian pupils *away from* their village communities.

Three years after the founding of the Carlisle Indian Industrial School, U.S. President Chester Arthur established the boundaries of the Hopi Reservation in 1882. As a result of Arthur's executive order to form the Hopi Reservation, government officials became increasingly involved in Hopi affairs and rekindled efforts to force Hopi children to attend day schools and the Keams Canyon Boarding School. The U.S. government constructed the boarding school in 1887 on the Hopi Reservation to teach children basic grammar, arithmetic, and vocational skills and to break down Hopi culture, language, and religious practices. By requiring Hopis to speak only in English and telling the children that their Hopi ways kept them from succeeding in life, school officials attempted to assimilate Hopi people into mainstream white society. The U.S. government's systematic approach to assimilate Hopis and weaken Hopi culture did not take place without Hopi resistance. As indigenous people, Hopi leaders, mothers, fathers, and other community members resisted with their words, prayers, thoughts, and actions. Some Hopi parents scorned white officials for their conduct, while others hid their children when Indian agents and Navajo police conducted roundups and forced the children to attend U.S. government schools.[6]

In 1902, while the situation on the Hopi Reservation intensified over the mandatory enrolment of Hopi children at U.S.

government schools, the Office of Indian Affairs opened Sherman Institute, an off-reservation Indian boarding school in Riverside, California. Schools such as Sherman Institute were created to weaken American Indian cultures and to provide Indian pupils with skills that would be useful to them in American society. In this regard, vocational education at Sherman Institute created an Indian working class that was meant to contribute to the labor needs of Indian and white communities. Founded on principles that were deeply rooted in the supposed superiority of American culture, the education at Sherman Institute aimed at transforming Indian pupils to think, behave, work, and look less like Native people, and more like white Protestant Americans. Government officials did not consult Native leaders, parents, or educators when they created academic and industrial curricula at Indian boarding schools. They instead followed presumptions that considered Indian people to be inferior to white Americans.

Indian parents certainly understood the U.S. government's agenda in sending their children to off-reservation Indian boarding schools. However, many parents wanted their children to succeed in a world of Anglo-American people, which necessitated their exposure to a Western education. As historian Michael C. Coleman points out: "Indian parents, and occasionally grandparents or tribal leaders, often *encouraged* young Indians to seek a school education, in order to secure a livelihood in the modern world or to become mediators between their peoples and American society."[7] Indian students needed to know about Native and non-Native worlds, and some of their parents wanted them to go to school with open minds, willing to accept beneficial aspects of white society. In Hopi culture, the idea of using the best of Hopi and white culture was not a foreign concept. In the summer of 1890, after Kikmongwi (village chief) Loololma from Orayvi and other Hopi leaders boarded a Atchison, Topeka, & Santa Fe Railroad in Winslow, Arizona, and traveled to Washington DC to speak with Commissioner of Indian Affairs Thomas J. Morgan, Loololma advocated that Hopi people needed to take advantage of the strengths of both cultures so they would learn to "survive" and excel in the world beyond the Hopi mesas.[8] As a result of Loololma's influence on his people, the village chief convinced some Hopi parents to send their children to the Oraibi Day School and the Keams Canyon Boarding School, but many Hopis did not support Loololma or the U.S. government's campaign to assimilate their children.

U.S. government policies that allowed for the removal of Indian pupils to off-reservation Indian boarding schools resulted in stress, anxiety, and internal divisions among Native communities. At the Hopi village of Orayvi on Third Mesa, one of three mesas on the Hopi Reservation, government officials urged parents and leaders to send their children to U.S. government schools, but many of the people refused to comply. In the early 1900s, tensions at Orayvi intensified over the school issue, and the people began to go against government officials and each other. Two Hopi factions emerged at Orayvi, which Indian agents and Christian missionaries called "friendlies" and "hostiles" based on their relationship with the U.S. government.

Although Hopis and non-Hopis alike use these terms to describe the Hopi factions, I have chosen to refer to the two groups as Hopi resisters and Hopi accommodators. These terms give Hopi and non-Hopi people a different way of describing and interpreting this important time in Hopi history. The terms "hostiles" and "friendlies" limit Hopi agency by confining Hopi choices and actions to a positive and negative binary. But the

Hopi people did not operate within this binary. Hopi accommodators considered the benefits of certain aspects of Christianity and U.S. government–run education. While government officials considered them to be "friendly," the accommodating Hopis strategically learned to adopt components of the so-called white man's way to suit their agendas on the reservation. They accommodated Western values and influences into Hopi culture, and they allowed their children to receive an education at on- and off-reservation Indian boarding schools. This was not a "friendly" act, but it was an act of accommodation that Hopis learned to refine throughout Hopi history.

The resisting Hopi faction saw little benefit in allowing American ways to enter Hopi society and culture. They resisted the U.S. government, Christian missionaries, and those Hopis who chose the accommodating route. Some readers may consider the resisting group to be the more traditional of the two, but the ideas of both resisting and accommodating have always been critical aspects of Hopi history and society. In this regard, Hopis functioned according to Hopi culture when they pushed back against the U.S. government and each other, and it was equally Hopi-like for Hopi accommodators to adopt, adapt, and accept change for what they believed benefited their people.

During this time in history, similar factions arose among Native communities throughout North America. But at Orayvi, tensions surrounding the two factions reached a crisis point that resulted in drastic and immediate consequences for the Hopi people. On September 8, 1906, Kikmongwi Tawaquaptewa,[9] leader of the accommodating faction at Orayvi, and Youkeoma, leader of the Hopi resisters, settled their dispute by staging a tug-of-war between the two opposing groups. Men from each faction gathered outside Orayvi, drew a line of cornmeal on the ground, and attempted to pull the opposing chief to the other side of the marker. Both men agreed that whichever side lost the battle would be required to leave the village. Commonly referred to as the Orayvi Split, the Hopi division was a turning point in Hopi history and had a direct impact on Hopi children and the number of Hopi pupils who went to off-reservation Indian boarding schools.

Two months after the Orayvi Split, government officials turned on Tawaquaptewa for illegally forcing the resisters out of the village and sent the thirty-four-year-old village chief and nearly seventy Hopi pupils from Orayvi to Sherman Institute.[10] The U.S. government required Hopi parents to sign their child's school application, usually with an "X",[11] which granted permission for their child to go to school. Government officials also sent Tawaquaptewa's wife, Nasumgoens, and infant daughter, Mina, along with Frank Seumptewa, from the village of Moencopi, and his wife, Susie, and their children, Ethel and Lilly, to Sherman Institute. Although Indian leaders such as Lakota Chiefs Spotted Tail and Red Cloud visited off-reservation Indian boarding schools in the late nineteenth century, their stay at the schools did not last longer than a few weeks. Tawaquaptewa and Seumptewa remained at Sherman Institute for nearly three years. Commissioner of Indian Affairs Francis E. Leupp sent the Hopi leaders to Sherman Institute to learn English and to appreciate the white American culture. But Tawaquaptewa arrived at Sherman Institute as a representative and leader of his people, and he continued his role as kikmongwi and elder with the Hopi pupils at the school.

From 1907 to 1909, the *Sherman Bulletin*, the official student-written school newspaper, recorded several occasions where Tawaquaptewa was a role model for the Hopi students at Sherman

Institute. For instance, on April 24, 1907, the *Sherman Bulletin* observed that Tawaquaptewa often called his "Hopi followers" together to give them "good advice." The Hopi pupils responded by not "hanging back" but instead pushed "rapidly ahead" in their industrial and academic training. Kikmongwi Tawaquaptewa also led the Hopi pupils at Sherman Institute in song and dance. One of these events took place at the Glenwood Hotel in Riverside where Tawaquaptewa and eight Hopi boys sang two songs in Hopi about the "growing and maturing" of corn.[12] School officials used the Hopi singings for entertainment purposes, but Tawaquaptewa and the other Hopi pupils sang their songs to reaffirm and express their identity as Hopi people, and to share their culture with non-Hopis in the greater Riverside area.

In addition to singing their Hopi songs, the pupils learned to appreciate other forms of music. At the Indian school in Riverside, teachers introduced Hopis to music by Bach, Beethoven, and Mozart. Students such as Bessie Humetewa from the Hopi village of Bacavi performed in the school's mandolin club, while Victor Sakiestewa from Orayvi played the clarinet in the Sherman Institute band. Having been raised in a culture that valued song and dance, the Hopi pupils went to Sherman Institute with an eagerness to try different instruments and genres of music. Alongside their involvement in music, Hopi pupils used their artistic talents to advance at the school and to contribute to their school community. In May 1923, the *Sherman Bulletin* reported that a *Riverside Press* reporter noted that Hopi pupil "Homer Cooyawyama, Sherman's talented artist, is about to enter upon a career that may make him famous." The reporter commented that one of the "leading artists" in Laguna Beach, California, had "become interested" in Homer and wanted to "take him to his studio" at the end of the school year. According to the reporter, Homer "painted the stage scenery" in the school's auditorium, which "attracted considerable attention from tourists and others, many of whom" thought it showed "much talent."[13] Homer's love for art originated from his community on the reservation.

For Hopi pupils such as Homer, their education did not begin at Sherman Institute or other U.S. government–run schools. Hopi education is among the oldest forms of education in the Americas, and Hopis brought their cultural knowledge with them to advance at the school.[14] In Hopi culture, elders instructed children in song and dance and shared stories that had life lessons. Hopi uncles taught their nephews the act and purpose of hunting and planting, while Hopi mothers, grandmothers, and aunties instructed girls to be powerful women in Hopi society. At an early age, Hopi children were taught to value hard work, and to shun laziness.[15] "Get up before the sun rises," Hopi parents often told their children, "the sun has many things to accomplish throughout the day, and it need not waste its time and energy on getting you out of bed."[16] Having been instructed in Hopi education and cultural values, Hopi pupils went to Sherman Institute with an eagerness to excel and to obtain the best that the school had to offer.

Following the pattern established by the ancient Hopi clans, Hopi pupils traveled to the Indian school in Riverside and encountered a place that was deeply embedded with religious ideologies and practices. Although government officials established Sherman Institute to operate as an industrial trade school, where pupils spent half of their day in the classroom and the rest of the day in a trade shop, farm, or ranch, officials also stressed instruction that was based on Christian principles and encouraged Hopi pupils to participate in Christian organizations. School officials used Christianity as a tool to civilize and assimilate Hopi pupils and they wanted Hopis to take the Christian faith home with them to convert their families on the reservation. Some Hopis, such as Polingaysi Qoyawayma and Effie Sachowengsie from Orayvi, embraced Christianity at Sherman Institute and adapted their Christian faith to fit with life on the reservation. Others, such as Don Talayesva, a Hopi pupil from Orayvi who attended Sherman Institute from 1906 to 1909, conformed to Christian behavior in front of school officials, but rejected Christianity and denounced the so-called white man's religion once they returned home. Hopi students such as Don adapted to the religious life at Sherman Institute and gave the appearance of accommodation by going along with the Christian instruction. Internally, however, many Hopis did not convert to Christianity.

Hopi students returned home from Sherman Institute in various ways. School officials usually did not allow or provide the means for students to return home during the summer or Christmas break. This meant that Hopi pupils typically did not return to the reservation until they had spent three or more years at the school. Hopi runaways, or "deserters,"[17] as school officials called them, also played a small but important role in the Hopi school experience. Some Hopi boys, and a very few girls, ran away from Sherman Institute. Some Hopis longed to be away from the harsh discipline at the school. Samuel Shingoitewa, a Hopi pupil from the village of Moencopi who attended Sherman Institute in the 1920s, once remarked to his family that after school officials punished him for an infraction and humiliated him by taking away his "stripes" on his school uniform, he hitched a ride on a Santa Fe train and returned to the Hopi mesas.[18] But not every Hopi student returned home alive. For other Hopi pupils, particularly those who attended the school in the early twentieth century, illnesses such as tuberculosis, whooping cough, influenza, typhoid, and pneumonia shortened their stay at Sherman Institute. Although deceased pupils were usually buried at the school's cemetery, some of the students returned home in a wooden coffin.

The Hopi boarding school experience at the Indian school in Riverside has various layers of meaning for Hopi people. For some Hopi students, Sherman Institute provided an escape from poverty and disease on the reservation. Other Hopis considered Sherman Institute to be a military compound where school officials told the students how to behave, talk, work, and think. Samuel Shingoitewa recalled that one of his most memorable experiences of the school was witnessing its regimented military structure upon his arrival. Students walking in formation and the constant roll calls and bugle sounds did not reflect life on the Hopi Reservation. "It was a government military school," he remembered, and "during the week you wear GI clothes, and then Sundays we wear blue uniforms."[19] Although no one perspective can adequately speak on behalf of all Hopi people, the Hopi boarding school experience was neither completely positive nor entirely negative. For many Hopis, the education they received at Sherman Institute never assimilated them into white American society as fully as it did pupils from other indigenous communities. This can be attributed to several factors. Unlike some other Native nations, the Hopi people have always remained on portions of their ancestral lands.[20] The Spaniards and the U.S. government did not succeed in forcefully removing them from their mesas, and therefore the essence of Hopi culture has survived to the present. In the early 1900s, Hopis continued to practice their ceremonies, speak their language, and vary rarely intermarried with the white population in Arizona. Furthermore, when Hopis returned to the reservation after their stay at Sherman Institute, the pupils came home to a culture and society that remained intact. Like other Hopis who attended different off-reservation boarding schools, the Hopi pupils at Sherman Institute did not abandon their indigenous education. Instead of allowing their boarding school experience to destroy the Hopi way of life, Hopis at Sherman Institute maintained the integrity of their culture, made accommodations to succeed at school, and used the skills they learned to contribute to their village communities.

This book, which examines one tribe's experience at an off-reservation Indian boarding school, places the history and culture of the Hopi people at the focal point of the narrative. It asks how a student's culture and tribal history influenced their experience at an Indian school, and builds upon the contributions of other scholars to uncover the complex ways that Hopi history and culture intersected with U.S. government policies.[21] Apart from providing the reader with a historical narrative, this book challenges the notion that a study on the Indian boarding school experience must be understood primarily through a defined framework of Indian education policies. Community-specific books begin with the history and culture of Native people and attempt to determine how students understood their unique experiences at Indian boarding schools as Zunis, Navajos, Apaches, or other Indian people. When government officials initially sent Indian students to federal off-reservation Indian boarding schools, they believed that Native cultures hindered the so-called progress of Indians and they wanted the pupils to leave their tribal identities behind on the reservation. Community-specific studies push back against this colonial practice. They highlight Native agency and explore the many ways that Indian pupils brought their Indian identities to school and how they responded to their boarding school experience as people from indigenous communities.

Recent studies of the Indian boarding school experience have focused on Indian health, literature, sports, and the ways Indian pupils "turned the power" at schools designed to destroy their culture and identity as American Indian people. A term used by historians Clifford E. Trafzer, Jean A. Keller, and Lorene Sisquoc, "turning the power" describes the ability of Indian people to turn the boarding school experience to their advantage.[22] This phenomenon enabled Native students to create an educational experience that benefited not only themselves, but also their communities. Students "turned the power" at Indian boarding schools in the nineteenth and twentieth century, and their achievement demonstrated the ability of Indian pupils to adapt, survive, and excel within a foreign and culturally hostile environment. At schools such as Carlisle, for example, officials did not allow students to speak their Native languages, dress according to their Native customs, or reflect any aspect of their indigenous heritage. Jacqueline Fear-Segal has demonstrated that even though Superintendent Pratt argued that Indian people had the same "intellectual capacity as whites," he nevertheless considered Indian cultures to be a hindrance to the American ideals of "progress" and "civilization," and he openly punished and humiliated Indian pupils who broke school policies.[23] Consequently, many Indian pupils resisted by running away from Carlisle and other Indian schools, while others pushed back in their thoughts or prayers, or with their silence. Under these and other less traumatic conditions, Indian students turned to the familiar and drew upon their culture to provide them with strength and confidence to face life's challenges.

In this book I examine the ways Hopis "turned the power" at Sherman Institute, and I build upon the work of many scholars including those who have written about the mandatory enrollment of Hopi students at U.S. government schools. In August 1979, historian David Wallace Adams published one of the first academic accounts that referenced the Hopi boarding school experience, "Schooling the Hopi: Federal Indian Policy Writ Small, 1887–1917." In this essay, Adams examines the role of federal Indian policy in the removal of Hopi students to off-reservation boarding schools. While providing information gleaned from U.S. government reports, newspaper articles, and Hopi hearings conducted by the Bureau of Indian Affairs, Adams' inclusion of the Hopi voice came primarily from three Hopi accounts: Polingaysi Qoyawayma's *No Turning Back*, Don Talayesva's *Sun Chief*, and Helen Sekaquaptewa's *Me and Mine*. These texts have become standard sources for researchers to use when comparing Hopis at Sherman Institute with other Indian pupils at different schools. Building on Adams's scholarship and Margaret D. Jacobs's article, "A Battle for the Children: American Indian Child Removal in Arizona in the Era of Assimilation," this book extends one step further by interpreting the Hopi experience at Sherman Institute through a Hopi cultural and historical framework.

Before Hopi pupils attended Sherman Institute in 1902, they had been educated in the ways of Hopi culture. Children learned lessons from their parents and other village members. Most importantly, Hopi pupils learned to think and behave like Hopis, which strengthened their identity as they traveled from the reservation to receive an education beyond the mesas. Not every Hopi pupil enjoyed their time at Sherman Institute, but many Hopis incorporated their culture to succeed in music, agriculture, trade, sports, and language acquisition. By learning English, Hopi pupils were empowered with an additional mode of communication and they learned to navigate in a world of Indian and non-Indian people. In this way, Hopis turned the U.S. government's institution of assimilation into their own and used the education at Sherman Institute to contribute to their tribe and village communities. Most importantly, the Hopi pupils continued the cycle of Hopi tradition, and returned to the Hopi mesas with new responsibilities as Hopi people.

Education
beyond the
Mesas

1. Hopi Resistance

In the summer of 1540, a group of Hopis from the village of Kawaiokuh on Antelope Mesa looked over the mesa's edge and observed a band of people they had never seen on their land.[1] The Hopis had encountered a Spanish exploratory party of seventeen cavalrymen, a small number of foot soldiers, a few Zuni guides, and a Franciscan priest named Juan de Padilla. Led by Pedro de Tovar, a lieutenant in Vasquez de Coronado's expedition to the southwest,[2] the Spaniards arrived in "Tusayan," or Hopi country, expecting to find gold, but instead they discovered homes made of stone, steep rock cliffs, and small fields of corn.[3] Closely observing the "strangers at their doors," the Hopis at Kawaiokuh looked at the men and their horses with amazement, but their curiosity quickly turned to concern and the people sounded an alarm throughout the villages.[4] Hopi leaders instructed their warriors to arm themselves and confront the intruders at the base of the mesa.[5] When the warriors approached the Spaniards, Tovar, through a Zuni interpreter, explained to the Hopis that they came on friendly terms, but the Hopis told the intruders to leave their land, and they drew a line in the dirt and instructed Tovar that he and his men could not cross beyond the marker.

When some of the Spanish "soldiers made motions to cross the line," Hopis hit one of their horses with a wooden "club," which caused commotion in both parties.[6] As tensions between the Hopis and Spaniards escalated, the Catholic priest grew impatient and called on Tovar to annihilate the Hopis. Tovar responded by ordering his soldiers to attack, and several Hopi warriors were killed. Realizing that the Spaniards would not hesitate to kill, the people at Kawaioukuh gathered food and other gifts and offered them to Tovar and his men. The Hopis allowed the Spaniards to enter their villages and agreed to trade with them. The Spanish expedition did not conduct itself like the Utes, Navajos, or other tribes that Hopis fought in the past; Tovar came to the Hopi mesas with powerful weapons and horses that quickly covered great distances, and the Spanish spoke a language that Hopis did not understand. But the Hopi people outnumbered the Spaniards. At any moment warriors from each of the villages could have joined together and killed the foreign intruders. However, the Hopis calculated the risks of forcefully resisting the Spaniards and chose, for the time being, a nonviolent approach.

The Hopi-Spanish encounter in 1540 was a turning point in Hopi history that foretold a wave of explorers and Christian missionaries who demanded that the people embrace Christianity and education in European ideals and values. Catholic clergy insisted that Hopis become educated in Christianity. From 1628 through 1633 Spanish missionaries forced Hopis to build three large churches at the villages of Orayvi, Awat'ovi, and Shungopavi. At Awat'ovi, Catholic friars required that Hopis attend Christian gatherings where priests educated Hopi children and other "neophytes" in the "catechism" and "rules and lore" of the Catholic religion.[7] Catholic missionaries also committed horrendous acts against the Hopi people. For example, historian Robert Silverberg noted that "when a friar caught a Hopi in 'an act of idolatry' at Oraibi in 1655, he thrashed the man until blood came, then poured burning turpentine over him. The man died; when the Indians complained, the friar was transferred to a different district."[8] In 1680, after priests abused and persecuted Hopis for practicing their own religion, Hopis despised the Spaniards, killed the priests at Awat'ovi, and destroyed the village.[9] After Catholic missionaries attempted to reestablish a Christian stronghold in the village, the Hopis destroyed Awat'ovi again in 1700. The people understood these acts of rebellion to be their contribution to the Pueblo Revolt of 1680, an event that united the Pueblo people to rid their communities of Spanish occupation. These acts of Hopi resistance kept the Catholic Church from regaining a strong presence on Hopi land.[10] As Hopi historian Lomayumtewa C. Ishii observes: these events, especially the final destruction of Awat'ovi, "marked a transition in Hopi history where outside European influence temporarily came to an end."[11]

Between 1680 and 1700, the Hopi people "maintained their independence" from Spanish control and even signed a treaty with the king of Spain that stipulated that they would not be subjected to his authority or be required to cease the practice of Hopi religion.[12] Although some Spanish missionaries visited the Hopi people from 1700 to 1745, the priests converted few Hopis and the Catholic Church failed to secure a substantial dedicated Hopi following. Generally speaking, the Hopi people despised the Catholic missionaries and detested their presence in their villages. In June 1776, for example, Catholic missionary Father Garces intruded upon Orayvi and the people wanted "nothing to do with him" and refused to give him a hospitable reception.[13] From 1776 to the 1850s, white explorers and fur trappers, U.S. government officials including surgeons and military personnel, and other Christian missionaries made their way to the secluded villages on top of the Hopi mesas.[14] In 1858, a group of Mormons led by Jacob Hamblin began a series of missionary activities that included several trips to the Hopi mesas in a fifteen-year period. Initial Mormon reports described Hopis as an "isolated people unspoiled by contact with other whites."[15] A year after their arrival on the Hopi mesas, Mormons taught a small group of Hopi children the "Deseret Alphabet," an English alphabet created by Mormons to increase literacy among their converts, and missionaries reported that they often heard Hopis reciting the alphabet throughout the villages.[16]

In the 1870s and 1880s, U.S. government officials relied on missionaries to provide information on Hopi affairs and to be good influences on the Hopi people. Since Protestant organizations controlled the schools in Hopi country in the 1870s, a Western education for Hopis was largely synonymous with a Christian education. In 1875, Navajo-Moqui[17] (Hopi) Agent W. B. Truax argued that the ignorant and superstitious Hopis ought to be given the opportunity to be brought to the "light of civilization and Christianity." According to Truax, this could only be accomplished if Hopis had access to the Bible and to a Western form of education. Truax believed that Hopi school attendance would increase if Hopis embraced Christianity and eliminated Navajo raids on Hopi land, which were a constant distraction to the children at Hopi day schools. Truax further argued that the problems caused by the Navajos could only be eliminated if the U.S. government created a separate Hopi Reservation.[18]

Some government agents opposed Truax's call for a Hopi Reservation. In 1878 Indian Agent William R. Mateer, along with other government officials, recommended that the U.S.

government remove Hopis from their mesa-top villages and relocate them on land near the Little Colorado River.[19] Government officials hoped that this would solve the Navajo problem, since the removal of the Hopi people would dissuade the frequent Navajo attempts to raid and pillage Hopi villages. Agents also argued that the traditional government in the Hopi villages proved problematic in securing Hopi school attendance. Basing his views on Christian morals and teachings, Mateer noted in 1878 that the "mode of living, huddling in villages, each house communicating with each other, induces promiscuous intercourse to such an extent that many" Hopis were infected with sexually transmitted diseases.[20] Mateer's description of Hopi villages as brothels gave support to the idea that Hopis should leave their villages and live separated from one another at the bottom of the mesas.[21] In spite of agent and Hopi protest, government officials formulated policies to secure a Hopi reservation four years after Indian Agent Mateer's recommendations to the contrary. On December 16, 1882, President Chester A. Arthur issued an executive order establishing the boundaries of a 2.5-million-acre Hopi Reservation in northeastern Arizona.[22]

In June 1890, nearly eight years after President Arthur established the official boundaries of the Hopi Reservation, Kikmongwi Loololma, four chiefs from other Hopi villages, and a white tradesman named Charles Keams traveled to Washington DC to ask Commissioner of Indian Affairs Thomas J. Morgan for help with Navajos who had raided their villages and destroyed their crops. After listening to the Hopi chiefs, Morgan recommended that the Hopis leave their homes on the mesas and disperse throughout the Hopi Reservation to prevent additional Navajo advancements.[23] Commissioner Morgan believed that if the Hopis lived at the bottom of the mesas, the Navajos would be less inclined to raid Hopi corn and bean fields. Morgan also encouraged the chiefs to convince Hopi parents to send their children to government schools. Although the Hopi leaders traveled to Washington to speak with government officials about their conflict with the Navajos, Morgan used this opportunity to convince them that submission to the U.S. government, particularly in regard to the issue of education, was in the best interest of the Hopi people.[24] In a further attempt to convince the Hopi chiefs that they should send their children to school, Morgan and other government officials strategically planned their trip home to include stops at the Carlisle Indian Industrial School in Pennsylvania, the Haskell Institute in Lawrence, Kansas, and the Albuquerque Indian School in New Mexico.[25]

Impressed with what he saw on his journey to Washington, Loololma returned to the Hopi Reservation and called a meeting in one of the kivas at Orayvi with leaders from the other villages. Loololma told the Hopi leaders about his trip and described how the white man used technology to grow "acres and acres" of corn. Loololma described that the white man grew corn that was twice the height of two Hopi men standing on top of each other. He told them about Fort Leavenworth, a military prison in Kansas, and how government soldiers had the capability to kill a man instantly with a pistol if he did not follow their orders. Although Hopis possessed some guns, Loololma's words reminded the people that U.S. government soldiers had more guns than the Hopis. After talking at length about his trip, Loololma asked those in the kiva to say how many white men they believed there were. None of the Hopis responded to Loololma's question. To demonstrate his point, Loololma grabbed handfuls of sand in a pit from the center of the kiva and slowly poured the grains of sand back into the pit and told the Hopis: "This is how many white men there are, and many more." He then asked the men in the kiva to state the number of Hopis who lived on the reservation. All of the Hopis present had a rough estimate, but none responded. Loololma reached down into the pit and took a pinch of sand and said, "That's how many Hopis there are."[26] Loololma then told the people not to "be afraid of the days to come." He explained that the "pahaana [white man's] way of life" was inevitable and that the Hopi people "must accept that." Although he recognized this certainty, he assured his Hopi followers that they could still "survive as a people" by learning the "white man's tongue" and the way he thinks. Loololma told them to grow familiar with the white man's ways so they could also "survive with it."[27]

Loololma's willingness to accommodate the wishes of government officials outraged several Hopis at Orayvi and other villages. Many years before Anglo-Americans arrived on Hopi land, Hopi elders prophesied that a white man would return to Hopis as their brother, and some Hopis equated white government officials with the expected "white brother."[28] In his examination of Hopi religion, John D. Loftin suggests that Loololma momentarily held to this belief, but so-called traditional Hopis, under Kikmongwi Lomahongyoma, rejected this conclusion.[29] Disagreements over Hopi prophecy, Christianity, and the U.S. government's policy of mandatory Hopi schooling led to the emergence of the resisting and accommodating Hopi factions. Government agents considered Loololma to be the Chief of the "Friendlies," and referred to Lomahongyoma as Chief of the "Hostiles," which defined Hopis in a way that did not help matters, but rather made the situation worse. Consequently, as Hopi artist Fred Kabotie observed, Hopis referred to themselves as "Hostiles" and "Friendlies" and started to act accordingly.[30]

Although disputes between the Hopi groups began before the 1890s, tension over Christianity and mandatory schooling escalated as government officials forced Hopi children to attend schools, including the reservation's only boarding school at Keams Canyon.

When government officials constructed the Keams Canyon Boarding School on the Hopi Reservation in 1887, Moqui Indian Agent S. S. Patterson reported that while Hopis at Orayvi "despised the face of the white man," Loololma still sent "two of his own children to the school," and promised to enroll additional Hopis from the village.[31] Loololma's willingness to comply with government officials angered Lomahongyoma and intensified the division between the two groups. Government officials believed that a compliant Indian chief such as Loololma could influence other Indian pupils to a greater degree than white government agents. In 1889, Commissioner Morgan noted that the plan for Indian education ought to make adequate "provisions" for the advanced education of an elite group of Natives who had a "special capacity or ambition, and [were] destined" toward leadership positions. Furthermore, Morgan commented that "the work of education should begin with [Indians] while they are young and susceptible and should continue until habits of industry and love of learning" took the "place of indolence and indifference."[32]

Morgan's policy on Indian education had a direct impact on Hopi parents, children, and village leaders. In 1890, Commissioner Morgan invited chiefs from each of the Hopi villages to attend a meeting at the Keams Canyon School. Not every village chief participated in the discussion, but those chiefs who met had one primary issue on their minds: the forced removal of Hopi children to U.S. government schools.[33] At the gathering,

Commissioner Morgan and other government officials attempted to convince the Hopi leaders that the U.S. government did not have a hidden agenda in requiring their children to attend school. Agents explained that education benefited Hopis by providing them with knowledge and skills to "meet the great, unavoidable problems of the future," and most importantly to ensure the "preservation of the Indian race."[34] But Hopis knew that the U.S. government created on- and off-reservation boarding schools to weaken Indian cultures and that government officials would go to great lengths to secure Hopi school attendance, even withholding "government [food] rations" for those who refused to send their children to school.[35] As historian Margaret D. Jacobs points out, "when authorities could not compel Indian people to send their children to boarding schools, many officials resorted to brutal means to achieve their ends."[36] Few things could have been more brutal than withholding food.

Shortly after the Hopi leaders met with the government officials, Commissioner Morgan and General Alexander McDowell McCook instructed the superintendent of the Keams Canyon School, Ralph Collins, to "gather into the schools all the Indian children he could find of school age."[37] Morgan's order went against the wishes of several Hopi parents and leaders and added to the tensions between Hopis and government officials. By June 1891, the situation over U.S. government-run schools intensified.[38] In a *Los Angeles Times* article dated June 27, 1891, a reporter noted that the "medicine men of the Moqui tribes" are "bitterly opposed to education, and they are determined to keep the Indian children out of school." According to the *Times* reporter, Hopi medicine men realized that once Hopi children became educated in U.S. government schools and learned about Western remedies and cures, their "power over the Indians will come to an end."[39] But the Hopi medicine men were not intimidated by government officials nor by the education taught at off-reservation Indian boarding schools. Their powers were deeply rooted in Hopi spirituality, and they knew that the effectiveness of their powers were not dependent on whether Hopi children received an education beyond the mesas.[40]

U.S. government soldiers such as Collins did not understand or value Hopi culture. They did not stop to consider the unseen forces at work when they attempted to subdue the Hopi resistance. Instead, Collins and his men responded to the Hopi situation as though it were simply another military campaign. Frustrated with the Hopi resistance, Collins notified Commissioner Morgan that Hopis at Orayvi "threatened to kill the whites and forcibly take their children from the school." In response to Collins's plea, Morgan sent military reinforcements and instructed Collins to arrest the Hopi instigators until the situation could be settled. Less than a week later, Lieutenant L. M. Brett and twenty men on horseback arrived at Orayvi and found a number of Hopis gathered together on the "flat house tops armed with rifles and bows and arrows." As the men approached the village, the Orayvi War Chief "defiantly rejected the offer of a parley, and threatened to open fire on the cavalry if they did not leave." Seeing that he would not be able to force the Hopis to comply with his orders, Brett and his men left the village and returned to their military post at Fort Wingate near Holbrook, Arizona.[41]

Hopis at Orayvi celebrated their victory but realized that military officials would return with more troops and weapons. When Brett informed General McCook about the drama that unfolded at Orayvi, McCook immediately relieved Brett of his command and ordered Lieutenant Colonel Henry C. Corbin to gather additional troops who were prepared to destroy the village with "two 3-inch Hotchkiss guns," which had the capacity to fire forty-three rounds of ammunition per minute.[42] Ready to demolish the structures and kill the people of Orayvi, Corbin led the expedition of two hundred men, including a few Navajos, from Holbrook to Orayvi.[43] Once Corbin and his men arrived at the village, the Hopi resisters assessed the situation and chose not to fight when they saw how many American troops had come to invade their village. When Corbin realized that the Hopis had taken this nonviolent approach, he arrested eight of the Hopi instigators, but "all refused to talk except one who said they were prepared to fight, but had no conception that Americans could bring more than thirty or forty soldiers against them." Shortly before Corbin left Orayvi, he gathered the people of the village together and explained to them the seriousness of their actions, and told them that instead of getting in the U.S. government's way, they should all go back to their peaceful ways of life.[44]

Corbin's paternalistic attitude provides a telling commentary on the way government officials related to what they saw as their Hopi wards. Seldom speaking to Hopis as equals, government officials considered Hopis to be lesser human beings, with the mental and social capacity of a child. Although some government agents valued and admired specific aspects of Hopi culture, the majority believed that Hopis, like every other indigenous people, were less intelligent, civilized, and sophisticated than white people. Government officials blamed the Hopis' noncompliant attitude on a misguided perception that Indian people could not think rationally without the enlightening influences of a Western education. In an article published in the *Chicago Daily Tribune* in 1884, the author referred to Indians as "adult children" who needed to be taught morals, good character, and industrial training.[45] Similarly, government officials saw Hopis as mentally immature children who needed an education at off-reservation Indian boarding schools. Therefore, U.S. government policies encouraged the removal of Hopi youth to schools, but many Hopis and some white individuals disagreed with this approach.

In September 1891, Edward B. Green, chief justice of the Indian Territory in present-day Oklahoma, ruled that the U.S. government had no authoritative power to kidnap Indian children and place them in American schools without the written permission of their parents. Following Green's ruling, he immediately "ordered an Indian boy named Thomas Lincoln to be released from Chilocco Indian School [in Indian Territory], and restored to his parents in the Iowa country." When news of Green's decision reached Commissioner Morgan, Morgan announced that he would "appeal the case and carry it up to the Supreme Court of the United States." The decision was important for the U.S. government's Indian education program, and Morgan feared that if Green's ruling became law at the national level, "every Indian school in the land" would be "emptied," including the Keams Canyon Boarding School and Hopi day schools.[46] Morgan's concern that Indian schools everywhere would be shut down implies that the majority of Indian pupils who attended schools in the late nineteenth century did so without their parents' consent. Although Chief Justice Green's decision did not have legislative support in Washington DC, it sparked a debate across America on whether the U.S. government should force Indian children to attend school. Historian Margaret D. Jacobs observes that "even some government officials questioned the wisdom of forcibly removing children from their homes to attend boarding schools."[47] In 1883 Thomas Donaldson, a government census agent, asked: "Shall we be compelled to keep a garrison of 250 to 300 men of the Moqui pueblos in order to educate 100 to 200 children at a distance from their homes? We began with soldiers and Hotchkiss guns. Are we to end in the same way? Such civilizing has not heretofore been a pronounced success."[48]

In January 1894, Moqui Indian Agent Lieutenant E. H. Plummer wrote Commissioner Morgan and told him that when he visited the Hopi villages, Hopi leaders and parents failed to convince him with their "half promise" that they would send their children to government schools.[49] During his visit to the Hopi villages, Plummer relied on an interpreter, a Hopi student who returned home from Haskell Institute, an off-reservation Indian boarding school in Lawrence, Kansas. The Hopi pupil was likely from Orayvi, part of a group of five Hopi males whom Superintendent Collins sent to Haskell in 1892.[50] The Hopi boy learned English at Haskell and proved valuable to Indian agents and the Hopi people. The Hopi interpreter told Plummer that some Hopis "preferred to have the [Navajo] policemen come after the children." Consequently, Plummer sent Navajo police to the reservation to show the strong hand of the U.S. government, but Hopi parents and leaders remained unimpressed with their tactics. Plummer informed Commissioner Morgan that it was "reported" to him that "soldiers must be sent to force the children" to attend the Keams Canyon Boarding School. "I must say," noted Plummer, "that I do not believe that this method should be pursued, if soldiers are sent I believe it should be to arrest and confine the headmen who are responsible for the children not being sent to school." Plummer argued that forcing Hopi children to school at that time of the year would be impractical and undesirable on many fronts. In January 1894, two feet of snow covered the path to Keams Canyon, and the temperature dipped to "17 degrees below zero." Instead of suggesting that government soldiers require Hopi children to attend school, Plummer asked Commissioner Morgan if he could instead withhold "annuity goods" and suspend "work on houses" to slowly weaken the Hopi resistance. Under the Rules for Indian Schools of 1892, the U.S. government allowed Indian agents to keep food and other goods from Indian people if they did not comply with federal policies.[51] Plummer also noted that the boarding school at Keams Canyon was already overcrowded, and a severe outbreak of mumps had overtaken the school.

Although Plummer believed he could convince Hopis to send their children to school without using government troops, his successor, Major Constant Williams, "promptly recommended" that General McCook send troops to Orayvi shortly after he took command in the Fall of 1894.[52] On November 16, 1894, McCook responded to Williams's request and dispatched soldiers and a detachment that specialized in operating Hotchkiss guns to Orayvi. Early the next morning, Captain Frank Robinson and a group of soldiers left Fort Wingate, 150 miles southeast of Orayvi. Habema (Heevi'ima), war chief of the Hopi resisters, sent warriors to intercept the troops and tell Robinson and his men to "hasten on" to Orayvi, as "poisoned arrows and Winchesters galore" awaited them.[53] As the troops approached the village from the north, Habema and his Hopi followers had every intention to fight, but when they saw the Hotchkiss gun "quietly awaiting the liberation of its rain of death," the Hopis decided not to proceed with violence. Williams and his men interpreted Habema's reluctance to fight as a sign of weakness, but Habema understood the situation and opted for a nonviolent resolution. In response to Habema's unwillingness to engage in open conflict, Major Williams arrested eighteen of the Hopi resisters, including Habema and Lomahongyoma, and marched the Hopi prisoners to Fort Wingate. Upon reaching their destination, military officials realized that Potopa, a Hopi medicine man known as "one of the most dangerous" of the resisters, had outsmarted the soldiers and "escaped capture." Anxious to rid Orayvi of all resisting leaders, officials sent Sergeant Henry Henser back to the village to capture Potopa.

When Henser returned to Orayvi and confronted Potopa, the Hopi medicine man "climbed up a ladder, and dashed down" into one of the village kivas. Once inside the kiva, Henser encountered a Hopi priestess who was tending a fire in the center of the kiva.[54] When the priestess saw Henser, she repositioned herself near a curtain at the back of the kiva and hid a doorway to a sacred chamber. With a "vicious look in her eye," the priestess blocked Henser's path and the medicine man ran into the chamber. Pushing the priestess out of his way, Henser proceeded through a "series of winding passages" that extended from the main section of the kiva. After several minutes passed, Henser noticed red material from a blanket sticking out from a crevice in the chamber wall. When Henser tugged at the blanket, Potopa tumbled out from the crack and the two men wrestled each other. As Henser and Potopa fought, the priestess rushed to Potopa's defense and stabbed at Henser with a "handful of poisoned arrows." Unable to penetrate Henser's military uniform, the priestess grabbed a bow and drew an arrow to Henser's head. As the priestess was about to let go of the arrow, a Hopi chief, possibly Loololma, rushed into the kiva and stood in front of her and knocked the bow from her hands. Although killing Henser would have prevented the immediate threat of Potopa's arrest, it would have led to greater problems for the Hopi people. The chief realized that government officials would avenge the death of a member of their military personnel and therefore chose to stop the killing. In doing so, the chief avoided further conflict and certain disastrous retaliatory consequences.

When Henser regained control, he tied Potopa's hands and arrested him. The next day, Henser, his men, and the Hopi prisoners walked in a single line down the mesa cliffs with an armed soldier assigned to each prisoner. In addition to the mounted troopers, "six privates and three non-commissioned officers" rode on the "flank a few yards to the right of the prisoners." Writing about their return trip to Fort Wingate, *Los Angeles Times* reporter George H. Guy noted that the Hopis run "better than they can do anything else," and they thought nothing of the 150-mile journey to Fort Wingate. According to Guy, who compared the Hopi prisoners to animals, "whenever the horses trotted," the Hopi prisoners "kept up with them with the greatest ease, for miles." After Henser and the Hopi resisters arrived at Fort Wingate, government officials interrogated the prisoners. Finding the resisters guilty of preventing their children's attendance at U.S. government schools, officials deported the resisting "ringleaders," including Habema and chief Lomahongyoma, to prison on Alcatraz Island in the San Francisco Bay in November 1894.[55]

Whereas many Hopis vehemently disagreed with the U.S. government's decision to send their leaders to Alcatraz, Guy portrayed the arrests and the removal of Hopi resisters as a series of positive events. Guy commented that since officials sent the Hopi resisters to Alcatraz, the Hopis' will to resist was undermined, which supposedly resulted in "profound peace in the reservation." But Hopi resistance toward government officials, Christian missionaries, and the U.S. government's Indian education policies did not cease when the nineteen Hopi resisters left the reservation for Alcatraz. Government officials only arrested leaders whom they identified as troublesome; therefore many Hopi resisters remained on the reservation. Furthermore, the forced removal of some resister leaders to Alcatraz angered several Hopis and intensified their feelings of bitterness and resistance toward the U.S. government.

Guy also congratulated government officials for ending the situation at Orayvi "without the loss of a single life." Giving no credit to the nonviolent approach of the Hopis, Guy focused on the U.S. government's role in settling the problem. Guy concluded that the "moral of this little campaign" showed that it was a further advantage to the United States "to have frontier military posts," and to maintain "men in command of our soldiers who have level heads as well as brave hearts; men who, while full of fight, prefer to secure bloodless triumph to scoring a more showy dramatic victory at the cost of the precious lives of the troops." Although newspaper commentators believed that sending the Hopi resisters to Alcatraz would end Hopi defiance against the U.S. government, Indian Agent Constant Williams concluded that peace and stability on the reservation had arrived for only a season, and he did not assume that it would last for any length of time.[56] In the same year that Williams recorded his outlook on the situation at Orayvi, Samuel L. Hertzog, superintendent of the Keams Canyon Boarding School, reported that as a result of sending the Hopis to Alcatraz, Hopi resistance was rendered ineffective and would cease if government officials did not allow the "leaders" to return home before they learned their lesson.[57] However, although government officials sent nineteen of the most influential resisters to Alcatraz, other noncompliant Hopis remained on the reservation and continued the resistance at home. In the absence of older leaders, younger Hopis took leadership roles and continued the fight.

Less than a year later, government officials released the Hopi prisoners at Alcatraz and returned them to the reservation in September 1895. Government agents, school administrators, and missionaries anxiously waited to see how the former Hopi prisoners would respond to mandatory school attendance. According to Ralph Collins, the new superintendent of the Keams Canyon School, prior to the return of the prisoners, Hopis on the reservation started a rumor that the U.S. government was indifferent to whether Hopi children attended school. Consequently, pupils whose parents did not want them to enter the schools remained at home. Collins noted in his report that this "feeling was greatly strengthened" once the Alcatraz prisoners returned home and claimed that government officials had told them that they did "not have to send any" of their children to school.[58] Indian agents, or other officials, may have told the Orayvi prisoners, either before they left for Alcatraz or during their time of imprisonment, that their children did not have to go to the reservation schools. When the prisoners came home, they reminded government officials of their promise, but Indian agents and school superintendents denied that this agreement had taken place. Government officials believed that the inferences propagated by the resisters would only be remedied by forcing their children to attend school.[59] This caused leaders from the resisting faction to increase their resistance against government agents and Indian policies.

Reporter George H. Guy commented that although ninety Hopi children attended the Keams Canyon School and had taken "kindly to the general course," Lomahongyoma, chief of the resisting faction, believed that the Hopi "youths were becoming too learned" and feared that their "sympathies would be weaned away" from the Hopi people and that they would "grow up with a white man's heart." Lomahongyoma argued that Hopi children had managed "very well without the white man's learning in former days, and he proposed that they should do so now." As more Hopis agreed to comply with government officials, Lomahongyoma attempted to forcibly prevent Hopi parents from sending their children to school, and when this failed, Lomahongyoma "seized their lands and stole their crops." Lomahongyoma then surrounded "himself with a large following of the turbulent element in his community" and prepared for a "bloody campaign" against the government.[60] Although willing and able to fight, Lomahongyoma and his followers did not resort to violence. Influenced by the U.S. government's use of Navajo policemen and superior weaponry, Lomahongyoma followed the example of previous Hopi chiefs who chose nonviolent methods to ensure Hopi survival. Government officials interpreted this nonviolent approach as a sign of Hopi compliance and cowardliness. Hopis had contemplated the consequences of killing U.S. government employees in the past, but Lomahongyoma's choice not to resist by force had its own ramifications, which involved the continual removal of Hopi pupils to the Keams Canyon School and reservation day schools.

While some Indian communities demonstrated little opposition to Congress's attempt to make Indian education mandatory in 1891, others adamantly opposed U.S. government schools and rejected colonial forms of education.[61] Even some white government officials voiced concerns over the U.S. government's removal of Indian pupils to off-reservation Indian boarding schools. In December 1892, John G. Rockwell, a member of the Indian Affairs Committee, remarked that Indian communities wanted and needed a "good system of primary schools, to which they may send their children, and at the same time have their help at home."[62] In March 1893, less than two years after Congress required that all Indian children receive an American education, the U.S. government constructed the new Oraibi Day School, a small one-classroom school designed to assimilate and prepare Hopi pupils for future attendance at off-reservation Indian boarding schools.[63] In spite of the opposition from Hopis at Orayvi, government officials continued their educational agendas and plotted ways to secure children of resistant Hopi families to attend the school.[64] Within its first year of operation, G. W. Goodman, superintendent of the Oraibi Day School, reported that an average of thirty Hopi students attended the school, and none of the students belonged to families of Hopi resisters.[65]

Although Hopi enrollment at the Oraibi Day School grew with children from the accommodating faction, government officials found it increasingly difficult to persuade resisting parents to allow their children to attend school. At Keams Canyon School in 1896, Collins, frustrated with noncompliant Hopi parents, lamented that he did not have an effective approach for dealing with the resisters, except to "let them personally alone, treat them kindly and justly, and put their children in school by force."[66] Contrary to what he wrote in his report, Collins did not let the Hopis alone, nor did he treat them with kindness and justice. Instead, Collins came from a type of U.S. government agent that forced their way into Hopi homes, threatened Hopis with violence, and dragged their children to school. Hopis detested this uncivilized and unruly behavior, especially parents from resisting families who were forced to send their children to on- and off-reservation Indian boarding schools.

The removal of Hopi children to reservation schools also strained the relationship between parents and their children.

When government officials forced the daughter of a leader of the Hopi resisters to attend the Keams Canyon School in 1894, the girl's father missed his daughter so much that he often visited her at school. While her father admitted that she was "happy, and gaining in knowledge," he was unrelenting in his objection to government schools. When the girl returned to the reservation her father tried to keep her from returning to school, but the girl seemed to enjoy her experience at the school, and she desired to go back the following year. Seeing that her father would not let her return in the fall, the girl ran away to school, and when she returned home a year later, her father "tore her school clothes into shreds, abused her shamefully, and told her that if she ever went to school again she need never return home." Defying her father's wishes, the girl ran away again and eventually married a former Hopi student from an accommodating family and lived in an American-style home in the Hopi village of Kykotsmovi.[67] The tensions Hopi pupils experienced with their parents continued throughout the twentieth century.[68] When Hopis attended the Keams Canyon School and off-reservation Indian boarding schools such as the Carlisle Indian Industrial School and the Phoenix Indian School, many who returned home found it difficult to readjust to life on the reservation. Several factors contributed to this reality. Hopis who went to boarding schools learned to live away from their parents and gained a greater sense of independence. Some Hopis willingly embraced the lessons taught at off-reservation Indian boarding schools, and when they returned home they encountered great divisions among their people regarding the relative merits of Western ways and Hopi ways.

By the late 1890s and early 1900s, partially due to a stream of new superintendents and government agents who had little or no experience working with Hopi people, friction between Hopi adults and government officials had escalated on the reservation. In October 1899, twenty-six-year-old Charles F. Burton became the new superintendent of the Keams Canyon School.[69] During Burton's four-year tenure, Hopis suffered immensely. The Western concepts of assimilation and acculturation that fueled Burton's policy of Hopi education set him at odds with the resisting faction on the reservation. In 1900, Burton reported that the Hopi resisters proved to be a "serious drawback to the progress of civilization." He noted that the resisters refused to "send their children to school" and severely criticized his administration of Indian education policies. Burton insisted that the Hopi resisters be "forced to send their children to school," but as long as a group of Hopis resisted American forms of education, the superintendent lacked the authority he fervently desired.[70] Shortly after Burton commented on the noncompliant Hopi resisters, he released a second report stating that with "only a very slight show of force," he and the day school teacher, Herman T. Kampmeier, went to Orayvi with "two policemen and brought away eight of the hostile children" to the school.[71] Anthropologist Peter M. Whiteley noted that "Burton's 'slight show of force' came to be a regular feature" during his four years as superintendent, and it showed his unwillingness to deal with Hopis in a civilized manner.[72]

Hopi parents were not the only ones who resisted Burton's methods of securing Hopi compliance. In his autobiography, Edmund Nequatewa recalled that when he was a student and ran away from the Phoenix Indian School in 1902 to return to the reservation, Burton sent Hopi and Navajo police to subdue him. After the police captured twenty-two-year-old Edmund near Shipaulovi on Second Mesa and took him to Keams Canyon,

Burton told Edmund that he had to return to Phoenix.[73] However, Edmund chose to disobey the superintendent and informed him that he refused to go back. Edmund's noncompliant attitude outraged Burton. Superintendent Burton told Edmund that if he did not reenroll in the school he would place Edmund in restraints and throw him in a wagon. Seeing that Burton was frustrated with the him and the situation, Edmund agreed to the superintendent's orders, but told him that once he arrived at the school he would run away again. After hearing Edmund's intentions, Burton advised Edmund that when the Hopi pupil returned to Phoenix, Burton would instruct school officials to lock him in the school's guardhouse. Edmund eventually did return to the Phoenix Indian School, but only after the school's Superintendent of Industries August F. Duclos promised that he would not be punished for running away.[74]

White day school teachers also voiced their concerns about Burton and his method of securing Hopi school attendance. In June 1903, Belle Axtell Kolp submitted an affidavit of her experience as a schoolteacher at the Oraibi Day School from 1902 to 1903. Kolp reported that she had witnessed the cruel behavior Burton and others demonstrated toward the Hopis at the school. According to Kolp, whenever school officials punished or threatened Hopi pupils, the school's principal, John L. Ballinger, told the Hopis that he was only following Washington's orders. Ballinger insisted that government officials had sanctioned his use of force, which demonstrates how some school officials took their association with the U.S. government as a license to act in a dictatorial fashion. Ballinger did not want to face the consequences of his actions, and he blamed his behavior on the U.S. government.[75]

When Kolp arrived at the day school in 1902, the school had 125

Hopi children and one teacher for each of the two classrooms. Upon her resignation in 1903, 174 pupils attended the school. However, school officials still had not hired a third teacher to handle the increased enrollment. Kolp recalled that at least twelve Hopi children were younger than four years of age and some could not "walk the mile which lay between" Orayvi and the day school. In her affidavit, Kolp noted that government officials forced these Hopi children "from their homes by an armed body" of government employees and Navajos, "not for the purpose of 'making better Indians,' but for the benefit for those in charge."[76] According to Kolp, Ballinger and his wife did not have a genuine desire to educate Hopis in the ways and customs of American society. Instead, the Ballingers wanted additional government funding, improved salaries, and a heightened sense of prestige. Although the day school had existed since 1887, Ballinger sought to replace it with a boarding school, which would allow him the opportunity to obtain more supplies and a greater salary. In addition to an augmented income, the presence of a boarding school guaranteed Ballinger a personal clerk, an appointment his wife was sure to receive. In 1903, Ballinger's wife made $30 per month as a school cook; as a clerk, her salary would have increased to $100 per month. However, as a result of a rise in Hopi enrollment at off-reservation Indian boarding schools in 1906, Ballinger's plan did not come to fruition.[77]

Although Hopi pupil attendance at the Oraibi Day School increased, the absence of children from the resisting Hopi families caused Ballinger to intensify efforts among the Orayvi people. On February 2, 1903, Ballinger formed what he called a "raiding party," or "round-up." "Physician Murtaugh, Carpenter [Peter] Stauffer, Blacksmith Copeland, and a Squad of Navajo" police raided Orayvi to kidnap children and force them to school.[78]

Ballinger sent armed Navajos to Orayvi that night, and the rest of the men, including Burton and Stauffer, joined the raiding party on top of the mesa at 5:30 the following morning. When the men arrived at Orayvi, snow was falling and blanketed the ground. Once the men located a few Hopi children, Ballinger instructed the children to walk the trail to the day school while armed Navajo policemen watched to make sure that they did not deviate from the path.

On February 4, 1903, school officials counted 150 Hopi children in attendance at the day school, a figure that angered Ballinger, who expected more students as result of his raid. Unwilling to settle for meager results, Ballinger and Burton organized a second roundup party and increased the number of armed Navajo policemen in his posse. In the early morning hours of February 5, 1903, Kolp noted that Ballinger and his men made a "clean sweep" of Orayvi and "dragged" men, "women and children" from their beds and houses. Government officials did not allow the women or children to take a "few articles of clothing" before they headed down the mesa; many had little to eat that morning and wore no shoes.[79] Historian Donald E. Miller once remarked that when U.S. government agents raided Hopi villages, "the women shuffled their children from house to house trying to conceal them." A number of the children "hid in dark unused rooms behind great stores of corn," and waited until the agents left or discovered them in their hiding spots.[80] When government officials captured the Hopi pupils, they forced parents and grandparents to carry their children who could not walk down to the "school building, through the ice and snow." Some of the children wore no clothes,[81] and when they arrived at the day school, Ballinger and Burton forced the children to stay "there all day, until after six in the evening." Before Burton allowed them to leave, he told the parents and grandparents that the children had to come each day that school was in session. Burton told them that even if it was stormy outside, or if the children could not walk, they had to carry them and return for them when the school dismissed at the end of the day. Furthermore, Burton threatened Hopi parents and grandparents and told them that if their children did not attend school, the pupils would be removed to an off-reservation Indian boarding school.[82]

Kolp's accusations ignited an investigation of Burton and Ballinger by the Sequoya League, an organization developed in 1903 by Charles Lummis, editor of *Out West Magazine* and special advisor to President Theodore Roosevelt, to promote the rights and causes of Southwest Indians.[83] Commissioner William A. Jones appointed Indian Inspector J. E. Jenkins to oversee the investigation along with a "competent representative" of the league.[84] Established to "assist Indians in common-sense ways," the Sequoya League accused Burton of being an "unsuitable person" for the position of Agent.[85] In addition to doubting his qualifications, the league noted that Burton's tenure was marked by "physical violence," and that Hopis feared and detested him as an "unfeeling, unwise and despotic oppressor."[86] Furthermore, a reporter for the *Washington Post* noted that the Sequoya League charged Burton of "incompetency to civilize and educate the Indians, arbitrary and despotic conduct, and violation of the rules of the service."[87] When the Sequoya League completed its investigation less than a year later, it concluded that Burton violated the rule that forbade mandatory "hair-cutting" of Hopi men and failed to notify the Indian Office of Kampmeier's poor behavior.[88] The Sequoya League gave Burton a minor reprimand for his actions against the Hopi people. In October 1903,

Inspector Jenkins "fully exonerated Superintendent Burton from the charges" and noted that "none of the persons making the charges has ever been on the Moqui reservation."[89] Although Burton was not convicted of his crimes, the league succeeded in removing Burton from his post on the Hopi Reservation. By November 1904, the U.S. government reassigned Burton to be the superintendent of the Grand Junction Indian School in Colorado, and the former superintendent of that school, Thomas G. Lemmon, replaced Burton as superintendent on the Hopi Reservation.[90]

In the early twentieth century, Hopi leaders, parents, and children experienced the consequences of U.S. government policies and the imposition of American values on Hopi culture. Contrary to a report in the *Chicago Daily Tribune* that described Hopis as "weak," "spiritless," and people who "never cared to fight,"[91] the Hopi resisters plotted and pushed back against the U.S. government and exerted great agency. For the time being, the accommodating Hopis allowed their children to attend the nearby Hopi day schools and the Keams Canyon Boarding School, where they were able to keep track of their children's progress and well-being. Hopi pupils returned home each day from the day schools to their village communities and Hopi parents often visited their children at the reservation's only boarding school in Keams Canyon. But these acts of Hopi accommodation were not enough to appease the demands of the U.S. government. Soon, government officials would ask and require Hopis to accommodate even more.

2. Policies and Assimilation

The forced removal of Hopis to reservation schools did not fully satisfy the U.S. government's assimilation or acculturation agenda. Government officials desired that Hopis would be grafted into American society and leave their indigenous ways behind. In the early twentieth century, the U.S. government sought to destroy Hopi and other Indian cultures with a civilized form of education.[1] Although reservation schools served as a major step in that direction, government officials, including day school teachers, believed that Hopi culture hindered the lessons taught at schools located on the reservation. This belief, coupled with the schools' close proximity to Hopi villages, families, and leaders, presented an obstacle in convincing children to appreciate the supposed superiority of white American culture. For many Hopi pupils, their formal exposure to a Western society and education ceased when they completed their course of academic and industrial instruction at day schools or the Keams Canyon Boarding School. Consequently, government officials believed that Hopis needed to expand their education beyond the mesas and sought to further the assimilation and acculturation process by sending Hopis to off-reservation Indian boarding schools.

Hopis believed that white government officials were ignorant of Hopi culture and values, but government officials and

Christian missionaries viewed Hopis as uneducated people who needed to be saved from their uncivilized and devil-like ways. The opinion that American Indians needed salvation from their savage modes of living and thinking stemmed from beliefs rooted in colonialism and racism. In 1893, the Ladies' Union Mission School Association, a Christian group from New York that attempted to proselytize and civilize the Pima and Maricopa Indians of Arizona, noted that while the "Indian" belonged to the "great human family," he was "below his white brother in mind, morals and heart culture."[2] To Christianize and civilize the Hopis and other Indians, the U.S. government developed off-reservation Indian boarding schools and demanded that Hopis attend, regardless of their personal desire to go. Often, in spite of parent and student disapproval, government officials forced Hopi pupils to leave their families and homes for schools such as the Carlisle Indian Industrial School, the Phoenix Indian School, and Sherman Institute.[3]

David Wallace Adams correctly observed that the "boarding school, whether on or off the reservation, was the institutional manifestation of the government's determination to completely restructure the Indians' minds and personalities."[4] In this regard, boarding schools served as battlegrounds for the minds and affections of Indian pupils. White men, many of whom held to Christian ideologies, drafted Indian education policies and established laws that paved the way for Hopis and non-Hopis to attend off-reservation Indian boarding schools. Individually as well as collectively, they determined what was beneficial for the indigenous peoples of North America. Government leaders did not consult Hopi leaders when they constructed Indian schools, nor did they seek the expertise of Hopi educators when they formulated curricula that affected Hopi children and communities.

Instead, white educators and government bureaucrats made decisions for a people they knew very little about with the goal of weakening Hopi culture through their assimilation and acculturation policies. As historian Jacqueline Fear-Segal noted, "discussion of Indian Schooling amongst whites never heeded or included the Indian voice," and "schemes to embrace Indians within United States society were framed by white concepts and offered on white terms."[5]

This manner of acting to civilize the Indian was largely propagated by a change in the accepted scientific and educational philosophies of the day. In the early twentieth century, race theorists challenged the prevailing anthropological notion that "progress was a natural human condition."[6] Social scientists disagreed with evolutionists such as Lewis Henry Morgan and argued that "non-white peoples had little chance of joining a 'civilized' society led by their racial superiors."[7] Initially, government officials believed that Indians would never become civilized unless they completely assimilated into white society. Historian Frederick E. Hoxie observed that many white Americans believed that the "differences between Indians and whites were great. Native societies were not in 'transition' to civilization, they were adapting slowly—if at all—to the forces of modernity." Again Hoxie noted that some white officials held that the primitive Indian "would cling to his old ways for as long as he could," which made the process of assimilation an "exceedingly problematic enterprise."[8]

In his introduction to Edwin L. Calcraft's *Assimilation Agent*, historian Gary C. Collins noted that "Indian assimilation constituted a hard-fisted canon that proselytized stripping Indian people of their 'barbarism' and remaking them in the 'civilized' image of white American society."[9] However, in light of the scientific and academic skepticism of previously accepted race theories, government officials questioned the effectiveness of a total assimilation approach. Since the total assimilation approached proved impractical, the U.S. government switched to the policy of acculturation that focused more on assimilating Indians by using Native culture and the environment to accelerate the process.[10] Ralph Linton, a prominent American cultural anthropologist, defined acculturation as "phenomena" that occurred when a gathering of people with "different cultures" came into "continuous first-hand contact" with each other. According to Linton, this constant contact resulted in "subsequent changes in the original culture patterns of either or both groups."[11] Although Linton's definition of acculturation left the possibility that both cultures could change, white Americans expected acculturation to apply only to Native ways.

The philosophical concepts of Indian assimilation and acculturation had several key promoters in the U.S. government. Captain Richard Henry Pratt, a strong advocate of assimilation and founder of the Indian school at Carlisle, learned much of his philosophy of assimilation from previous interactions with black troops that he commanded in the U.S. Army. Historian Robert Utley observed that according to Pratt, once the system of slavery "transplanted [the slave] from his Native habitat and tribal affiliation into a new cultural environment" the slave adapted a "new language, new dress, and new customs."[12] Consequently, slaves began to act and think less like primitive African savages, and more like American citizens. Pratt used the slave experience as a model for Indian assimilation.[13] This analogy, however, did not convince some white Americans who believed that Pratt's theory failed to take into consideration the supposed difference between the "Red man" and the "Negro." In March 1886, a *New*

York *Times* reporter commented, "There is perhaps a degree of docility, imitativeness, and adaptability in the humbler black which the red man does not usually possess."[14]

Government officials closely connected Indian assimilation with the U.S. government's desire that Indians contribute something useful to American society. This mentality originated many years before the construction of the first federal off-reservation Indian boarding school. In 1818, the House Committee on Indian Affairs told Congress that if the government put the "primer and hoe" into the hands of Indian children, they would "naturally, in time, take hold of the plough; and, as their minds [became] enlightened and expand[ed], the Bible [would] be their book, and they [would] grow up in habits of morality and industry," and "become useful members of society."[15] Government officials wanted Indians to abandon their cultures and practices, for "Indianness" had little value or usefulness in American society.

Although government officials implemented an educational system on the Hopi Reservation, some believed that their practices and methods were substandard. In June 1902, one of the grievances expressed by Herman Kampmeier, a teacher at the Oraibi Day School, focused on insufficient school facilities available for training Hopi boys in industrial education. Kampmeier complained that the "one great irremediable drawback" to the Oraibi Day School was that it had become "impossible" to give the boys adequate "industrial training," which in Kampmeier's opinion was "paramount to everything else in an Indian school."[16] In his examination of the Rainy Mountain Boarding School in Oklahoma, Clyde Ellis noted that "off-reservation boarding schools emphasized industrial and domestic training, but at levels higher than their reservation counterparts. Instruction was better, facilities were generally superior to anything found on reservations, and students were the best the other schools had to offer."[17] While the Oraibi Day School provided the foundation for an American education, the school did not train Hopi pupils in industrial education to the same degree as off-reservation boarding schools, especially one such as Sherman Institute. Since a large percentage of industrial education involved farming, the limited resources of land, seed, and machinery at the Hopi day schools posed a serious problem to the U.S. government's assimilation agenda.[18]

Providing Indian pupils with a useful education was a major component in Pratt's understanding of off-reservation Indian boarding schools. While serving as superintendent at Carlisle, Pratt argued that the system of gathering Indians on their land only produced "inactivity on reservations." The Indian's supposed laziness and primitive behaviors accorded with the belief that the only good Indians are dead ones. According to Pratt, "idleness and ignorance had destroyed" other Indian nations, and due to the U.S. government's failure to incorporate Indians into American society, Indians retained their tribal identities, self loyalty, language, and the "rights and orgies of their savagery." Pratt's answer to the "Indian problem" was to provide Indian pupils with a practical education that was conducted away from indigenous communities.[19]

While Pratt implemented Indian policies at Carlisle, few government officials influenced early twentieth century Indian education policies more than Commissioner of Indian Affairs Francis Ellington Leupp. During Leupp's tenure as commissioner from 1905 to 1909, the issue of Indian education demanded much of his attention. According to Leupp, educating Indians in Anglo-American values and culture preserved Indian people from "extinction."[20] Although Hopis valued education, the traditional forms of education that Hopis practiced in their village communities did not satisfy the U.S. government's education or assimilation goals for Hopi people. Government officials such as Leupp believed that several obstacles hindered the transformation of Indians, including Hopis, to behave like civilized American citizens. One primary hurdle surrounded the supposed mental capabilities of Indians as compared to their "white brothers." In July 1907, at the Indian branch of the National Education Association Convention held in Los Angeles, California, Leupp told his audience that the "Indian is really an adult child," and although "he has a man's physique," he nonetheless has "the mentality of a boy about 14 years old."[21] Leupp's opinion of the mental capacities and intelligence of Indian people mirrored those of other government officials. Leupp's paternalistic attitude saw Indians as children who could not think rationally as adults do. Leupp believed that if Indians did not receive help from the U.S. government, Indians would remain in a state of savagery and would be unable to proceed in a progressive and civilized world.[22]

Although Leupp favored day schools to off-reservation boarding schools,[23] the latter served as laboratories for the development and implementation of Indian education policies that Leupp and other government officials supported. One of the many institutions for civilization and progress was the Perris Indian School, an off-reservation Indian boarding school near Riverside, California. In 1892, the Office of Indian Affairs allocated funding for the construction of the Perris Indian School, which enrolled 8 students during the first year of operation. By 1902, the school had a yearly enrollment of 350 pupils.[24] Government officials constructed the Perris Indian School with the premise that an adequate water supply from the local San Bernardino

Mountains would be available. Primarily an agricultural institution, the Perris School depended on large amounts of water to maintain the school's growing population and farm. When water shortages arose in 1897, government officials considered abandoning the Perris site for a more suitable location for the school.

Plans to close the Perris Indian School outraged some people in the Perris community. In January 1898, the residents of Perris gathered to frame a "petition and demonstration to the Indian Bureau to prevent" the school's removal. Many of the residents at the meeting disapproved of the school's superintendent, Harwood Hall, for "reporting so unfavorably of the soil and conditions." They further said that in light of Hall's "brief residence" in Perris, he lacked the qualifications to determine the "capabilities of the valley." Other residents commented that had Hall "made a little investigation of the orchards in the valley," he would "not have reported the valley barren." Those at the meeting overwhelmingly agreed that the water supply, soil quality, and the educational welfare of the Indian pupil were not the real reasons for Hall's insistence on moving the school to Riverside. Instead, the Perris community accused the school's administrators and teachers of caring more about their "social enjoyments, which would be more extensive near some large city or town," than the education of their "Indian wards."[25] While many people in Perris tried to convince government officials of the abundant water supply at the school, Estelle Reel, superintendent of Indian schools from 1898 to 1910, concluded that the lack of water necessitated the "removal of the school to another location."[26]

Considered by one *Los Angeles Times* newspaper reporter to be "one of the most absurd, as well as reprehensible, propositions" intended to "throw a sop of public money to a Southern California town," the decision to move the Indian school from Perris to Riverside outraged the Perris community. In April 1900, news coverage of the proposal focused on the evil influences a large city such as Riverside would have on Indian students. The *Times* reported that "even so moral a place as Riverside, where the only saloons are drug stores, could not avoid having now and then a hoodlum or a wayward youth from the wicked town of San Bernardino stray that way, corrupting with his bubonic plague [the] habits [of] the guileless Indian boys and girls."[27] In November 1900, Commissioner of Indian Affairs William A. Jones reported in his annual address that "owing to the unfavorable location at the site it has been decided that the Indian school at Perris, Cal., cannot be made into an industrial school for Southern California," a plan that the government had initially considered. Convinced of the poor and inadequate conditions in Perris, Jones informed his audience that the Indian Appropriation Act "for the fiscal year 1901" included a proposal to erect a new school in Riverside, "provided that a suitable site can be obtained there for a reasonable sum."[28]

A few months after Commissioner Jones' annual address, Superintendent Hall and other officials secured an alternate site for the school campus. On May 18, 1901, A. C. Tonner, assistant commissioner of Indian affairs, laid the "corner stone of the main building" at the new school location in Riverside.[29] Located six miles from downtown Riverside, Sherman Institute encompassed a forty-acre lot accessible by "street car direct from the city." Government officials chose the site "because of its excellent climate, picturesque surroundings, culture and refinement of its citizens and the sympathetic interest taken in the Indian boy and girl by the community." The school originally had nine buildings, which Indian students and U.S. government workers constructed according to a Spanish Mission architectural style to complement the buildings in the surrounding area.[30] Hopi students who attended Sherman Institute in the 1920s remembered the first time they saw the Spanish Mission buildings. Marsah (Talasitiwa) Balenquah, a Hopi pupil from Bacavi who attended Sherman Institute from 1920 to 1934, recalled that the buildings at the school were "something else," and looked so different from the stone houses on the reservation.[31] School officials named the school after the Chairman of the Committee of Indian Affairs of the House of Representatives James Schoolcraft Sherman, not General William Tecumseh Sherman. Considered by some to be a genuine friend of the Indian, James Sherman later became vice president under President William Howard Taft from 1909 to 1912.[32]

In 1902, Romaldo Lachusa, a California Indian, was the first student to enter the school. Only one Hopi enrolled at this time, Chas Frederick, but in July 1902, a band of several Pima Indians from Arizona were the first group of Indian pupils to arrive from the southwest. Under the direction of Superintendent Hall, the school's first-year population exceeded 150 pupils, and a year later, the student count rose to 300. In 1903, sixteen-year-old Maude Tsapawba from the Hopi community of Toreva on Second Mesa entered Sherman Institute as the school's second Hopi student. Between 1904 and 1905, the number of pupils at Sherman Institute nearly doubled to more than 500.[33] During this period, ten Hopis attended the school, including Harry Chosnintewa-McLaw and Saul Halyne from Toreva, and Adolph Hayeauma, the only Hopi pupil from Orayvi.[34] In addition to the Indian students, "seventy five men and women" worked as "instructors in the different departments or as teachers in the school."[35]

Hall was delighted with the increase in student population, but it created logistical problems including severe overcrowding issues. In September 1904, Hall "turned away more than 200 Indian children" who sought admission at the school.[36] With 135 Indian pupils in attendance at the Indian school in Perris and 400 pupils at Sherman Institute, Hall found it difficult to admit additional students when the U.S. government provided funding for only 400 students. Several pupils turned away from Sherman were former students who arrived a few weeks late for school, only to discover that Superintendent Hall had given away their spots.[37] By the end of 1905, construction on all eleven buildings, which included the student dormitories, was nearly finished. With the completion of the school in 1906, Hall enrolled 600 students for academic and industrial training.[38]

To assimilate Hopis into American society, school officials insisted that Hopi and other Indian students learn the English language. Although many of the Hopi pupils were instructed in English at various reservation schools, including the Oraibi Day School, Toreva Day School, and Keams Canyon Boarding School, the ability to speak and read English was a critical hurdle for Hopi students to overcome.[39] Becoming proficient in a new, different, and difficult language entailed more than memorizing vocabulary and rules of grammar. David Wallace Adams observed that for Indian pupils, learning English required an innovative "way of thinking, a new way of looking at the world."[40] By studying English, Hopi understanding of American culture expanded, which left an impression on their minds that allowed them to comprehend the world and their own culture through both Hopi and Western perspectives. Government officials understood the connection between language and culture and recognized the potential of language to transform Indian pupils. Furthermore, as Amelia V. Katanski notes, non-Indian reformers believed that the "English language itself apparently possessed qualities that individuated its speakers, removing them from tribal communalism and bringing them one step closer to individual civilization."[41]

Although the Hopi people of Arizona and the Pueblo Indians of New Mexico received U.S. citizenship through the Treaty of Guadalupe Hidalgo in 1848,[42] government officials believed that certain characteristics of American citizenship needed to be developed and refined at Indian schools. Closely connected with the U.S. government's ultimate desire that Hopi students would behave and think more like American citizens, Superintendent Hall expressed hope that "Indians as a distinctive people" would "finally be lost" and that "future generation[s]" would not be "known as Indians, but all classified as American citizens."[43] Hall's sentiments mirrored the beliefs of other school officials, including Jessie F. House, a regional superintendent of Indian schools in South Dakota, who told a reporter from the *Kansas City News* that providing Indians with an American education would eliminate all "tribal Indians" by the year 1928.[44] In June 1907, while conversing about the Indians of the West, Commissioner Leupp commented that the "attitude of the government toward the American Indian" was no "longer one of paternalism." Instead, the new approach sought to "place the Indian in a position where he" would become a citizen and useful worker.[45] Government officials routinely emphasized the importance of hard work among Indian people, and even argued that Indian students must be trained to fulfill other roles besides farming. For example, at the Lake Mohonk Conference in 1908, an organization that Cherokee historian Tom Holm describes as exerting "growing political power" in Indian affairs at this time,[46] Robert

G. Valentine remarked: "In every Indian there is a workman if you can only get at him. This is testified to by the examples from twenty-seven kinds of work on which Indians are engaged within the Indian Service and from the forty different kinds of work on which they are engaged outside of the service on equal terms with white men. This is a good argument against the old idea that all Indians could and should become farmers."[47]

Government officials and other reformers believed that some Indian people would not become respectable American citizens unless they read, wrote, and spoke the English language. Therefore, the overriding emphasis of the curriculum at Sherman Institute focused on the elements required to reach full American citizenship. Teachings deemed practical, such as farming, cooking, and other industrial skills, had a fundamental role at Sherman Institute, as teachers interwove industrial training in the curriculum at each level. The subjects taught at the Indian school in Riverside resembled the curriculum used at the Hopi Reservation day schools, with daily classroom activities that varied by grade. In the early 1900s, nine grade levels had been developed at the Indian school in Riverside. The grades ranged from the primary to the eighth grade, with an additional advanced grade for students who wanted to continue their education. School officials considered eighth grade to be the final year of training, where students participated in skill-oriented learning. The younger students did not have the extent of industrial education that the older students received at the eighth and advanced grade levels.[48] A small number of Hopis who attended Sherman Institute between 1906 and 1909 returned to the reservation before they completed their education, and later asked to finish their industrial education at the school at the advanced grade level.[49]

In 1907, the *Sherman Bulletin* observed that school officials divided the primary pupils "into two sections—one just beginning to learn English and the other finishing the first reader." The ages of the students did not correspond to traditional grade levels; the average age of the second grade pupils was eleven years old. Arithmetic in the second grade classroom consisted of subtraction and the multiplication of numbers between one and three.[50] Although teachers often recited arithmetic problems verbally in the classroom, teachers required students to create problems on their own. In addition to math, school officials instructed Hopi pupils in reading and spelling, which they learned by writing and reciting words on the chalkboards and from books. Similar to the ways teachers taught white children in the public schools, the teachers at Sherman Institute incorporated songs and "interesting little stories" into the curriculum. The primary pupils sang child melodies and played games that enlivened and entertained the Indian students at the school. These activities attracted the attention of Hopi pupils who came from a culture that valued music and story telling.[51]

In the third grade, school officials used similar methods to teach Hopi pupils the same subjects found at the second grade level. Students in the fourth grade learned division problems and focused on life situations that involved the purchase and sale of goods. School officials at Sherman Institute and other off-reservation Indian boarding schools did not want their students to return home and be swindled by white traders, ranchers, or any person who sought to take advantage of Indian people. At Haskell, Myriam Vučković notes that Indian pupils "learned how to count bushels of wheat, how to calculate their worth, how to build buildings with mathematical precision, how to manage financial obligations, and how to avoid being cheated by the local trader."[52] Teachers emphasized the correct formation of sentences and encouraged students to learn words that went along their industrial training. School officials also required students to participate in writing exercises, which at times involved copying quotes from former presidents of the United States and other high-ranking government officials. One of the quotes came from Commissioner Leupp, whose saying, "The foundation of everything must be in the development of character," was used in a fourth grade classroom in September 1907.[53] At no point in the early twentieth century did teachers at Sherman Institute highlight sayings or quotes from Indian leaders. Teachers at the school administered writing exercises to the pupils to reaffirm American and Protestant values, not pride in their Native identities.

The fifth, sixth, and seventh grade classrooms at Sherman Institute provided the students with instruction in mathematics, language, spelling, composition, history, and geography. Teachers in the eighth grade and the advanced grade levels required students to use their math skills to calculate business documents and to perform other work that they considered important to a modern day farmer. These students learned number combinations up to twenty, and the teachers encouraged the pupils to calculate numbers problems out loud and on paper. School officials incorporated object lessons that included familiar household items. While this practice took place at all grade levels, it became more pronounced in the upper grades. By the time the Hopi pupils reached the eighth grade, the focus on correlating academics with industrial training intensified. At every possible juncture, teachers designed lessons to incorporate aspects of industrial training. School officials used this technique to attract and generate a desire in students to hone and practice these skills. Students read stories about farmers, blacksmiths, and shoemakers, and they constructed basic sentences and drew pictures, such as plows, farms, and saddles, that related to their industrial education. The domestic arts, such as sewing, cooking, and cleaning, were also prevalent in girls' education.[54]

The instruction at Sherman Institute covered traditional academic subjects such as math, spelling, and writing, but government officials created the school to teach Indian pupils industrial trades that they could use on the reservation. School administrators at Sherman Institute considered vocational training to be a major reason for the school's existence, and they designed the curriculum to direct the attention and energies of students toward industrial vocations. In addition to supplementing the curriculum with references to industrial occupations such as plumbing, teachers at Sherman Institute provided students with a hands-on training program. In 1907, Superintendent Hall commented that this program included instruction in farming, "blacksmithing, wagonmaking, carpentering, harnessmaking, shoemaking, tailoring, engineering, and all activities pertaining to work of boys."[55] Four miles from the school campus along the south end of Magnolia Avenue, the Sherman Ranch was intended to correct the inadequacies of similar programs found at reservation day schools. School officials more than compensated for the level of training found among the day schools, and Superintendent Hall eagerly placed as many Hopi pupils at the Ranch as possible.

Viewed by school officials as a "little training school in itself," the Ranch incorporated academics and manual labor to advance the U.S. government's policy of practical education. Hopi boys at the Ranch learned to be good American farmers, and teachers gave Hopi girls the skills needed to become skilled farm wives.[56] Covering approximately one hundred acres, Hall described the Ranch as "one of the finest bodies of land in California," located "under the most ample and largest irrigating system in southern California."[57] The boys at the Ranch were "responsible for tending the livestock, preparing the soil for planting and planting the necessary grains and vegetables. The girls' duties were those deemed necessary to running a farm household. They were taught to make butter, milk a few cows, care for some poultry, and raise vegetables necessary for the farm meals."[58] School officials wanted Hopi girls to think of themselves as future farm wives, and not as Hopi maidens. By building upon the abilities Hopis first acquired on the reservation, school officials intended the domestic and industrial instruction to assimilate Hopis into American society in a manner that would produce little resistance among the Hopi people.

Superintendent Hall often showcased the student's industrial and domestic abilities at the annual graduation commencement ceremonies. In June 1908, a *Los Angeles Times* reporter noted that at Sherman Institute the "graduating exercises" followed "original and different lines" than those commonly used at schools for white students. Rather than using a fixed program of memorized readings, students demonstrated their talents at dressmaking, "blacksmithing, harness making, cooking and engineering." Although commencement ceremonies did involve a few recitations, they focused on practical themes and included programs with the titles "What the Indian Most Needs" and "Industrial Education of the Indian."[59] Visitors at commencement thought highly of the school's industrial- and domestic-based programs. The sight of Indians in formal attire reciting patriotic poems and displaying domestic talents pleased white Americans who

believed that school officials had made progress in their attempts to civilize the Indians. Indian pupils took great pride in
their accomplishments at Sherman Institute, and many Hopi
pupils wanted to succeed at the school.[60] Former Hopi pupil
Samuel Shingoitewa recalled how proud he was to receive the
title "Expert Harness Maker" while a student at Sherman Institute in the 1920s.[61]

While the boys at the Indian school in Riverside worked in the
school's harness shop, Indian girls participated in programs
intended to provide opportunities to "soak up the dominant
American culture."[62] Closely connected with the domestic
training at Sherman Institute, the school's Outing Program
secured employment for girls and young women to work in
white-American homes in the Riverside area. David Wallace
Adams noted that the Outing Program in its "purest form was
designed to place select students for extended periods of time
in middle-class farm households, where, in exchange for their
labor, students would earn a small wage and, more importantly,
come to know firsthand the daily expectations, values, and life-
ways of their patrons."[63] But, as Adams points out, the Outing
Program "degenerated" into one that provided white families
with "cheap Indian labor." In 1917, Hopi pupil Myra Sacha-
manema from the village of Toreva worked for a white woman
named R. N. Ross in Corona, California. Although Myra only
made $4.00 per month, Ross tightly controlled the money that
Myra earned, and even deducted money from her wages if she
needed new shoes, clothes, or desired transportation to return
to the school.[64]

The idea behind the Outing Program did not originate at Sherman Institute or other off-reservation Indian boarding schools.
Historian Margaret Connell Szasz noted that in the seventeenth

century, Englishmen advocated that Algonquin children live in English homes to receive exposure to Christianity and "civility."[65] During the 1900s, school officials at Sherman Institute viewed "Outing" as a way to fulfill Riverside community's growing labor needs. Through the Outing Program, girls cooked, cleaned, washed, and took care of children for white families. School officials wanted their Indian pupils to be exposed to American influences; however, pupils usually ended up working as domestic servants. In his examination of the Phoenix Indian School, historian Robert A. Trennert Jr. observed that although government officials established outing programs at off-reservation boarding schools to "promote rapid assimilation, it evolved into a method of supplying cheap labor to white employers."[66] In the early twentieth century, Hopi girls in the Outing Program worked at least eight hours a day, six days a week, and received $10.00 or less per month. Instead of paying the pupils directly, the employer sent the money to the school, where officials kept some of the earnings and placed the rest in the student's bank account.[67] In 1908, sociologist Fayette Avery McKenzie not only advocated for outing programs, but favored the adoption of Indians by white families. "If more children could be sent to the non-reservation schools," wrote McKenzie, and "through them into white families, and if they could go earlier and stay longer, the Indian problem would be resolved so much the sooner." McKenzie further noted "it would be even better" if "many children could be sent out into [white] families ready to adopt them."[68]

McKenzie's desire for Indian pupils to live with white families echoed the sentiments of government officials in Washington DC. In 1910, former Commissioner Leupp called Pratt's establishment of an outing program at Carlisle to be his "great monument of his life work." Leupp referred to Pratt's manner of running the school's outing program as an "inspiration" that "brought the young Indian into contact with the big white world." Leupp based some of his support of the outing program on a young Sioux that he met who attended an off-reservation Indian boarding school in the fall and winter and worked on a "white man's farm" during the summer. Leupp recalled that the time the pupil spent on the farm "wore off much of his natural shyness, and taught him that there were some white people and white ways worth knowing—a fact which he had always heard denied on the reservation."[69]

In the early twentieth century, the Indian school in Riverside was one of the largest off-reservation Indian boarding schools in North America and served as a flagship Indian school for the U.S. government. Superintendent Hall wanted the public to regard Sherman Institute as the epitome of all boarding schools. Initially the school's student population came from Southern California, with only a small number of Hopis in attendance. By 1906, the Hopi population at the school increased from ten students to more than seventy. This occurred not as a result of Hall's enrollment strategies, but was due to circumstances at Orayvi that Hopi accommodators and resisters ultimately controlled.

Although all Hopis valued education, many Hopis at Orayvi did not approve of the Americanized education offered at reservation day schools and off-reservation boarding schools. Hopis detested school officials who would not allow their children to speak Hopi and opposed U.S. government attempts to undermine the authority and centrality of Hopi culture through Indian schools. Concerned that the assimilation of Hopi children into mainstream American society would have a negative effect on the Hopi people, Hopi parents and village leaders at Orayvi not only opposed the U.S. government but resisted each other, as no definite consensus on the school issue was present among the people. By the early twentieth century, the internal Hopi division intensified and Hopi leaders concluded that due to the constant friction the two factions could no longer live in the same village. Listening to the pleas of Christian missionaries and addressing the situation as Hopi people, leaders and elders of Orayvi agreed to settle the dispute according to Hopi customs, which did not involve guns, knives, or other weapons intended to kill. Their solution to the problem would have a major impact on Hopi society and directly affect the future of Hopi children at off-reservation Indian boarding schools.

3. The Orayvi Split and Hopi Schooling

On September 8, 1906, shortly after the sun rose over the Hopi mesas, the two Hopi factions gathered outside Orayvi and engaged in a tug-of-war that forever changed the future of the Hopi people.[1] While more than five hundred Hopi men gathered outside the village,[2] Hopi leaders poured a line of cornmeal on the ground and the two groups positioned themselves on each side of the marker.[3] Leigh J. Kuwanwisiwma, whose grandfathers participated in the Hopi dispute, recalled that Tawaquaptewa (leader of the accommodators) and Youkeoma (leader of the resisters) stood "chest to chest" near the center of the line while their followers pushed and pulled them from behind.[4] Attempting to keep their leader from crossing over the line, the Hopi factions understood that whichever group lost the confrontation would be forced to leave the village. Many Hopis received injuries when others pulled, pushed, grabbed, or scratched them in the commotion. Furthermore, children who observed the battle from a distance saw their fathers, uncles, and grandfathers shoving each other from opposite sides. Kuwanwisiwma noted that the battle "went on for hours" until the accommodating Hopis pulled Youkeoma over the line and demanded that every resisting Hopi family leave the village. Hopis whose family members lived at Orayvi during this time recalled that men, women, and children wept as their relatives quickly gathered their belongings and left for a campsite two miles west of Orayvi. A few hours later, some of the resisting Hopi families returned to the village for food and clothes, but the Hopi accommodators told them to "get out" for they had "no business" at Orayvi anymore.[5]

The Hopi separation stands out in Native American history as a representative situation brought upon American Indians through the imposition of U.S. government policies that had significant, lasting consequences for Indian communities. The Hopi split resulted in rapid change for all Hopi people, particularly for the children who grew up in the drama. One of these children was six-year-old Na-kah-who-ma, also known as Fred Kabotie, whose family was among the resisting families at Orayvi.[6] Fred was originally from the village of Shungopavi, but his family followed Youkeoma to Orayvi when he was small. Not long after the split, government officials required Fred to attend the Santa Fe Indian School in New Mexico. At the Indian school in Santa Fe, Fred's fifth grade teacher, Elizabeth W. DeHuff, encouraged and nurtured his artistic talents.[7] Fred would later become one of the great Hopi artists of the twentieth century.

As demonstrated in the life of Fred Kabotie, Hopi divisions did not result in only negative consequences. In Hopi culture, divisions are thought to bring about good, eliminate evil, and fulfill Hopi prophecy.[8] Whether contention over spoken words, ill thoughts, or opposing opinions, Hopi divisions develop for a reason and purpose that is often not realized until many years have passed. While causes for this particular split are numerous, one cause was a recent smallpox epidemic that ravaged Hopi villages and left many Hopis outraged at the deadly effects the disease had on their people. In December 1898, less than four years before government officials began classes at Sherman Institute, smallpox broke out throughout the villages on First Mesa. When news of the virus reached G. W. Hayzlett, Indian agent of the Moqui Indians, Hayzlett immediately stationed a group of Indian police between Second and Third Mesa to prevent the spread of the disease. The police consisted of several Navajo men who had been involved with the forced removal of Hopi children to U.S. government schools. Once the Navajo police established a quarantine, Hayzlett instructed Samuel E. Shoemaker, "head farmer" in "charge of the Moqui Indians," to immediately go to the villages and assess the situation.[9] Attempting to eradicate the epidemic, Shoemaker and other officials burned the clothes of infected Hopis and fumigated their homes.[10] Many resisting Hopis refused to comply with U.S. government physicians, interfered with officials by not obeying their commands, and insisted that Hopis abandon Western practices of medicine for traditional Hopi remedies.[11] For more than a thousand years, Hopi medicine men had cured all sorts of ailments through prayers and ceremonies, and they called on the people to once again rely on their culture. In his examination of U.S. government physicians and the Navajo people, historian Robert A. Trennert Jr. observed that, "unlike the Hopi traditionalist, Navajos actively sought out [smallpox] vaccinations," which "prevented the debacle" that occurred among the Hopis in 1898.[12]

Worried that the resisting faction would create further problems with government officials, Hayzlett called on the Office of Indian Affairs for "military assistance" and requested enough soldiers to subdue the resisters.[13] Officials in Washington permitted Hayzlett's request and sent a group of thirty soldiers on horseback from Fort Wingate, New Mexico, to the First Mesa villages in Arizona. When they arrived on Hopi land, they found several resisting Hopis who refused to be washed in an acid-based water solution and who rejected the U.S. government's provision of new clothes. Eventually, U.S. government troops restrained the noncompliant Hopis without injury and arrested "eight of the leaders" of the resisting faction. According to Hayzlett, "had it not been for a few of such leaders," no "serious" trouble would have been incurred.[14] Although officials had supposedly convinced the majority of the Hopis that the "civilized mode of treatment for the sick" was superior to their tribal remedies, they told them that if "another outbreak of the disease" occurred, they should submit and "receive treatment" from health officials.[15]

By April 1899, over 600 Hopis on First and Second Mesa had been infected with smallpox, and 187 of them had died.[16] Hopis from both factions suffered from the disease, although a greater number of resisting Hopis died in the epidemic. A quarantine protected Hopi children who attended reservation schools from the smallpox outbreak, but when government officials allowed the children to return to their villages several months later, some discovered that their parents or other family members had passed away.[17] Although the U.S. government's account of the 1898 Hopi smallpox outbreak is partially addressed in the Annual Report of the Commissioner of Indian Affairs in 1899, Hopis have preserved their own memories of the event in oral and written forms. Edmund Nequatewa, a former Hopi student who attended the Keams Canyon Boarding School in 1898, remembered that when the epidemic reached Second Mesa, U.S. government agents "condemned" the entire reservation and established a boundary between the school and the villages. Edmund recalled that Navajo policemen went "back and forth day and night" and refused to permit people to travel beyond their homes.[18]

As a result of the U.S. government's mandatory quarantine, school officials did not allow Edmund's grandfather to visit him at the Keams Canyon School until the following year. When Edmund returned home in the summer of 1899, he saw many Hopis who were infected with smallpox and commented that their "faces were all speckled" and difficult to identify. Edmund's immediate family was spared from death, but his aunts succumbed to the disease.[19] Albert Yava, a Hopi-Tewa from Hano on First Mesa, also attended the Keams Canyon School when smallpox reached the villages. Albert remembered that government officials "isolated the schoolchildren" to keep them away from family members who had been infected with the disease. On Second Mesa, so many of the Hopis became ill that only a small number of people remained to bury the dead. Albert recalled that Hopis who were well enough to assist the dead "disposed of the bodies" by placing them in "rock crevices." When Albert returned home in 1899, he realized that many people had perished, and those Hopis who survived "struggled to get enough [food] to eat."[20]

The epidemic weakened the already deteriorating relationship between the Hopi resisters and the accommodators. While government officials blamed the high number of Hopi deaths on the noncompliant resisting faction, some Hopi resisters held that Hopi spirits punished them with smallpox for the Hopi accommodators' decision to send their children to U.S. government schools and accept American ways. In Hopi culture, breaking traditional laws or teachings results in consequences such as illness and death. Although Kikmongwi Loololma rejected this interpretation of the epidemic, Chief Youkeoma used his belief that the disease was a form of retribution to strengthen his case against the Hopi accommodators and the U.S. government. The

Hopi accommodators used smallpox to their advantage, as well. Helen Sekaquaptewa recalled that when the epidemic came to Shungopavi, the accommodators seized the opportunity to take "matters in their own hands" and "forced several of the most difficult resisting families out of the village." The exiled Hopis "went over to Oraibi where they were welcomed and taken in by the Oraibi" resisters.[21] This increased the resisting population at Orayvi in size, influence, and strength, which furthered the division among the people and set the stage for the final act of separation at Orayvi in September 1906.[22]

Between 1900 and early 1906, tensions at Orayvi increased between the two factions.[23] Anthropologist Richard O. Clemmer noted that after the smallpox epidemic ended in 1899, the Hopi resisters "began holding their own ceremonies at Oraibi, making their own paraphernalia and persisting in their opposition to the schools."[24] When Kikmongwi Loololma died in 1904, Tawaquaptewa, "one of [Loololma's] eldest sister's sons,"[25] became Loololma's successor and knowingly "inherited the quarrel" between the two factions.[26] The resisters at Orayvi considered Tawaquaptewa to be weaker than Loololma, and they used this change in leadership as a strategic opportunity to invite additional Hopi resisters from Shungopavi to live at the village. Although Tawaquaptewa was against the "invitation" of additional resisters, Youkeoma encouraged his followers to ignore Tawaquaptewa and welcomed a number of resister families from Shungopavi to live in Orayvi.[27] Orayvi's thousand residents were deeply divided as the two chiefs openly opposed each other.[28]

Since the establishment of the Hopi Reservation in 1882, the U.S. government's interest in Hopi affairs had grown. As the tensions at Orayvi escalated, Indian agents on the Hopi Reservation kept government officials in Washington DC apprised of the situation. A few months prior to the Orayvi Split, Commissioner Leupp traveled to Orayvi and attempted to gain information on the situation between the resisters and the accommodators. After an unsuccessful conversation with Youkeoma, Leupp tried to meet with Tawaquaptewa. At night, three Hopi men followed Leupp down the path that led from Orayvi to a "principal cottage at the foot of the mesa." When Leupp arrived at the cottage, the three men forced their way into the house and, upon lighting a small torch, Leupp realized that the men included Tawaquaptewa and "two of his supporters." Leupp recalled that one of the Hopi men spoke English and volunteered to serve as their interpreter. Tawaquaptewa spoke first and told Leupp that he would like to ask him a few questions without the presence of white men and Hopi resisters. Tawaquaptewa asked Leupp about his role in the U.S. government. Leupp responded that he was the commissioner of Indian affairs, "in charge of the people of his race all over the country," and that he had come from Washington. When Tawaquaptewa asked why Leupp had visited Orayvi, Leupp told him that he wanted to witness with his "own eyes the condition of the Oraibi Indians—how they were living, how white employees of the government were taking care of them, and so on."[29]

The commissioner's words did not sit well with Tawaquaptewa, for Tawaquaptewa hoped that Leupp intended to end the conflict between the resisters and the accommodators. Leupp informed Tawaquaptewa that he did not mean to solve the quarrel for it would take more time than he had to spend. Instead, Leupp wanted Tawaquaptewa and Youkeoma to settle their "difference" as white men settled their "disputes," which involved "talk[ing] things over," and solving their problems with each other, instead of "falling back, like so many little children, upon the government." According to Leupp, Tawaquaptewa desired to know when the commissioner would get rid of the Hopi resisters in Orayvi and "send them away to a distant place" so that the Hopis could "divide their land and other property" among the accommodators. Leupp assured Tawaquaptewa that he did not plan to punish the Hopi resisters. The Hopi chief, however, did not believe the commissioner, and he told Leupp that he was skeptical of his reply. Tawaquaptewa knew that Indian agents kept officials in Washington informed about the situation at Orayvi and realized that Leupp had more knowledge about the Hopi conflicts than he indicated. In spite of this, Leupp insisted that he would not take action, and rebuked Tawaquaptewa for not trusting him.[30]

When Tawaquaptewa heard Leupp's response, he and the other Hopi men left the house with a "rather discouraged air." Frustrated with the "ignorant" Tawaquaptewa, Leupp traveled back to Orayvi to strategize with government agents whom Leupp believed to be "intelligent" white people. Following a discussion with government officials whom Leupp viewed as superior to the Indians, the commissioner concluded that only a show of military force would alleviate the tensions between the resisting and accommodating factions.[31] Leupp's plan for resolution through the use of military force did not reflect the advice that he gave Tawaquaptewa to discuss things with Youkeoma as levelheaded men and to settle the dispute in a civilized manner like white Americans. It should also be noted that Tawaquaptewa, not Leupp, made the initial effort to meet and talk with the commissioner and that the two Hopi factions eventually settled their problems without using weapons. In this regard, the Hopi groups acted more civilized than Leupp.

After Leupp visited the Hopi Reservation and then the Pacific Northwest, he returned to Washington DC and wrote about his visit among the Hopis. "The Indians at Oraibi Agency, in Arizona, are somewhat hostile in their attitude," said Leupp. The commissioner remarked that since Hopi men work during the day, the "meeting had to be at night." Leupp described that he "climbed up to their dwelling place, with the scene lighted by only the stars, and listened to their grievances."[32]

Although much has been written on the Orayvi Split, including Peter M. Whiteley's two-volume account in 2008, additional documents have since emerged that shed light on Youkeoma's interpretation of the event. In 1911, government officials from the U.S. Army and the Indian Service interviewed Youkeoma in a kiva about his understanding and recollection of the Hopi division.[33] In the interview, Youkeoma recalled that he was chief throughout Burton's administration, and that he had been one among several resisting Hopis whom Collins arrested in 1894.[34] When U.S. government agents attempted to send Youkeoma's children to school, Youkeoma adamantly refused to comply and stated that he had to follow the traditions of the Hopi people. Seeing that Youkeoma honored Hopi ways and did not submit to the wishes of the U.S. government, many Hopis from the resisting faction chose him as their leader, which he accepted in accordance with Hopi custom.[35] In Youkeoma's opinion, the "new ways" of the white man would not survive; only ancient Hopi customs lasted forever.

This manner of thinking influenced Youkeoma's understanding of the Hopi dispute, and it provided the conceptual framework for his dealings with the U.S. government. Youkeoma believed that regardless of what happened in this world, Hopi traditions would endure. In spite of Youkeoma's belief that Hopi traditions would not cease, Youkeoma also lived in the present and found himself deeply concerned over issues that involved government-run education and the U.S. government's attacks on the Hopi way of life. Believing that the U.S. government wanted Hopis to "go back to the bad ways of the underworld," Youkeoma argued that government officials in Washington should not have molested Hopis, but should have encouraged them to live their lives according to Hopi ways.[36]

A day after the Hopi people declared Youkeoma to be chief, Herman Kampmeier, a teacher at the Oraibi Day School, forced his way into Youkeoma's house and asked the chief to send his children to school. Youkeoma declined to do so, and in response, Kampmeier dragged the chief "out of the house" and "threw" him "down to the second story." Once Youkeoma picked himself up, Kampmeier took Youkeoma to where the other government officials and Christian missionaries had gathered. Heinrich Voth, A. H. Viets of the Oraibi Day School, and Navajo police held Youkeoma down while Kampmeier cut his hair and told him that they no longer considered him to be a Hopi chief.[37] Angry at Youkeoma's noncompliant attitude, government officials sent the chief and the Hopi pupils to the Keams Canyon School, where they repaired roads for three months.[38] Although Youkeoma did not reveal the exact reason why officials insisted on sending him to Keams Canyon, U.S. government agents and missionaries may have wanted to prevent him from causing additional trouble with compliant Hopis or government officials at other villages.[39]

When Youkeoma returned to the village of Shungopavi on Second Mesa, Indian Agent Theodore G. Lemmon sent Navajo police to arrest Youkeoma and convince him to send his children to government schools. As the Navajo police arrived at Shungopavi, Youkeoma and the other resisting leaders fled into a kiva. When Lemmon told the Hopi men to exit the kiva, the men insisted on remaining inside. Realizing that the resisting Hopis did not intend to come out, Lemmon instructed Navajo police to detach the top door of the kiva. Youkeoma and the other men eventually emerged, but they refused to give up their children. Once Youkeoma climbed out of the kiva, Navajo police clubbed him unconscious and he remained in that state for many hours. That evening, as soon as Youkeoma regained consciousness, he returned with his nephews to Orayvi.[40] From Orayvi, Youkeoma organized the Hopi resisters and increased efforts to challenge government officials and their perceived allies, the Hopi accommodators.

In the first week of September 1906, Youkeoma assembled his followers together and told them that Hopi prophesy had foretold that the accommodating Hopis would be forced out of Orayvi without injuries or weapons. Youkeoma instructed his followers not to hurt anyone, even if the opposition attacked them with guns, clubs, or knives.[41] In the days just prior to the split, missionaries asked the Hopi accommodators to refrain from using weapons, as this would cause excessive bloodshed and distress among the people. However, some accommodators, unaware that Youkeoma had told the resisters not to use force, worried that Youkeoma and his followers would use wooden bats and did not want to face them unprepared. Seeing the potential for a disastrous outcome, missionaries implored Youkeoma and Tawaquaptewa to meet to resolve the situation.

The two chiefs agreed to convene at a small home at Orayvi. When Tawaquaptewa entered the house, he told everyone who was not Hopi to leave. About twelve Hopis remained in the house. Tawaquaptewa then questioned Youkeoma about his future plans for the resisting faction. Specifically, Tawaquaptewa desired to know if Youkeoma intended to keep the Hopi resisters from Second Mesa at Orayvi. Tawaquaptewa feared that the increased number of resisting Hopis in Orayvi would deepen the tensions between the two groups. Furthermore, Tawaquaptewa worried that there would not be enough food in the village for additional families. Youkeoma confirmed that his followers from Second Mesa would remain with him at Orayvi. This information did not surprise Tawaquaptewa, but it validated what he already knew to be true. Tawaquaptewa told Youkeoma that he and his fellow Hopi resisters would not be welcomed in Orayvi, but would be driven out of the village by him and the accommodating Hopis.[42]

As the meeting intensified, Tawaquaptewa's right hand man, Frank Seumptewa from Moencopi, grabbed Youkeoma and threw him off his chair and onto the floor.[43] Two men from the resisting faction immediately stood up and tried to block the entrance of the door. The situation worsened, and fighting ensued as the accommodating Hopis sought to force Youkeoma and his group out of the village. Youkeoma recalled that a great "struggle resulted" as both sides kicked and hit one another with tightly clenched fists. The fight continued outside, and when Tawaquaptewa and his band finally managed to drive the resisting Hopis north of Orayvi, well outside the village, the two groups argued about Hopi ways and customs. Youkeoma shouted that Tawaquaptewa was "no longer Chief" and therefore he "had no right to the lands" at Orayvi. Youkeoma then bellowed that Tawaquaptewa and the accommodating Hopis would be forced to abandon Orayvi as well, because it had been foretold in a prophesy that when a great division occurred among the people, the village of Orayvi would no longer exist.[44]

According to Youkeoma, the conflict ended when he, not Tawaquaptewa, drew a line on the ground and stepped over it, which signified that he and the other resisters agreed to leave Orayvi of their own volition.[45] Youkeoma's recollection of the event did not acknowledge a violent struggle in the final moments of the standoff. This interpretation placed Youkeoma in complete control of the situation. By Youkeoma's account, he willingly stepped over the line to end the feud. As Helen Sekaquaptewa remembered the event, after the fervent argument, when Youkeoma etched a line in the sandstone just outside of the village, he challenged Tawaquaptewa by saying, "Well, it will have to be this way now. If you [are able to] pass me over this line, then I will walk." According to Sekaquaptewa, Tawaquaptewa "immediately jumped to the challenge" and the two chiefs physically pushed each other back and forth until the accommodating Hopis successfully exerted enough strength to pull Youkeoma over the line.[46]

Within minutes of the Hopi battle, Tawaquaptewa and his band forced 102 resisting families to leave the village.[47] As Youkeoma left Orayvi, he told the accommodating Hopis that they had been "following the Witch" (Tawaquaptewa) and had been diminished into the wicked ways of the Underworld where people of evil hearts remained.[48] After cursing the accommodating Hopis, the resisting band traveled nearly four miles to Hotevilla on Third Mesa, chopped down several cedar trees to make room for their shelters, and set up camp.[49] That night, the resisters gathered around a fire and several Hopis asked Youkeoma what would happen next. Youkeoma told his followers that U.S. government soldiers would "come and take him prisoner or kill him." Youkeoma instructed the Hopis to not "follow him unless brave enough to stand the consequences"

and declared that he would never "part from his old Hopi traditions."[50]

On September 9, 1906, one day following the split, Superintendent Lemmon responded to the situation at Orayvi by recom-
mending to Commissioner Leupp that the Hopi resisters build
"two villages" on opposite ends of the reservation. He further
suggested that government officials remove Tawaquaptewa and
Youkeoma to a location off the reservation, perhaps a prison,
where they would not be able to instigate additional troubles.
Lemmon also noted that the U.S. government should establish a
"smaller village" for the most "superstitious" Hopis (resisters),
and that all of the religious leaders ought to be eliminated from
these villages. He added that in his opinion, the priests who
were the most conservative and therefore the most problematic
to the U.S. government's efforts needed to be disposed of to
maintain control in the resisting Hopi community. As long as
the priests remained in the village, the ability of white agents
to maintain peaceful relationships among the Hopis would
diminish. Therefore, Lemmon declared that only the "more
intelligent" or progressive, accommodating Hopis, should be
allowed to dwell in a superior community, while the ignorant
and resisting Hopis had to reside in a lesser village.[51]

Shortly after Lemmon's report, Matthew Murphy, superintendent of the Western Navajo agency, offered his recommendation
for the Hopi situation. As an Indian agent with the U.S. government, Murphy's sphere of authority included Moencopi, a satellite village of Orayvi, and the close association between the two
villages provided him with inside knowledge of the events that
had developed on Third Mesa. In his statement, Murphy advised
government officials to eliminate Tawaquaptewa's chieftainship.
Murphy further suggested that an "Indian judge be appointed

by the superintendent in charge, subject to the approval of the Commissioner of Indian Affairs."[52] Murphy intended to break apart the practice of chieftainship within Hopi society. In the early twentieth century, government officials attempted to appoint Hopi judges at the villages to administer U.S. government policies and to secure Hopi compliance. Officials believed that they had given Hopi leaders power to act as judges over their people, but this authority existed before Europeans and white Americans arrived on Hopi lands. Furthermore, Murphy reported that the U.S. government should exile Youkeoma and the other Hopi resister leaders off the reservation, and that their banishment should last indefinitely. Finally, and most devastating to Hopi society because of its communal understanding of land ownership, Murphy recommended that after the resisting faction acknowledged the authority of the Indian judge, the U.S. government should immediately survey parcels of land at Orayvi and prepare to distribute individual allotments.[53]

In the month following the Orayvi Split, government officials did not bother the resisting Hopis at Hotevilla. By mid-October, however, armed soldiers bullied Hopis with weapons, threats, and demands. Helen Sekaquaptewa remembered that she and other Hopi resisters at Hotevilla "awoke to find" her "camp surrounded by troops" accompanied by Superintendent Lemmon. The superintendent informed the men of the village that "it was a mistake to follow" Youkeoma in ignorance, and that the "government had reached the limit of its patience." Their children, Lemmon told them, "would have to go to school."[54] Edmund Nequatewa recalled that some of the Hopi resister children who moved to Hotevilla had already been enrolled at the Oraibi Day School. When government officials tried to force the children to return to the Oraibi Day School, their parents refused to comply and stated that since they no longer lived at Orayvi, they did not have to send their children back to the school. But the soldiers and Navajo policemen possessed guns, and despite their protests, some of the people at Hotevilla believed they had no choice but to cooperate with government officials.[55]

In late October 1906, U.S. government agents stationed near the Oraibi Day School called on Tawaquaptewa to give his opinion about the Hopi division. When officials asked Tawaquaptewa through an interpreter why he forced Youkeoma and the resisters out of Orayvi, Tawaquaptewa explained that "before the white men had built schools, everything had been going all right."[56] Once the U.S. government constructed schools, and required Hopi children to attend these schools, Hopi factions developed and tensions between the two groups intensified. Since Youkeoma refused to comply with the wishes of the U.S. government, Tawaquaptewa blamed him for the problems that led to the Orayvi Split and, ultimately, gave Youkeoma's noncompliance as the reason for driving him out of the village.[57]

That same month, Supervisor Reuben Perry visited Hotevilla with Tawaquaptewa. According to Hopi oral tradition, Perry "set up a duel" between Tawaquaptewa and Youkeoma to weaken the influence and beliefs of both chiefs. Older Hopis recalled that Reuben gave Tawaquaptewa a loaded pistol and told him to shoot Youkeoma, but Tawaquaptewa refused to murder the resisting chief. Anthropologist Peter M. Whiteley observed that "Perry's intention, apparently, was to publicly expose the unwillingness of both leaders" to kill one another and to "undermine their authority."[58] Hopi informants at a Hopi Hearing in 1955 recalled that Perry told Tawaquaptewa and Youkeoma that "from that day on," they were no longer chiefs, and could never again be known as "leaders of their people."[59] Perry did not understand that, as a non-Hopi, he did not have power to remove either man from his position.

On November 4, 1906, Perry and a group of armed soldiers gathered around Hotevilla and captured eighty-two of the children from resisting Hopi families. Against the wishes of their parents, Perry forced the children to the Keams Canyon School and arrested fifty-three of the Hopi resisting men who refused to allow their children to be taken away. When Perry told the Hopi men that he would allow them to return to Orayvi if they agreed to send their children to school, twenty-five reluctantly agreed to his proposition.[60] At that time in Hopi history, life was extremely difficult at Hotevilla. Living in makeshift tents, eating little food, and not knowing what U.S. government agents would do next, the Hopis who consented to Perry's proposition did so to survive. Perry ordered the men to sign a contract written in English to demonstrate their compliance. The agreement stipulated that the resisters could remain in Orayvi as long as they lived in "peace and harmony" with the accommodating faction and permitted their children to attend school until they reached twenty years of age. Furthermore, it mandated that the Hopi resisters had to "submit and obey" U.S. government commands and to help bring "justice" to noncompliant Hopis who strayed from the articles that were set forth in the agreement.[61]

Shortly after Perry required the Hopi resisters to sign the contract, government officials arrested Youkeoma and sixteen other resisting men and imprisoned them at Fort Huachuca in southern Arizona, where they remained until October 1907.[62] In the same year, officials sent a "dozen or more men in their early thirties" from Hotevilla to the Indian school at Carlisle.[63] One of the Hopis who went to Carlisle was Louis Tewanima, the great long distance runner from Second Mesa. Government officials considered Tewanima and the others to be promising leaders. Many of these men were married and had children, yet government officials forced them to attend the school for five years.[64]

Officials dealt with Tawaquaptewa in a similar manner: they sent him to the Indian school in Riverside to break down Hopi culture by attempting to assimilate a Hopi chief into American society. According to Commissioner Leupp and other government officials, Tawaquaptewa had gone against the U.S. legal system and acted in an un-American fashion when he demanded that the Hopi resisters leave the village,[65] because in American society, it was against the law to forcibly remove a white family from their home. Officials determined his guilt, rather than a trial by his peers. Government officials turned against Tawaquaptewa, attempted to strip him of his chieftainship,[66] and threatened to send him to a military prison if he did not willingly attend an off-reservation boarding school.[67]

When government officials, including Commissioner Leupp and President Theodore Roosevelt,[68] forced Tawaquaptewa to choose between the Phoenix Indian School and Sherman Institute, Tawaquaptewa chose the Indian school in Riverside because many children of the resisting Hopi families attended the Phoenix school. He wanted to avoid further and unnecessary conflict and trouble that would surely emerge if he resided at the same school as the resisting faction. Tawaquaptewa desired that the transition to life off Hopi land would be as smooth as possible for the Hopi children, and so he chose to be exiled at Sherman Institute, not at the Indian school in Phoenix.

The division at Orayvi affected more than Hopi leaders, parents, and adult members of the Hopi community. Tensions between children of the two factions also escalated and became evident at the reservation schools. Helen Sekaquaptewa recalled that the "attitude of the parents carried over to their children," which was evidenced "on the school [play]grounds." The children from accommodating families made fun of the children from resisting families, called them names, and refused to allow them to participate in games. Helen remembered that when she and the resisting children walked up the trail to Orayvi after school, accommodating children waited at the top of the mesa and attacked the resisting children with rocks.[69] The drama that unfolded on the reservation caused children to remain fiercely loyal to that side chosen by their families, and this allegiance did not stop at the boundaries of the Hopi Reservation. Tawaquaptewa realized that many parents from the accommodating faction would later opt to send their children to the school that he chose; therefore he needed to select a school that would give the children the optimum ability to thrive and succeed without the pressures of resisting friction. Government officials also realized that if they placed accommodating children with resisting children at the same school, it would result in problems among the students. To ensure that the resisting children would not have a negative influence on the accommodating children, and to prevent further divisions among the pupils, officials placed the two groups at different schools and honored Tawaquaptewa's request to be placed with the Hopis at Sherman Institute.

Although rarely observed, the U.S. government's policy of allowing the presence of Indian chiefs at off-reservation boarding schools was not an entirely new practice. In August 1888, Crazy Head, a leader of the Crow Nation, enrolled at Carlisle, where officials noted that his "record as a warrior and ability as a chief are quite well known by many of the boys at the school from different tribes."[70] Sent to Carlisle to learn the "white man's ways," Crazy Head also had a positive impact on the Crow students at the school.[71]

When government officials sent Tawaquaptewa to Sherman Institute in November 1906, the Orayvi chief followed in the footsteps of Crazy Head, who used his power and influence to support and encourage those pupils under his care. But Tawaquaptewa was more than a leader to the Indian pupils at Sherman Institute. He came to the Indian school in Riverside as an elder and as an individual who provided the Hopis and other Indian pupils with wise counsel and perspective. He had learned how to deal with government officials and Christian missionaries in the past. He knew how to navigate in and around U.S. government Indian policies, and he understood the importance for Hopi children to receive an education beyond the mesas. Although Tawaquaptewa understood that government officials had sent him to school to learn English and appreciate the supposed superiority of American culture, he chose to enroll at Sherman Institute to encourage and lead the Hopi pupils under his care. In this regard, Tawaquaptewa continued as kikmongwi at an institution that was designed to destroy Hopi and other American Indian cultures.

4. Elder in Residence

In November 1906, two months after the Orayvi Split, government officials took advantage of the turmoil on Third Mesa and sent nearly seventy Hopis from Orayvi to Sherman Institute. Wearing tattered clothes, "cheap shoes, homemade flour sack shirts" and worn out pants, the "wild-looking band from the mesas" reflected an image and people the U.S. government intended to change.[1] And change they did. Under the umbrella and protection of Indian education, the young Hopis from Orayvi entered a school that altered the way they saw themselves, their people, and the world in which they lived. But unlike the first Hopi who came to Sherman Institute in 1902, the students who traveled by wagon to Winslow, Arizona, and then boarded a Santa Fe train to Southern California in 1906 did not endure the academic and cultural challenges alone. Accompanied by their kikmongwi, Tawaquaptewa, his wife, Nasumgoens, their daughter, Mina, and other Hopi leaders, the pupils had the stability, encouragement, and influence needed for their survival and success.[2]

With the headline "Mokis at Last in School," the *Los Angeles Times* reported that Tawaquaptewa had "adopted the Sherman uniform in place of the richly embroidered blanket, buckskin leggings and moccasins which he wore upon his arrival at the school." To create room for the Hopi students, Superintendent Hall sent "fifty boys and girls of mixed Indian blood" back to their reservations. Possessing at least one-fourth "Indian blood," these students could legally attend a federal off-reservation Indian boarding school, but schooling the Hopis had become a major priority for the U.S. government. The newspaper account stated that the "experiment of educating the Moki Indians at the school is being watched with particular interest, as they are one of the most primitive tribes in the United States, clinging to the same modes of living they are believed to have followed a thousand years ago." The reporter described the Hopi students as "primitive," but the pupils would prove their intelligence and abilities and demonstrate agency at the school with their kikmongwi present to help them navigate and excel in this new environment.[3]

The Hopi pupils composed a large tribal representation at the school of six hundred, second only to the so-called California Mission Indians.[4] For many of the Hopi students, Sherman Institute became synonymous with the "land of oranges," a term used by Hopi pupils to describe the abundant orange groves in Southern California. In the early twentieth century, Hopis circulated stories on the reservation about the oranges at the school, and how the exotic fruit "existed by the wagon load."[5] Hopi student Polingaysi Qoyawayma from Orayvi recalled that teachers at the Oraibi Day School showed a group of Hopi youth pictures of orange trees that stood "heavy with fruit." Teachers told the children that oranges in Riverside looked like "peaches on the Hopi peach trees, only much larger."[6]

With an estimated five hundred people in Orayvi after the split, hardships on families and the community resulted when the pupils left for school. Primarily an agricultural society, the people of Orayvi relied on the annual harvest of corn, beans, various types of squash, and wheat for their survival.

Families on the reservation needed every available hand to plant and harvest their crops. In the social world of the Hopis, boys worked alongside their fathers in the fields; once the boys left for school, their fathers no longer had their seasonal help. Hopi mothers lost their daughters' help to the school's Outing Program. Apart from the physical hardships resulting from their children's absence, parents prophesied and worried that their children would be overtaken by the white man's culture and want nothing to do with the Hopi way. For some, this worry came true, but most Hopi students returned home to contribute to their family and village community.

In 1906, Indian education in the United States focused heavily on industrial training. Influenced by policies drafted by Superintendent of Indian Schools Estelle Reel, the Office of Indian Affairs urged school superintendents and teachers to "eliminate from the curriculum everything of an unpractical nature" and to modify "instruction to local conditions and immediate and practical needs of the pupils."[7] Indian boarding schools did not exist to create Indian scholars, medical doctors, professors, lawyers, or future business leaders. Instead, U.S. government policy directed Indian education toward the practical, emphasizing skills that would be useful for Indian students once they returned to the reservation. For Hopi students at Sherman Institute, their practical education involved various industrial programs. School officials instructed Hopi pupils in agriculture and leather- and metalworking and reinforced the importance of work and the value of earning and saving money.

Along with the industrial training, government officials educated Indians "along natural lines," which stood in contrast to the complete transformation approach found in Indian education during the 1880s and 1890s. Encouraging teachers to take from Indian culture only that which encouraged the learning of white civilization, the Office of Indian Affairs expected teachers to have a basic knowledge of Indian ways and develop lessons accordingly, bearing in mind that the "value of education to any child" would be "measured by its usefulness to him in later life."[8] This change in methodology did not come quickly to Sherman Institute, as "several of the teachers" at the school failed to "realize the importance of adapting the instruction to meet the needs of their pupils."[9] The amount of Hopi culture incorporated into the curriculum largely depended on the teacher. Although school officials allowed Hopi culture in the classroom if it took the form of Hopi arts or crafts, it never became a major element at the school. Instead, school officials required teachers to center their instruction on academic subjects, such as math, history, or English.

Tawaquaptewa had, at best, a very basic understanding of English when he arrived at Sherman Institute in 1906.[10] Although he had conversed with government agents and missionaries on the reservation, he did so with the help of an interpreter. Tawaquaptewa knew the power of language and he knew that Hopi success depended on the ability to communicate with white government officials, Christian missionaries, traders, and tourists. What Tawaquaptewa lacked in English grammatical skills, he quickly made up for during his three-year stay at the Indian school in Riverside. Learning English "in less than five months," Tawaquaptewa motivated his Hopi followers at the school. In response, Hopi students made "mark[ed] improvements in their language lessons" and outpaced other pupils in language acquisition.[11] With a "mature mind and determination to master" the English language, Tawaquaptewa "expressed a strong desire that all the Hopi pupils" would follow his example in each of their academic and industrial endeavors.[12]

The younger Hopi pupils attended class together, but Tawaquaptewa and his wife, Nasumgoens, belonged to a class designed to teach adult students. Although school officials still considered them "primary pupils," and adult students practiced the "same lines in spelling as the regular primary" classes, in math they incorporated "number work" and used "familiar objects and materials for exercises."[13] By using objects and materials familiar to the older students, teachers related lessons in math with life situations on the Hopi Reservation. For some of the students, knowledge of basic math was valuable for agricultural purposes, especially when Hopi farmers sold crops and purchased seed on the mesas. As time went on, math skills assisted Hopi men and women when they made and sold their beautiful art and crafts to white tourists visiting the reservation.

Standing Rock Sioux writer Vine Deloria Jr. once remarked that for Native people, "elders are the best living examples of what the end product of education and life experiences should be." Deloria observed that the "elder exemplifies both the good and the bad experiences of life, and in witnessing their failures as much as their successes we are cushioned in our despair of disappointment and bolstered in our exuberance of success."[14] At Sherman Institute, Tawaquaptewa clearly wanted the Hopi pupils to witness and learn from his success in both industrial and academic programs. Five months after Tawaquaptewa arrived in Riverside, the *Sherman Bulletin* reported that "in light of the large amount of school material yet to be mastered, Chief Tawaquaptewa," a member of Mrs. Harvey's adult class, made "remarkable progress."[15] In a letter to Commissioner Leupp dated February 4, 1907, Superintendent Hall commented on Tawaquaptewa's progress and stated that the "Chief has impressed everyone here as being a mighty good character—so anxious to do what is right."[16] Hall frequently corresponded with Leupp about Tawaquaptewa's progress. Leupp insisted that Hall keep him informed on Tawaquaptewa's performance, both academically and in his overall attitude. Leupp realized early on that Hopi cooperation at the school depended on Tawaquaptewa's positive leadership. Regardless of the U.S. government's assimilation and acculturation agenda for Tawaquaptewa, the Hopi leader applied his chieftainship to each Hopi student at the school. In April 1907, the *Sherman Bulletin* reported that Tawaquaptewa frequently called his "Hopi followers together" to give them "good advice." He told the Hopi "boys and girls to enter into everything heartily in connection with the school," to "secure the best that Sherman [had] to give." Consequently, the Hopi pupils did not "hang back," but pushed "rapidly ahead." With "great respect for their Chief and confidence in his counsel," the Hopi followers listened to Tawaquaptewa at school in the same manner as they did at Orayvi.[17]

Along with his involvement in academics and industrial training, Tawaquaptewa demonstrated his leadership with the Hopi pupils in music and dance. At Sherman Institute, music centered on American and European selections that ranged in genre from classical to religious to American patriotic compositions.[18] In addition to using music to assimilate and further demonstrate the superiority of American culture, school officials regularly incorporated music for entertainment purposes, often including Hopi pupils. In March 1907, Tawaquaptewa and "eight of his followers" sang a Hopi song in the school's auditorium. As an impressed audience looked on, the program began as a Hopi boy kept a steady beat on a drum. With a school banner in his hand, Tawaquaptewa led the small procession of Hopi singers into the auditorium, singing and dancing with "signal ease and excellent time." Those who witnessed the event noted that Tawaquaptewa was "fascinating in the animation, grace and agility in which he kept time to the perfect rhythm of the music."[19]

Two months after entertaining the audience in the school's auditorium, Tawaquaptewa and his followers performed the Eagle Dance, a dance commonly done by several Pueblo Indian communities of the southwest, including the Hopis. Tawaquaptewa "took his place at the drum" and "ten singers carrying rattles" aligned themselves on each side of him. The *Sherman Bulletin* noted that "after a few weird strains to the beat of the drum, two small boys as heralds entered" the auditorium and positioned themselves on each side of the stage. The boys then whirled a "stick attached to a string," to "imitate the disturbance of the elements." As the performers whirled the stick, four boys dressed as eagles entered the auditorium and joined the dance. Fellow students commented that the Hopi boys performed the dance with fascinating rhythm, "grace," and "agility." At the request of Tawaquaptewa, each outfit used in the Eagle Dance came from Orayvi,[20] and consisted of complete and fully authentic pieces, which included:

4 woven scarfs,
4 narrow woven belts,
6 skirts for dancers,
4 skins to wear on back,
8 beads for wrists (white)
8 eagles' wings for arms,
  Enough eagles' tails for four dancers,
  Short feathers for around neck and back,
10 gourds or rattles,

4 red horse hair Kachinas,
8 little round rattles for knees,

Hopi Names,—
4 garsh gnuh nah (horns)
1 ah tay he (blanket)
8 hrun qua
8 (Anklets) non ho gas me[21]

In addition to the Hopi outfits, Tawaquaptewa requested that his brother Talasquaptewa send his "silver belt, ear rings, shoes and beads," and asked his wife's sister Nevahmoieunih to send "red, yellow, and blue" Hopi bread called piki, which is often eaten during ceremonies and special gatherings.[22]

Tawaquaptewa's willingness to allow Hopi music at Sherman Institute may have resulted from the influence of Natalie Curtis, a white ethnographer who worked with Tawaquaptewa personally at the school to preserve traditional Hopi songs. Historian Harry C. James remarked that Curtis "possessed an amazing faculty for gaining the respect and cooperation of the Indians with whom she worked. This was certainly true of the Hopi who always spoke of her affectionately as 'The Song Woman.'"[23] In 1908, Curtis visited Tawaquaptewa at Sherman Institute and noted that, "of all the Hopi poets, none sings a gladder song than Tawakwaptiwa. He is one in whom the gift of song wells up like living waters, a Hopi untouched by foreign influence, the child of natural environment, spontaneous, alert, full of life and laughter."[24]

Curtis' work with the Hopi people did not begin with Tawaquaptewa, but with Kikmongwi Loololma. Near the end of Loololma's life, Curtis urged him to preserve the songs of his people and had told him that the "Hopi children are going to school; they are learning new ways and are singing new songs—American songs instead of Hopi. Some of the children are very young—so young that there have been, perhaps, but three corn-plantings since they came into the world. These little ones will never sing the songs of their fathers. They will not sing of the corn, the bean blossoms, and the butterflies. They will only know American songs."[25] Although American songs were in abundance at Sherman Institute, Hopi pupils also proudly sang songs of their own in the Eagle Dance and set a precedent for Hopi music at the school for years to come.

More than a hundred years later, Hopi students continue to sing and dance their traditional songs at Sherman Institute, now called Sherman Indian High School. The path established by Tawaquaptewa in 1906 continues today, and it reflects a trend that came about at most of the off-reservation boarding schools at some point. The U.S. government had established the boarding schools to assimilate Indian students, but those very students used the boarding school as a place to preserve and protect their own cultural ways. While Tawaquaptewa and other Hopi students learned English, American songs, and played instruments to the music of European masters, they also instructed each other in Hopi words, songs, and stories. Tawaquaptewa taught the Hopi children to conduct the Eagle Dance, and he encouraged the youth by his actions and words. He helped preserve the Hopi way through an institution designed to destroy it.

Superintendent Hall's tolerance of Hopi culture at Sherman Institute may appear to be an anomaly. The U.S. government had instructed Hall to weaken American Indian cultures through the boarding school, but the superintendent outwardly encouraged Tawaquaptewa and the students to converse, sing, and dance in the Hopi way. Hall allowed the Hopis to share their culture through song and dance to promote Sherman Institute as a progressive and enlightened institution. Hall hoped to advance the school as an academic and industrial-based institution, and himself as a visionary administrator who saw value in Native cultures. Furthermore, Hall hoped that the patrons who witnessed the Hopi dancers would contribute money and resources to the institution, or hire Indian students to work in their businesses, schools, or homes. In essence, Hall used Hopi songs and dance to publicize Sherman Institute and to further the larger educational aims of the school. Some administrators may have felt that the use of Hopi songs and dances might prove dangerous to government objectives, but Hall felt completely in control and believed that his agendas overruled the objections of others.

In the months following the Eagle Dance, Hopi pupils had additional opportunities to demonstrate their culture to the school and to the local community. Superintendent Hall routinely called upon the Hopi Singers to provide entertainment at formal occasions, including the annual conference of the National Education Association (NEA) held in Los Angeles in July 1907.[26] Conducting the Eagle Dance before thousands of U.S. educators, Tawaquaptewa led the Hopi dancers and singers in Hopi songs while wearing traditional Native clothes.[27] Prior to the NEA Convention, Superintendent Hall wrote Estelle Reel and told how the "singing and dancing" to be performed by the Hopis at the Convention, was "better than anything" he had "witnessed or heard among any Indians."[28]

The Hopi Singers brought attention to more than Sherman Institute and Superintendent Hall. Each dance also provided the school and community a glimpse into the beauty and complexities of Hopi culture. The surrounding community initially looked at the Hopis as savage Indians, but Hopi songs, dances, instruments, and the colorful outfits worn by the Singers aroused the curiosity of Indians and non-Indians alike. When word of the Hopi Singers spread beyond the greater Riverside area, reporters and photographers from various Los Angeles newspapers begged Hall for permission to "take photographs of the Hopi eagle dancers." Publicity in the print media would have been good for the school and Superintendent Hall, but for reasons unknown, Hall refused to "give his consent."[29] Hall's refusal to allow reporters and photographers access to the Hopi Singers does not fit with his desire to present the school or himself in a positive light. Perhaps legal or school policy issues influenced his decision; perhaps he was fearful of exploiting the Hopis, or unwilling that daily school activity be disturbed by anxious reporters. Tawaquaptewa may have weighed in on the issue and asked Hall to prevent the reporters from taking photographs of dancers.[30] No documents have emerged to enlighten us on this point, but in Arizona many Hopis objected to photographers documenting their ceremonies. Even today the Hopi people explicitly forbid non-Hopis from taking pictures of their villages, kivas, and religious dances.[31]

Although the Hopi Singers consisted entirely of Hopi pupils, other musical groups at the school included students from different indigenous communities. Receiving less attention than the Hopi Singers, the Mandolin Club incorporated both Hopi and other Indian students and remained one of the largest musical ensembles at the school. Composed of thirty-seven "bright, charming girls," the Mandolin Club demonstrated their talents before "many noted people" and also performed alongside the Hopi Singers at the NEA Convention in 1907. Under the direction of music teacher Charles Weyland, the girls excelled at playing mandolins and guitars to entertain students, staff, and school visitors.[32] Mattie Coochiesnema, a Hopi pupil from Orayvi, played with the girls in the Mandolin Club. Mattie came to Sherman Institute in 1906. In March 1909, the school's newspaper reported that Mattie was "doing fine in the mandolin club" and that she wished "she could stay at Sherman all the time."[33] Mattie's desire to remain demonstrates how Hopi pupils eventually adjusted to the school. Time, along with friendships, the presence of older Hopi women, and shared experiences in groups such as the Mandolin Club, helped the Hopi girls to accept and think differently about their temporary California home.

Hopi students had additional opportunities to be involved musically at Sherman Institute. Dennis Talashoenewa, Archie Mashawistewa, Victor Sakiestewa, and Homer Homewyewa all played in the school marching band.[34] Hopis who participated in the Sherman Band performed at school events including football games, the Sunday roll call, and formal concerts. In a typical week, the band practiced "every evening from 6:30 to 7:30."[35] Students met individually with the band's director, Charles Weyland, for music lessons. Hopi pupils learned to play a variety of instruments. Pierce Hopi became proficient with the snare drum and Archie Talawaltewa rapidly learned to play the clarinet.[36] Many of the Hopi students performed with other musical groups once they returned to the reservation. In December 1913 one Hopi graduate, Victor Sakiestewa, asked the school's superintendent if he could return to the school to play with the band at the 1915 World's Fair in San Francisco.[37] In his remarkable study on American Indians and their use of music from 1879 to 1934, historian John W. Troutman noted that "boarding schools generated a national profile and entered the public consciousness in large part through the musical performances of the students; the highest-profile performances were those at world fairs and presidential inaugurations."[38] Although Victor did not play at the World's Fair, nor did he ever play for Sherman Institute after graduating, he used his music training to serve his community by performing in the Santa Fe Indian Band, which included Hopi, Navajo, and other Indian musicians.[39]

In addition to their involvement in music, Hopi students participated in games and sports. Since the school's founding in 1902, officials encouraged students to be involved in outdoor sports and recreation.[40] Viewed by Superintendents Hall and his successor, Frank M. Conser, to be essential for good health, recreation provided two necessities for Indian students: physical exercise and fresh air. At a time when tuberculosis threatened the student body and ravaged Indian communities in North America, medical officials believed that fresh air kept students healthy and strong, both mentally and physically.[41] Teachers encouraged students to participate in outside recreation, including basketball, football, baseball, and polo, as sports strengthened muscles and fostered team mindsets among Indian students. Along with the physical benefits, organized sports provided an opportunity for students to engage competitively with each other.[42]

As Hopi sport involvement increased at Sherman Institute, so did the risk of injury. Serious sport-related accidents involving Hopi students were rare. The most serious incident happened after Thanksgiving Day in 1907. In the school's recreation yard, John Pablo, a Pima Indian boy from Blackwater, Arizona, and two small Hopi boys enjoyed a game of football.[43] As one of the Hopi boys ran with the ball, John tackled him to the ground.

Unable to move, John lay paralyzed while his Hopi schoolmates attempted to help. When asked by his peers if he had pain, John replied that he did not have any pain whatsoever. Unknown to the boys at the time, John had severely injured his neck. After his fall, John "lapsed into unconsciousness and was removed to the [school's] hospital." Although school officials administered "restoratives and everything possible" to revive him, John died shortly thereafter. School officials did not blame the students for John's death. Instead, Superintendent Hall viewed the unfortunate event as an accident that occurred among a "crowd of young, inexperienced boys attempting to play" a game that both sides had only recently learned. News of John's death was a shock to the entire school. Superintendent Hall addressed the issue in the next Sunday chapel service, where he reminded the pupils that life hung on a thread, for in a "moment's time," a similar accident could happen to one of them.[44]

When Hopi pupils were not involved with sports or musical endeavors, they participated in the school's industrial program. While the Hopi boys labored in the fields, the Sherman Ranch girls received instruction in domestic training. In a report to the Department of the Interior in 1906, Hall described female involvement at the Ranch by explaining a number of different Ranch components: "the girls have a kitchen [and] garden, in which they raise vegetables for the farm table. They also milk a few cows, care for a limited number of chickens, turkeys and ducks," and look "after the feeding of a few pigs." Hall reported that the girls "do all the domestic work of the household," which included "canning the fruit, caring for milk, making the butter, and all work usually performed by the farmer's wife."[45]

The Hopi girls at the Ranch included Louisa Tawamana, who demonstrated how to make butter to an auditorium full of staff and students. Impressed with the "manner in which she handled the churn," Louisa's schoolmates called her an "expert," though they complained that her soft-spoken voice made it difficult for the audience to hear.[46] Other Hopis received praise for their abilities to cook and bake. Effie Sachowengsia received school-wide attention for her peach pie and Iolo Sewensie made a good impression on her peers with her cinnamon rolls.[47] Hopi boys also cooked and baked at the school. Herbert Homehongewa worked in the kitchen,[48] and Keller Seedkoema excelled in the school's bakery.[49] In Hopi culture, women typically cooked and prepared the food, while men planted and hunted animals such as deer, elk, and rabbits. At Sherman Institute, Hopi boys experienced roles usually reserved for Hopi women.

Hopi success at the school flourished with the encouragement and influence of additional Hopi leaders. When the Hopi pupils left for school in 1906, government officials also sent Frank and Susie Seumptewa, and their two children, Ethel and Lilly, to Sherman Institute to become familiar with American ways and to learn the English language. With Ethel and Lilly under the age of four, Susie spent most of her time tending to the needs of her children. Frank worked as a groundskeeper, so he may have had more contact with the Hopi pupils, especially the boys.[50] It should not, however, be assumed that Susie had little influence on the students. Using her ability to weave baskets and Hopi coil and wicker plaques, Susie became known throughout the school for her talent in basketry. Susie's abilities stood as an example for the Hopi and non-Hopi girls in the Needle Art Department whose beautiful display of Hopi plaques adorned the walls of the school's administration building, now used as the Sherman Indian Museum.[51]

Basket making also provided the Hopi girls with revenue.

In a letter to field matron Miltona Keith, Superintendent Hall noted that two Hopi women were "anxious to commence" basket making, and requested from Keith that she send a sufficient amount of material by railway express to be paid for by Hall's school account. Among the "paraphernalia necessary for the making of baskets," Hall requested that Keith send "green, red, blue, yellow, black" and mostly white yucca plant material along with "sticks for the center strands." Hall commented to Keith that the Hopi women would "make considerable money out of their baskets," for they would "have no trouble to find plenty of buyers."[52] On the Hopi Reservation, mothers instructed their daughters in the art and cultural significance of basket making. In the early twentieth century, Orayvi women traded their baskets for food and items such as pots and pans. Hopis at the Indian school in Riverside sold plaques to white tourists who visited the school throughout the year. Visitors could purchase authentic Hopi arts and crafts without needing to visit the Hopi Reservation. Susie's influence in basket making had a profound impact on the girls at the school, and one can only imagine what could have been accomplished had she remained for the entire three years.

Unfortunately for the Hopi students, Susie's stay at Sherman Institute lasted only four months. In March 1907, Susie became ill and left "with her two little girls" and returned to Orayvi.[53] Her husband remained until he completed his three-year term in June 1909. Three months after she returned home, Susie sent a letter to Hall with a message for the Hopi students. After inquiring how "all the Hopi children [were] getting along," Susie told the pupils how it pleased their parents to hear of their accomplishments at the school.[54] In August 1907, Susie attempted to return to the school, but Hall refused her readmittance, stating that the "doctor reports that one of her lungs is considerably affected [with tuberculosis], that under such conditions it would be only a question of a short time before she would have to be sent home again."[55] Fearing that tuberculosis would spread to other pupils at the school, Hall did not wish to admit Susie in light of her uncertain health condition.

The Hopi pupils occasionally received letters from home, such as the letters from Susie, but they more frequently wrote letters to their families on the reservation. On the last school day of each month, school officials required each student to write a letter to their parents or other members of their family. School administrators had Indian pupils write letters to improve grammar skills and to facilitate a familiarity with the English language. Letters also kept families informed of the student's health and school life.[56] Students had freedom in what they wrote, as long as the letters were "decent and respectable." The requirement to write home once a month was the bare minimum, for students could write as often as they wished. Administrators required students to provide substance in their letters, telling the students that short and pointless letters disappointed their families.[57]

A few examples of letters that Hopis wrote between 1906 and 1909 are recorded in the *Sherman Bulletin*. The excerpts provide a positive but not fully realistic picture of the attitude that Hopis had toward the school. Students rarely wrote material critical of the school or school officials, and even if Hopis had negative things to say, administrators would not have published such comments in the *Sherman Bulletin*. Teachers also screened each letter for grammatical errors, which may further explain the letters' positive tone. The examples, however, do appear to reflect the overall Hopi experience at Sherman Institute in the early twentieth century.

At Sherman Institute, school officials required that Hopi students write letters to their families in English. However, the vast majority of Hopi parents could not read or speak English. Since few government officials spoke Hopi in those years, the responsibility fell on Christian missionaries on the reservation to translate letters sent by Hopi students at Sherman Institute and other off-reservation Indian boarding schools. The letters Hopis sent to their parents varied in subject matter. Some of the students remarked that the Hopi pupils at the school worked and studied with much effort and commitment. Other Hopis commented on the school's beautiful "grounds and buildings" and referred to Sherman Institute as the "finest" school they had ever seen. Additional Hopi letters reported that "every Hopi girl and boy" was "doing well" and in good health.[58] After several days of rain in February 1908, Tawaquaptewa wrote to his family that he was "very glad for the white people that the rain had come again." The "heavy rainfall and abundant supply of water" in Southern California was a "novelty" for the Hopi students, who had never experienced that amount of rain on their dry and arid reservation.[59]

In December 1907, U.S. government field matron Miltona Stauffer, formerly Miltona Keith of Orayvi, along with her husband, Peter, visited the Hopi pupils at the Indian school in Riverside as part of their "annual leave of absence" to Southern California. In the early 1900s, the U.S. government hired women as Field Matrons to teach Indian women how to sew, cook, and raise children according to American customs. The Hopis at Sherman Institute knew the Stauffers from their prior work on the Hopi Reservation.[60] While Miltona labored among the Hopi as a field matron, Peter worked as a government mechanic. Both spoke Hopi, and they earned the respect of Hopis who belonged to the accommodating faction. When the Stauffers arrived at the school, the Hopi students received them "most joyfully" and Tawaquaptewa "threw his arms about Mr. Stauffer and embraced him, being so glad to see his old friend."[61]

Upon entering the school in 1907, the Stauffers seemed "much pleased at the happy, healthy appearance of the eighty Hopi children."[62] Although Hopi health at the school was generally good, Hopis, like other Indian students, suffered from illness. In November 1906, school officials diagnosed Jennie Tuvayyumptewa with "tuberculosis in the upper part of her left lung," and Victor Sakiestewa suffered from bronchitis. While Victor's illness did not appear to be serious enough to "interfere with his school work," school nurses closely monitored his condition and Superintendent Hall promised Victor that if his health worsened, he would be sent home.[63] Some of the severely ill pupils remained at the school's hospital until they recovered or died. In November 1908, Superintendent Hall noted that Hopi pupil Adam Nakhaha died of "heart failure caused by pneumonia" and that his classmates buried him in the school's cemetery.[64]

In a school health inspection conducted on April 20, 1909, officials reported that Tawaquaptewa was "well developed" and in "good health."[65] Although Tawaquaptewa never became seriously ill at the school, health officials diagnosed his daughter, Mina, with whooping cough in May 1907. As Mina's condition worsened, Tawaquaptewa quickly sent his wife and daughter on an Atchison, Topeka & Santa Fe Railroad train to Winslow, where family members met them and took them to Orayvi.[66] When Mina and Nasumgoens arrived at Orayvi, government officials detained both of them at their home to prevent the spread of whooping cough to others in the community. Shortly after they arrived at their village, Superintendent Hall allowed Tawaquaptewa a brief visit to Orayvi as part of a ploy by the U.S. government to increase Hopi enrollment. At Orayvi, trouble developed as many Hopis blamed Hall for the "detention" of Tawaquaptewa's "wife and child on account of whooping cough."[67]

When he heard about the controversy at Orayvi, Superintendent Hall wrote Tawaquaptewa and stated that he had nothing to do with detaining his wife and daughter, and explained that it had been "done by the order of the Physician," who "did not want the whooping cough to spread among the little children of Oraibi."[68] While placement of the blame for Tawaquaptewa's wife and daughter's detention remains questionable, the tension that resulted had a lasting effect on Hopi-government relations. Hopis at Orayvi may have spread rumors about Superintendent Hall to entice Tawaquaptewa and other Hopis toward anger and noncompliance. In the past, government officials had demonstrated how easily they detained Tawaquaptewa and his family at Sherman Institute, and it is possible that the Hopis thought that the government would detain the family on the reservation once they migrated home. Whether or not Tawaquaptewa accepted Hall's explanation is unknown. We do know that Tawaquaptewa cooperated with Hall and other officials, which in turn preserved Hopi pupil cooperation at the school.

While school officials at Sherman Institute gave Hopi pupils instruction in becoming good citizens, the U.S. government made similar attempts to Americanize their families on the reservation. In 1891, as a direct consequence of the General Allotment Act of 1887 (more commonly known as the Dawes Severalty Act) government officials surveyed Hopi land to distribute individual allotments.[69] Many Hopi people who lived on the reservation rejected the allotment of their lands, because as author Frank Waters once observed, "news that the government was going to give [the Hopis] land which they already owned seemed at once too ridiculous, insulting, and tragic to believe."[70] Hopi leaders, and most Hopis, opposed allotment because it threatened the social and religious structure of Hopi culture and the Hopi understanding of land ownership that was closely associated with Hopi clans. When surveyors came to the reservation and placed their stakes in the ground, Hopis routinely removed the markers after the officials left.[71]

In a letter dated June 7, 1909, Commissioner Leupp wrote Superintendent Conser regarding his concern over a "little trouble brewing at Oraibi owing to Tewaquaptewa's attitude toward allotment." Leupp stated that Tawaquaptewa had demonstrated the "ignorant Indian in him," and while such ignorance came as no surprise to Leupp, it nevertheless annoyed him and needed to be addressed. It was "generally understood through the pueblo," that Tawaquaptewa had "been instigating" his brother Talasquaptewa to advise the Hopis on the reservation "not to accept allotment." Leupp could "hardly conceive" that Tawaquaptewa was a "big enough fool to set himself up in opposition to the Government." In spite of Tawaquaptewa's attendance at Sherman Institute and having "seen a little of the world," Leupp did not "count on his having learned" any "wisdom."[72] Upon receiving Leupp's letter, Conser "immediately called" Tawaquaptewa into his office and "advised" Tawaquaptewa that he had received a letter from Commissioner Leupp that stated that Leupp was "disappointed because of the stories" that had come to his attention regarding Tawaquaptewa's attitude. After Conser "read the letter" and "explained" it at great length, Tawaquaptewa admitted that he had indeed "advised his brother against taking allotment," but assured Conser that he would begin to encourage his brother in the opposite direction.[73]

Even though Tawaquaptewa "talked quite favorably" of allotment after Conser read and explained Leupp's letter, Conser acknowledged that it was impossible to tell "just what position" Tawaquaptewa would take when he returned to the reservation.[74] It is doubtful that Tawaquaptewa would have demonstrated an attitude of noncompliance with government officials two weeks before he expected to return home to the Hopi mesas. He may have been concerned that Leupp, at the suggestion of Conser, would attempt to keep him at the school longer than originally agreed upon. Nevertheless, the "ignorant Indian" was more intelligent than Leupp or Conser realized.[75] Their attempt to assimilate the Hopi chief had failed.

Up until his death in 1960, Tawaquaptewa, struggling to maintain the leadership he once had at Orayvi,[76] claimed that Superintendent Hall tricked him into signing a statement that encouraged Hopi cooperation with the U.S. government.[77] Tawaquaptewa believed that Leupp and Hall took advantage of his beginner's knowledge of English while a student at Sherman Institute. Even though there were tensions between Tawaquaptewa and government officials, Tawaquaptewa refused to allow the problems to hinder his involvement with the Hopi pupils under his care. Always concerned about his Hopi followers, Tawaquaptewa faithfully fulfilled his obligation as kikmongwi and elder to provide the encouragement and leadership needed for Hopi success at one of the largest off-reservation Indian boarding schools.

In spite of the U.S. government's agenda to assimilate Indians and ultimately destroy Indian cultures, Hopi culture remained intact at Sherman Institute. Hopi pupils took a potentially disastrous time in their history and turned it toward the betterment of Hopi people. The very institution that the U.S. government had designed to civilize the Hopis became a powerful tool that Hopis used to preserve their culture. Hopi students refused to view themselves as victims held against their wills by the hand of the federal government. Instead, they followed the counsel of their kikmongwi and acted as Hopis even while others wanted them to behave like Anglo Americans. Hopi students at Sherman, by continuing to draw on their heritage, formed a new life in a pragmatic manner that benefited the Hopi people as a whole.

Some Hopi students became attached to their school and did not eagerly migrate home. But others welcomed their return to the mesas. In June 1909, a group of Hopi students from Orayvi returned home with their chief, Tawaquaptewa. Of the initial seventy-one Hopi students that arrived in November 1906, fifty-five returned to Orayvi in 1909. Most of them were boys. Although several of the pupils eagerly returned home,[78] twenty "of the Hopi children [had] requested permission to remain at the school another year." However, "every Hopi parent absolutely declined to consent to their children remaining" at Sherman Institute any longer.[79] Before he migrated back to the reservation, one Hopi student told fellow schoolmates: "We Hopis are about to leave Sherman. I will not forget my teachers, for they have been kind to me, and I will try to come back here next year."[80] Indian pupils continuing at the school wished that all of their Hopi friends would return the following year.[81]

In a similar fashion to how they first arrived at the school, the Hopi pupils left Sherman Institute on the Santa Fe train to Winslow, Arizona, where their parents met them and took them by wagon to Orayvi. Throughout their stay, the Hopi pupils grew to adore the school, and many spoke of the "purple and gold" in endearing terms. Most of the Hopis who returned home readapted to life on the reservation, but they never forgot about their school. Other students became restless and found it difficult to live as they once had. A year following his return, Victor Sakiestewa wrote to Superintendent Conser that he no longer wanted to live at Orayvi and asked permission to return to the school for another term. Willing even to pay his transportation costs, Victor represented a number of Hopi pupils who, once they experienced life beyond the Hopi mesas, came to appreciate opportunities that did not exist for them on the reservation.[82]

In the early twentieth century, the U.S. government invested a significant amount of time and money educating Hopi students at Sherman Institute.[83] Fearful of losing their investment as well as the progress believed to have been made with Hopi people, government officials labored to keep Hopi enrollment from declining. In an effort to secure future attendance, Conser frequently wrote former Hopi pupils on the reservation. The younger Hopis enthusiastically received Conser's letters and felt privileged and honored to have the superintendent's personal attention. Although Conser's correspondence proved fruitful in the years to come,[84] no one motivated Hopi attendance at Sherman Institute more than Hopis themselves, and nothing affected their experience at the school more than Hopi culture and the teachings they first received in their village communities.

5. Taking Hopi Knowledge to School

Education for indigenous people did not originate at U.S. government schools.[1] For the Hopi students who traveled with Tawaquaptewa to Sherman Institute in 1906, education began in their villages and centered on values that encompassed the beauty and complexity of Hopi culture.[2] Education on the Hopi Reservation involved instruction from family members or community elders. Hopi elders educated children through song, dance, story, prayer, and practical experiences. Elders instilled in children an appreciation for the Hopi way. Before Hopis attended U.S. government schools, used lead pencils, or sat at wooden desks, Hopi children received education on the mesas, in the fields, and within the walls of their stone homes. Helen Sekaquaptewa from Orayvi once recalled that Hopi children "had on-the-job training. Children learned to care for the sheep and raise corn in the day-by-day school of experience. Girls learned from their mothers to grind corn, prepare the food, and care for the household. Men and boys met in the kiva in winter time for lessons in history, religion, and traditions—all taught in story and song."[3] J. R. Miller, a historian of the Canadian residential school system, observed that "not all societies have schools, but all human communities posses educational systems." Miller further noted that "education, as distinct from schooling, has clear purposes whose achievement is essential for any collectivity to survive and prosper."[4]

In the "educational system" of Hopi culture, boys learned to be men by following the example of their fathers, uncles, and village leaders. Hopi men educated their sons and nephews in the purpose and act of hunting, farming, and activities that included religious responsibilities for the family, village, and clan. Similarly, Hopi girls learned to be mothers, home caretakers, basket makers, dancers, and powerful women in Hopi society from their mothers, aunties, grandmothers, and village and clan members. Education for Hopis did not begin at Sherman Institute, but with the Hopi people, and Hopis used their indigenous education to advance once they entered Western schools established by Christian missionaries and the U.S. government. In her examination of Indian education during the colonial period, historian Margaret Connell Szasz noted that "when Native American youth were educated in White schools—whether in colonial, nineteenth-, or twentieth-century America—they brought to those institutions varying degrees of native culture." Szasz further argued that "formal schooling" at places such as Sherman Institute or the Carlisle Indian Industrial School "often served as an overlay for the attitudes and perceptions of the world that they had already acquired within the family and the community."[5]

Throughout Hopi history, Hopi families and parents have played a vital role in the mental, social, and spiritual development of their children. Hopi education starts at birth and involves special naming rituals for the Hopi infant.[6] Family members give names to their children to associate them with their clan, things of nature, and the land, but government officials at off-reservation Indian boarding schools often stripped

Hopis of their names for Anglo names. David Wallace Adams noted that the U.S. government's name-changing policy resulted when teachers found it difficult to "pronounce" or "memorize" Indian names and that Commissioner Morgan insisted that Indians either abandon their names or choose their Indian first name as their surname to prevent confusion when they inherited allotments from family members.[7] Before Hopi pupil Victor Sakiestewa arrived at Sherman Institute in 1906, school officials at the Oraibi Day School changed his first name from Honwalpi to Victor and instructed him to replace his mother's surname with his father's name. Peers and teachers knew him as "Victor" at the Indian school in Riverside, but he kept his Hopi name, Honwalpi, as his middle name.[8] Polingaysi Qoyawayma had her name changed at the Oraibi Day School before she attended Sherman Institute with Victor in 1906. Teachers at the day school changed her name to Elizabeth White, and students at both schools referred to her as "Bessie."[9]

Although nearly every Hopi pupil who attended Sherman Institute between 1902 and 1929 had either been given or had chosen Anglo first names, many retained their Hopi surnames.[10] As an act of accommodation, Tawaquaptewa also changed his name at Sherman Institute. In June 1909, the *Sherman Bulletin* reported that "Chief Tawaquaptewa [had] decided to take on an American name."[11] According to the school's newspaper, Tawaquaptewa chose "Wilson" as his first name and kept "Tawaquaptewa" as his surname. From this time on, Tawaquaptewa was known as "Wilson Tawaquaptewa," a name that he kept until his death in 1960. Tawaquaptewa's willingness to change his name does not reflect the noncompliant attitude he showed after he returned from Sherman Institute, but while a student at the school, Tawaquaptewa always led the other Hopis by his example.

Along with providing them with a name, parents and other family members shared many stories with Hopi children. Hopis used stories to teach children about their culture and to remind them of their responsibilities to Hopi society.[12] Some stories described the origins of Hopi people and taught valuable lessons about life according to the Hopi way. Hopi artist Alph H. Secakuku from Supolovi on Second Mesa points out that Hopi stories are often told in the Hopi language and that "stories for children are usually in the simpler forms of parables" that "emphasize the importance of the past as a moral guide, and the maintenance of the high standards of Hopi life."[13] Hopi pupils at off-reservation Indian boarding schools shared their traditional stories with other Indian students. One story, "Jus-wa-kep-la," originated on the Hopi mesas and traveled with Hopi pupil Nora Homehoyoma when she left for Sherman Institute in the early 1900s.[14] School officials published "Jus-wa-kep-la" in the *Sherman Bulletin* in January 1912. Nearly sixty years later in 1970, anthropologist and ethnographer Harold Courlander published a similar version of the story, titled "Joshokiklay and the Eagle," in his account of the "tales" and "legends" of the Hopi people.[15]

In addition to "Jus-wa-kep-la," Hopi parents taught their children stories on how to overcome evil and the value of working with each other on common problems. Although officials at Sherman Institute encouraged pupils to achieve individual accomplishments, Hopi pupils came from a culture that elevated group cooperation. In March 1928, Hopi pupils at Sherman Institute published a story in the school's newspaper titled "Youth and Fire Boy and the Giant Elk" that spoke to this Hopi upbringing. In 1979, G. M. Mullett republished a similar story, titled "The Giant Elk," in her collection of Hopi Spider-woman stories.[16] However, Mullett does not provide an interpretation of the story or place "The Giant Elk" in a historical context.

Youth and Fire-Boy and the Giant Elk

There once lived an elk, who dwelt in a lush, protected valley near a Hopi village. The elk was broad shouldered and large in stature, comparable in height and mass to a tree or a house. He had horns that were gnarled and twisted like the branches of an old, weathered tree. Giant-elk did not eat vegetation, such as leaves and grass, but preferred to fill his belly with humans. His appetite for people was the reason he chose to live in such close proximity to the Hopi villages; he would lie in wait and capture any Hopis that came forth from their homes. Giant-elk's habit of consuming Hopis became so regular that the people in the village grew increasingly upset and knew that something must be done to protect their people, although no one was able to come up with a feasible plan to rid the valley of the man-eating elk. Finally, two boys in the village named Youth and Fire-boy decided that they could not stand idly by while Hopis lived in constant fear for their lives. They took their quivers of arrows and bows and set forth to hunt and kill Giant-elk.

As they traveled the short distance to confront their foe, Youth and Fire-boy met Mr. Mole, who asked where the boys were headed. When the boys told him about their plan, Mr. Mole fell to his knees and begged them not to go any closer to Giant-elk, for he saw that the boys were small and would quickly be overpowered and consumed by the elk. Hearing this, the boys proudly raised their heads and pulled back their shoulders, telling the mole that their quivers were filled with magic arrows, given to them by Spider-woman and that the weapons would not miss their mark. Youth and Fire-boy passionately explained that they needed to rescue their families from the constant terror and threat of death facing all in the village. Mr. Mole looked with great admiration on the two brave lads, and seeing that they would not be swayed from their mission, told them that he foresaw a problem even for their magic arrows. The mole revealed that the elk's hair was unnaturally coarse and thick, and would be impossible for weapons to penetrate. But the twins, determined to save their people, replied that they could not turn away, and determined to continue in their endeavor.

Mr. Mole realized the gravity of the situation the brave boys were about to face, and asked them to wait a moment to give him a chance to think. He leaned on a rock, closed his eyes, and tried to come up with a plan. At last, while the boys waited above ground, Mr. Mole rapidly dug four large underground chambers, each getting progressively deeper. He then dug small tunnels between the holes, connecting them together. When he finished, Mr. Mole told the boys to stay where they were, and he snuck forward on the trail to locate Giant-elk. He saw that the large creature was settling on the ground for an afternoon nap. Mr. Mole hurried back to the boys and ran down to the underground chambers, where he burrowed a tunnel leading to the surface, ending at the chest of the sleeping elk. The sudden movement under Giant-elk's heart awakened him, and he angrily reared his head and shouted, "Who are you, and how dare you awake me?" But Mr. Mole did not allow himself to show his fear, and quickly replied, "I am sorry to have woken you! Please do not be upset, for it is I, Mole, and I have long admired the soft, long fur on your chest. My children are in need of a warm bed, and I thought you would certainly not mind giving some of your beautiful hairs to me for this purpose." Appeased by the flattery, Giant-elk granted Mr. Mole permission to take his hair, but asked that he remove the hairs with a gentle hand.

After Mr. Mole acquired the hairs, he thanked Giant-elk and quickly ran back to the boys by way of the underground tunnel. He then came to the surface and told Youth and Fire-boy that there was an underground burrow that would lead them directly to the elk, and that there was a vulnerable patch of skin in the great foe's chest. Mr. Mole then instructed the boys to follow the tunnel and be certain that they aim their weapons at that one area of weakness on the elk. As the boys approached Giant-elk, they found him as Mr. Mole had described. The boys looked at each other, thought of how their families had suffered, and aimed their bows. Their aim was true, and the arrows penetrated deeply through Giant-elk's exposed skin. Giant-elk threw back his head and leapt to his feet in pain. He saw the boys peeking up through the burrow's entrance. Youth and Fire-boy rushed back through the tunnel, but Giant-elk dove in after them, using his powerful horns to rip and tear the tunnel open as he charged after them. As Giant-elk chased the boys, Youth and Fire-boy rushed to the first underground room and hurriedly crawled inside the small opening. Giant-elk was right behind, and he gored his massive horns in the opening and into the room, with the intention of spearing the twins. The room where the twins were huddled was too deep, however, and the elk was unable to reach them. Filled with anger, Giant-elk began to tear through the hole with more vengeance, and with great forceful heaves and grunts, quickly destroyed the first hole and began pushing through to the surface. The boys huddled as far back as they could, but saw the elk rapidly getting closer and thought that their demise was imminent. Just then, Mr. Mole arrived and pulled the boys to the second, third, and fourth hole, the last being deeper than all the others. As Giant-elk thrashed his horns through the fourth hole, tearing through the dirt to the sky and vehemently trying to reach the boys, he continued to bleed from his heart and finally collapsed to the ground, dead.

Youth and Fire-boy clung to Mr. Mole and repeatedly thanked him for his cunning scheme, quick thinking, and bravery. When the boys and Mr. Mole arose from the body, they were met by Mr. Chipmunk, who heard the large commotion of the final struggle and came over to investigate. Mr. Chipmunk saw the carcass of Giant-elk and immediately asked, "Is it possible that you are the ones who accomplished this incredible act of defeating our terrible enemy?" Fire-boy replied, "Yes, we were able to kill him, with the help of daring Mr. Mole. Now we wish to take some of the elk meat to our village to eat in celebration with our people, but we do not have a knife with which to cut it." Mr. Chipmunk, greatly impressed with the boys' humility and heroism, offered to cut the elk up with his sharp teeth. To show their appreciation, Youth and Fire-boy each took one finger and made a stripe of red elk blood down Mr. Chipmunk's back. Today, the two stripes made by Youth and Fire-boy are visible on the chipmunk, as a reminder of his help after the slaying of Giant-elk. When Mr. Chipmunk finished cutting the elk, the boys gathered the meat on their backs and made their way home. As they traveled back to their village, pieces of the meat they carried fell to the ground and transformed into Hopis that had been eaten by Giant-elk. Upon arriving at the village, the Hopis rallied around the boys and celebrated the victory with a great feast of corn, melon, stew, and piki. After many years of unrest, the village once again had peace, and the people were filled with thanksgiving and happiness.[17]

"Youth and Fire-Boy and the Giant Elk" teaches about several aspects of Hopi culture, including the special relationship Hopis have with animals. While living on the Hopi mesas, Hopi children saw chipmunks and moles on a regular basis. Hopis may have interpreted the foe in the story to be a representation of the trials or fears that they experienced in life. Furthermore, the story emphasized the lesson that often one or even two individuals cannot overcome trials without additional help. Youth and Fire-boy needed assistance, and they accepted Mr. Mole's aid to conquer their common enemy. The concept of working together to solve a problem is part of Hopi culture, and Hopi parents encouraged their children to accept and offer help by not allowing their pride to hinder a partnership with others.

In their collection of essays on the Indian boarding school experience, Clifford E. Trafzer, Jean A. Keller, and Lorene Sisquoc remind us that Native "storytellers" often "refer" to "negative forces as monsters." They note that for the pupils who attended Indian schools, the "English language, a foreign curriculum, and white officials represented monsters." Indian students combated these and other enemies through various forms of resistance. Some of these students, or "heroes," died fighting against the monsters they encountered at Indian schools, but many more survived and used their "newly acquired powers to do additional good for their people."[18] Hopi students encountered many "monsters" at Sherman Institute. Far from their village communities, Hopis relied on each other to overcome situations that otherwise may have "captured" or "swallowed" them up. In addition to the great hardships Hopi pupils experienced at the school, occasional—and at times violent—earthquakes frightened some Hopis about their temporary home in California.

Hopi pupil Marsah Balenquah recalled that one night in the 1920s she awoke from a strong earthquake that caused the walls in her dorm room to sway back and forth. The girls in the dorm screamed and ran into the hallway. Many of the girls searched for their dorm mothers, but all of the Hopi girls rushed to a common room and huddled together on a bed. Terrified at the shaking and sound of the earthquake, the girls cried and spoke to each other in Hopi and asked why they had ever left their homes for Sherman Institute.[19] That night the "monster" the girls encountered came in the form of a violent earthquake, but their foe did not overcome them. Comforting each other with Hopi words, the girls faced their fears and worked together to survive in a land far from home.

Hopis confronted other "monsters" at Sherman Institute that had far more serious consequences for the pupils. Dangers of all kinds surrounded the students. Indian pupils learned to make harnesses and build wagons in the school's industrial shop, cut pieces of wood with powerful electrical saws, and operate large modern appliances. Students did their best to operate the equipment safely, but serious accidents occasionally happened. In August 1910 fifteen-year-old Hopi pupil Bennie Pahsah [Tewanimptewa] from Moencopi was working in the laundry department when his "arm was caught in the centrifugal wringer." Superintendent Conser noted that the wringer "wrenched" Bennie's arms "so badly" that he feared that health officials would need to amputate.[20]

When Bennie's father, Frank Tewanimptewa, heard about his son's condition, he told Conser that he did not want the boy's arm to be severed.[21] But Conser, acting in a paternalistic fashion, disregarded the wishes of Bennie's parents and authorized the doctors at the school to cut off the arm between the "shoulder and the elbow."[22] Bennie's parents were heartbroken and upset that health officials amputated the arm. Bennie's mother, Tsuamana, was especially aggrieved by the situation. She accused

Conser of stealing Bennie's arm, and she demanded that he pay him monetary compensation for his loss. In a letter to Conser dated July 3, 1912, she told Conser that Hopi medicine men on the reservation could have healed the arm, and she expressed deep anger and disappointment in him for not allowing her son to come home prior to the scheduled amputation, which was a year and a half after the accident. "The boy went away well," Tsuamana told Conser, "and came home in such bad shape."[23] When Bennie's parents sent him to the "land of oranges" in the fall of 1909,[24] Hopi leaders Tawaquaptewa and Frank Seumptewa and their wives were no longer at the school, so the Hopi students were left to battle the "monsters" by themselves. Bennie faced a "monster" at Sherman Institute, but he survived the encounter and returned to the reservation in 1912.[25]

As well as bringing their traditional stories such as "Youth and Fire-Boy and the Giant Elk" to Sherman Institute, Hopi pupils came to the Indian school with a love and appreciation for music. In the early twentieth century, ethnomusicologist Natalie Curtis observed that the "music of the Indian is the spontaneous and sincere expression of the soul of a people."[26] Walter Hough once recalled that the music that "most attracted" his attention in "Hopiland" was the "various" songs for ceremonies, songs for "love, war, or for amusement," and songs "sung by mothers to their infants, or shrilled by women grinding corn." Hough further noted that in the land of the "Song Makers," the men sang "at their work" and the "children at their play."[27] Hopi poet Ramson Lomatewama once remarked that in Hopi culture, "we believe that when we sing songs, we are sharing our feelings of happiness with nature." Furthermore, Lomatewama notes that Hopis consider the corn plants to be their children, and when the Hopi farmers sing songs in their fields, it causes the corn to grow.[28]

Hopi knowledge and appreciation of music went with Hopi pupils to Sherman Institute. In the early 1900s, Hopi pupil Polingaysi Qoyawayma was instructed by her mother to sing many Hopi songs, and Polingaysi used her singing abilities to advance at Sherman. Polingaysi recalled that when she enrolled in school, her "strong lungs" immediately caught the "attention of her teachers." Although likely one of the smallest students for her age, Polingaysi had a powerful voice that made an impression on her classmates and teachers.[29] Soon musical opportunities became available for Polingaysi at the school. Government officials often incorporated music within the overall school curriculum, which gave the students an opportunity to share their talents with their peers, teachers, and people associated with the Riverside community. While some of the pupils at Sherman Institute welcomed the attention that came from performing, others reluctantly participated due to their shyness. When her teachers asked Polingaysi to "take a leading part in one of the school programs," the young Hopi girl was horrified at the thought of "making a mistake before an audience." Although sympathetic to her concerns, Polingaysi teachers firmly told her to overcome her anxiety. Polingaysi's "innate good sense and her love of music overcame her fears." By singing before large audiences, Polingaysi received "pleasure" by making others happy. Polingaysi used her singing ability to advance at the school, to overcome her sense of isolation, and to provide an avenue for expressing her feelings of joy and fear.[30] Polingaysi could have allowed her fears to overcome her, but her mother did not teach her to crumble when difficult situations arose. Instead, by using a talent first cultivated among her people, Polingaysi excelled at school and became an example for Hopi and non-Hopi students to follow.

The music trend at Sherman Institute was replicated by Hopi pupils at other off-reservation Indian boarding schools. Leigh J. Kuwanwisimwa recalled that when he attended the Ganado Mission School in Arizona, he took lessons in guitar.[31] Some Hopis became so proficient in music that they formed music ensembles or bands. Ivan Sidney, former chairman of the Hopi Tribe, along with other Hopis at the Phoenix Indian School, established the Hopi Clansmen, a band that played at school and non-school-related functions in the 1960s. In the early twenty-first century, Sidney reunited the Hopi Clansmen to play for the Phoenix Indian School reunions and at charitable events.[32]

Along with teaching through music and stories, Hopi adults taught their children many games that reminded Hopi children of life lessons. Although Hopi pupils participated in sports such as football, baseball, and basketball, they preserved and did not forget Hopi games and eagerly shared them with other Indian pupils at the school.[33] In November 1907, a group of Hopi boys introduced a spinning top game called riyànpi to their peers. Instead of using a string, the Hopi boys lashed at the spinning top with a cloth whip attached to a stick. Students at Sherman Institute reported that "all of the smaller" boys enjoyed the new game, and noted that the game required "no little skill."[34] Like other Hopi games, riyànpi improved and strengthened one physically, mentally, and spiritually. Hopi scholar and educator Willard Sakiestewa Gilbert from Upper Moencopi once observed that Hopi boys played riyànpi to improve their self-esteem and to demonstrate respect for their peers. In Hopi culture, girls did not play riyànpi, which explains why the Hopi boys and not the girls played the game and taught other boys at the school.[35]

The cultural purpose and reason for playing Hopi games on occasion conflicted with values reinforced at Sherman Institute.

School officials told the students that Americans valued winning and not losing. People in American society played games to defeat their opponent, not to show respect for the opposition. School officials instructed students to "fight for a principle, animated by an ideal." On the Hopi Reservation, the principles and ideals of playing games derived from the culture of the Hopi people. The American philosophy encouraged Hopi students to reject the education from their elders and to replace it with values esteemed by Western society. No longer in an environment or among a people who viewed games according to the Hopi way, the students at Sherman Institute learned that the "principle" worth fighting for was loyalty to the school, and the "ideal" that each should strive to gain was "success."[36]

At Sherman Institute, Hopi students relied on their cultural upbringing to help them learn new skills and embraced opportunities to integrate their indigenous ways with American ideologies and practices. In addition to incorporating their indigenous knowledge to the rigors of the school's academic and industrial-based programs, Hopi pupils returned to their culture in other activities such as games and sports. In his account of sports at Indian boarding schools, John Bloom keenly observed that "athletic contests, teams, and games existed at Indian boarding schools on a level of symbolic activity that was no less important than the day-to-day work and teaching that was done at these institutions."[37] The "symbolic activity" associated with sports fit with the assimilation agenda that officials implemented at Indian schools. The inclusion of sports for assimilation purposes, coupled with the fascination white Americans had with successful Indian athletes, made the school an ideal place for officials to develop football, basketball, baseball, and cross-country teams.

In addition to teaching them riyànpi, Hopi parents and elders encouraged their sons to be great long distant runners.[38] In his autobiography, Albert Yava (Hopi-Tewa) recalled that many years ago "men and boys from Oraibi used to run all the way to Moencopi" in the morning "to tend their fields there, and when they were finished they would run all the way back" that same afternoon.[39] The distance between Orayvi and Moencopi is approximately fifty-five miles, which meant that the men and boys ran over a hundred miles in one day. Hopis have always been known for their ability to run great distances, and their reputation as runners carried with them to various off-reservation Indian boarding schools throughout the United States. Louis Tewanima, the Hopi runner who attended Carlisle, is perhaps the most famous. Tewanima twice represented the U.S. and the Hopi people in the Olympic Games, first in 1908 in London and again in 1912 in Stockholm, where he won a silver medal in the 10,000-meter race. Although Tewanima has received nearly all of the publicity, other Hopi runners accomplished noteworthy achievements at different schools, including Sherman Institute.[40]

At the Indian school in Riverside, Hopis excelled in various running competitions. At the Sherman Institute Cross-Country Race in December 1922, "more than 1,000" spectators witnessed five Hopi pupils win "first places."[41] Led by Hopi student Loky Tewanimptewa, "who finished the three and three quarters miles in twenty minutes and 55 and one half seconds," the Hopi winners included James Humetewa, Thomas Humprey, Henry Humetewa, and Bruce Athutu. The "route taken by the [thirty] runners included a circuit" throughout Riverside that ended in front of the "grandstand" at the Chemawa park near the school. According to a *Riverside Press* reporter, the "race was a contest between the Hopis" and Navajos, although other Indian students participated in the event. The reporter further commented that according to "tradition, the Hopis have lived in the mesas of central Arizona for years and have grown their crops in the canyons below. This tribe of Indians is noted throughout the country for endurance and although the five men finishing first in yesterdays contest average less than 115 lbs and were small in stature, years of packing crops from the desert canyons to their mountain homes gave them the ability to out-run their Navajo rivals."[42] In spite of the report issued in the *Riverside Press*, Hopi running success at Sherman Institute did not develop as a result of hauling corn, beans, melons, and squash from the bottom of the "desert canyons." Long-distance running required training and a state of mind and being that involved every aspect of life. George Wharton James, a writer who often romanticized accounts about the southwest, correctly noted that it was not uncommon for an "Oraibi or Mashongavi to run to his home to Moenkopi, a distance of forty miles, over the hot blazing sands of a real American Sahara, there hoe his corn-field, and return to his home, within twenty-four hours."[43] For the Hopis, running was a trustworthy mode of transportation, and Hopi farmers relied on their ability to run to care for their fields.

The Hopi people believe they have an inseparable connection to the land, and in spite of a dry and arid climate, Hopis have successfully used ancient farming techniques. Apart from squash, beans, melons, grapes, peaches, apricots, and wheat, Hopis are best known for their corn. Corn has a central role in Hopi society, for the Hopi way of life revolves around corn.[44] In mid-April of each year, Hopis begin their first corn planting on fields located on and below the mesas. A second corn planting begins in May or early June, which Hopis consider to be the main corn crop. Varying in size from one-half acre to more than eleven acres, Hopi cornfields belong to individual Hopi clans and are passed down through the female lineage. Hopi agricultural success can be attributed to tried and tested methods, the ability to adapt to the environment, and Hopi ceremonies and prayers. Hopis have for generations used the dry farm technique with the seasonal planting of corn. Although some fields are located in close proximity to springs and washes, such as at Moencopi, Hopis have relied on the seasonal rains to water their crops. Once the corn plant emerges from the ground, the farmer protects the young plant, much as a Hopi mother takes care of her infant child, or a Hopi father cares for his young daughters.

Hopi boys brought this knowledge of planting and harvesting with them to the ranch at Sherman Institute and the farms located in the greater Riverside area. At times farm-related activities extended beyond the school's boundary. Depending on the location of the farms, local ranchers often hired Hopi pupils to work on their fields. With skills first developed on the Hopi mesas, Hopi students excelled at planting and harvesting and quickly familiarized themselves with new farming techniques in Southern California. At Sherman Institute, several Hopi pupils worked for Edgar Hazell, owner of the San Jacinto Ranch, and received noteworthy attention in the local newspaper. Hazell, a retired barrister from London and known as one of the most "successful ranchers in Riverside County," remarked to a *Riverside Press* reporter that the Hopi boys he employed made thorough, "trustworthy and efficient help."[45]

Hopis excelled at the ranch because they came to school already highly skilled in agriculture. Hopi archivist Stewart B. Koyiyumptewa from Hotevilla observed that this advantage separated Hopis from other Indian pupils who arrived at boarding schools with little or no knowledge of farming.[46] Whereas the Navajo students came to schools with an acute understanding of raising livestock, Hopi students' expertise was agriculture. Hopis transferred skills that Hopi fathers, uncles, and grandfathers had taught them prior to their attendance at U.S. government schools. On the reservation, Hopi children cleared fields, planted, hoed weeds, and harvested crops. In his autobiography, Don Talayesva recalled that "learning to work was like play. We children tagged around with our elders and copied what they did. We followed our fathers to the fields and helped plant and weed. The old men took us for walks and taught us the use of plants and how to collect them."[47] For Don and the other Hopi boys at the school, the lessons that their parents and elders had given them contributed to their success in each aspect of the school's ranch-related programs.[48]

Although school officials allowed Hopis to practice their songs, stories, dances, and art at Sherman Institute, Superintendents Hall and Conser's willingness to allow aspects of Hopi culture at the school had its limits: they had little tolerance for what they considered to be Hopi religion. School officials believed that this aspect of Hopi culture originated from Satan, and so they encouraged the students to replace their Hopi spiritual beliefs with Christian teachings from the Bible. Hopi pupils going to Sherman Institute arrived at an institution that was designed to assimilate them into Western society, a society whose citizenship was based on Christian ideals and values. Similar to when the ancient Hopi clans ventured beyond the mesas and met people who held to different religious beliefs and customs, the Hopis arrived at Sherman Institute and encountered a people from across the United States who had deep commitments to Christian beliefs and practices. But at the Indian school in Riverside, Christian ministers and teachers did not want Hopis and other Indian students to simply fuse Christian and Native religious teachings together. They wanted the pupils to abandon their indigenous beliefs for biblical doctrine and return to their communities as Protestant missionaries who would continue the process of assimilation and indoctrination with their people on the reservation.

6. Learning to Preach

On June 2, 1915, nearly six hundred Indian pupils gathered in the main auditorium at Sherman Institute. Eager to see their classmates graduate at the school's thirteenth annual baccalaureate ceremony, the pupils filed into the auditorium, quickly took their assigned seats, and waited for the service to begin. Although the students were accustomed to meeting in the auditorium for various events, the baccalaureate service held special meaning for the entire school; students and teachers alike looked forward to the service with great anticipation. In previous years, school officials at Sherman Institute had invited prominent government officials or educators to serve as the keynote speaker for the event, but on this occasion the school's superintendent, Frank M. Conser, called on Reverend Horace Porter to address the graduates and other students in the auditorium.

A Protestant minister and pastor of the First Congregational Church in Riverside, Porter was a familiar face to several of the students, including some Hopis who regularly attended his church. After expressing his gratitude for the opportunity to speak to the students, Porter told the pupils that he hoped that they would succeed in life and not forget the following three points: "First. You are workers. Second. You are workers together. Third. You are workers together with God!"[1] It was God, Porter told the students, who provided them with hands and feet to work with. Making his message tangible, Porter called on the Indian pupils to look at their hands and told them that their "hands [were] one of the most wonderful things in all the world." Porter reminded the pupils that with their "four fingers and a thumb" they made "bows and arrows and shoes and clothes and pictures and books and wagons and houses and bridges and automobiles and airplanes" all because God had given them the ability to work with their hands. Calling their attention to a Tallyho wagon made by former Hopi student Victor Sakiestewa, Porter asked the students, "Who made the wood? Who made the iron? God made the wood and iron. Who then made the Tallyho? Was it not made by God and Sakiestewa?" Porter's message portrayed God at work alongside the efforts of men and women. He challenged the students to realize that after they had completed their education at Sherman Institute and went "out into the great world again," they ought never to forget to be workers "together with God."[2]

For many of the Hopi pupils in the audience, going "out into the great world" meant returning home to the Hopi Reservation. Although some students remained in California or secured work in other parts of the country, the vast majority of the Hopi pupils migrated back home and away from the structured lifestyle found at the Indian school in Riverside. School officials and religious leaders realized that the baccalaureate service was one of the last opportunities for them to address the graduating class on religion and life beyond the school. For the students remaining at the school, Porter's message served as a reminder that the lessons learned at Sherman Institute, including what they had been taught about the Bible and Christianity, needed to return with them to their homes and village communities on the reservation. The school's success at assimilating Indians was gauged by the number of pupils who returned home and practiced the skills and knowledge acquired at the school. For students who actively participated in various Christian activities both on and off the school campus, religious officials such as Reverend Porter fervently hoped that they would live as Christians and share Christianity with their communities.

In the early twentieth century, government officials routinely exposed American Indian pupils to Christian teachings at off-reservation Indian boarding schools. Christian instruction at Indian schools served as an evangelistic tool for Protestant and Catholic clergy and played a significant role in the government's overall assimilation of Indian people. While off-reservation Indian boarding schools existed primarily to train Indian students in industrial trades such as farming and blacksmithing, school officials often encouraged Indian pupils to attend Christian gatherings, pray Christian prayers, and adopt, at least for a time, a cultural worldview based on the Christian Bible. At Sherman Institute, school officials incorporated the Christian faith in the school's curriculum, music instruction, and various activities on and off the school campus. Among those in attendance at the school, the Hopi pupils accounted for a significant portion of Indian students who experienced firsthand the U.S. government's attempt to assimilate them through a Christian education. While some Hopi students accepted the religious lessons and principles taught at the school, others rejected Christianity and refused to abandon or adapt their Hopi beliefs to fit with the Christian faith.

The U.S. government created off-reservation Indian boarding schools to destroy Indian cultures, train pupils in industrial trades, and further the ideals and values of white Protestant America. Christianity was only one of many tools the government used to accomplish these goals. In this regard, off-reservation Indian boarding schools did not operate solely as secular institutions, but neither did they function entirely as religious ones. Unlike the Bible-centered education Indian pupils received at Catholic Indian boarding schools such as Saint Boniface in Banning, California, or the Native residential schools in Canada, U.S. government schools merged Christianity with education to create citizens of Indian people.[3] Citizenship stood as the ultimate goal in the U.S. government's use of Christianity in the education of Indian pupils. In light of this, the officials realized that Indian people would not permanently change and become full citizens unless the U.S. government, through the institution of Indian boarding schools, separated Indians from their religious ways and replaced them with the Christian faith.[4] As Chickasaw historian Amanda J. Cobb once observed, "teaching the students white Christian traditions was not enough for missionaries; stripping the students of Native traditions had to happen simultaneously."[5]

The primary objective of Protestant and Catholic missionaries in sharing the Christian faith with Hopis was centered on an internal, spiritual transformation of the soul. Alongside this transformation, missionaries throughout Hopi history used Christianity to replace certain aspects of Hopi religious culture. Furthermore, in the late nineteenth and early twentieth century, philanthropists who financially supported American Indian education gained much of their "moral energy" from religious reformers who wanted America to consist primarily of (Protestant) Christian citizens. David Wallace Adams observed that philanthropists did not simply want to "snatch the Indians' soul from a hellish fate"; they adamantly believed that American citizenship could not happen apart from "Christian morality."[6]

In addition to religious reformers, Commissioner of Indian Affairs Francis E. Leupp significantly shaped the U.S. government's Christian education policies of the early twentieth century.[7] In 1905, Leupp wrote B. B. Custer, superintendent of the Indian School in Albuquerque, New Mexico, and outlined his Christian education policy at Indian boarding schools. Leupp told Custer that he grew up in the "old-fashioned notion" that the American government stood for "all religious faiths" and that the "separation of Church and State" was a primary principle in the United States' "patriotic creed." Leupp further commented that "any school system conducted at the public expense ought either to eliminate all religions" or "adopt one which will be as nearly universal as it can possibly be made." Leupp admitted to Custer that, had he established the first "Indian school system," he would have "cut it wholly free, as far as the Government's share in the training of the children was concerned, from any and all ecclesiastical connections."[8] However, Leupp clearly conveyed to Custer that he did not intend to "abolish religion from the schools, but merely confine the school's own teaching, as far as its spiritual phases were concerned, to good morals."[9] Indian boarding schools throughout the United States, including Sherman Institute, adopted Commissioner Leupp's Christian education policy.

Although Sherman Institute did not offer courses on the Bible or theology prior to the early 1930s, school officials encouraged Indian pupils to participate in various Christian activities. Christian events at the Indian school in Riverside included weekly Bible studies for boys and girls and chapel services held in the school's auditorium. In accordance with government policy, Leupp advocated that all "dogmatic religion" be left to missionaries and their organizations, whom Leupp gave the "freest access" to Indian pupils. Leupp insisted that school officials incorporate Christian principles in daily academic instruction. However, in areas such as evangelistic preaching and in-depth Bible study, he allowed Protestant and Catholic clergy to have full control. At Leupp's insistence, school officials at Sherman Institute limited Christianity in the classroom to universal moral values, which included "virtues of kindness; . . . self control of passions; charitableness of judgment and gentleness of speech and action; . . . cleanliness of body and mind; honesty and unselfishness" and all "elements of human conduct which [make] for better relations between fellow men."[10] Although not exclusively Protestant ideals, the virtues taught at the school reflected the teachings of most major Christian denominations in the United States.

At no point in the early twentieth century did government officials allow non-Christian religious groups to work among students at Indian schools. Religious principles and values "expressed and encouraged" at Sherman Institute were those of the Christian faith. In school applications from 1902 to 1929, every Hopi student checked "Protestant" as their preferred faith. The only other option would have been to check "Catholic," as school officials did not allow Native religion at the school (unless it took the form of Indian dances or songs for entertainment purposes) and did not even consider other world religions. When asked if any Hopi students attended Catholic services at the Indian school in Riverside, Bessie Humetewa from the Hopi village of Bacavi, a student at Sherman Institute in the 1920s, replied "No, all Hopi students only attended Protestant services."[11]

Humetewa's observation is best understood in light of past experiences Hopis had with Christian missionaries. Like many Indian students who attended off-reservation boarding schools in the early 1900s, Hopis had been introduced to Christianity by missionaries before the U.S. government forced them to receive an Anglo-American education. As Catholic clergy continued to bring Christianity to Hopis in the seventeenth century, some Hopis welcomed the priests, while others despised their presence and in 1680 forced the Catholic Church off Hopi land. Historian Harry C. James correctly observed that there was such a "distrust [and] hatred, of everything Spanish," that it "permeated Hopi thinking down through the centuries."[12] This negative and suspicious opinion of Catholicism went with Hopi pupils to the Indian school at Riverside; consequently, none who attended between 1906 and 1929 did so as Roman Catholics.

Protestant denominations such as the Mennonites also contributed to Hopi opinion of Christianity.[13] Prior to their attendance at Sherman Institute, no early twentieth-century Christian directly influenced Hopis more than Mennonite missionary Heinrich R. Voth. Born in Russia in 1855, Voth ministered to Hopis at Orayvi from 1893 to 1902. Shortly before he started his ministry on the reservation, Peter Stauffer, a fellow Mennonite, informed Voth that the Hopis needed "more than the white man's clothing, houses and education"; they needed the "Gospel of Jesus Christ."[14] During his nine-year stay at Orayvi, Voth earned the respect of many Hopis who conversed with him in their Native tongue. However, regardless of Voth's fluency in the Hopi language and understanding of Hopi culture, his evangelistic efforts did not produce any immediate Hopi conversions. Anthropologist Peter Whiteley noted that in his time with the Hopis, Voth did not secure one Hopi convert.[15]

The absence of Hopi conversions should not be perceived as a complete Mennonite failure. The Mennonites required all converts to make a public profession of faith via baptism by immersion as a testimony of their commitment to Christ. Unless a missionary baptized an individual, he or she was not considered a genuine convert. In the early twentieth century, some Hopis believed in the Christian god, but did not make a public profession of faith before their families or village leaders. A group of Hopis did participate in Christian services and actively attended church. Many Hopi children who attended Voth's congregation eventually enrolled at the Indian school in Riverside. Polingaysi Qoyawayma knew Voth personally and participated in his ministry prior to her arrival at Sherman Institute in 1906. Before she attended the school, Polingaysi enjoyed "attending religious services" led by Voth and the other Mennonites, "for she loved to sing."[16] The Mennonites taught Polingaysi and other Hopi children many Christian songs. More important from the missionaries' perspective, the Mennonites used songs and stories to introduce Hopi children to the Bible and the Christian faith. The religious foundation Voth and the Mennonites laid, particularly among the Orayvi children, carried with Hopi pupils to the Indian school in Riverside.[17]

Although the Mennonites earned the respect and friendship of some Hopis, Voth's ministry had its share of Hopi critics. In his autobiography, Don Talayesva recalled that when Voth and the "Christians came to Oraibi and preached Jesus in the plaza where the Katsinas danced," the "old people paid no attention" to them, but parents told their children "to accept any gifts and clothing" handed out by the missionaries. Don recalled that Voth "never preached Christ" to him alone; rather, he always talked about Christianity to Hopis in a group. In accordance with Christian teachings, which placed great emphasis on the life, death, and resurrection of Jesus Christ, Voth told Don and other Hopi children that Jesus was their "Savior" who had paid the price for their sins. Don recalled that to demonstrate the power of the Christian god, Voth instructed him and other Hopis to "ask Jesus for whatever" they wanted. For Don, oranges and "candy looked pretty good," and so he prayed for them just as Voth had instructed him to do. But when Don finished praying and fixed his gaze toward heaven, Jesus did not "throw anything down" to him.[18]

Voth told Don that the Hopi gods he believed in "were no good." However, Don did not listen to Voth, but sought the counsel of his Hopi elders who reminded him that "when the Katsinas danced in the plaza it often rained." The older Hopis in the village taught Don "that the missionaries had no business condemning [their] gods," for doing so "might cause droughts and famine." Don's distrust of Christianity transferred with him to Sherman Institute, where school officials and religious leaders attempted to convince him to abandon Hopi beliefs for the Christian faith.[19]

The U.S. government's desire that Hopi and non-Hopi Indian students abandon their traditional religions for Christianity was a necessary component of the education provided at Sherman Institute and other off-reservation boarding schools. In May 1909, the Sherman Bulletin included a short article that reflected the overall Christian tenor of the school. The article noted that "if the world is ever to be conquered for Christ it will be by every one doing his own work, filling his own sphere, holding his own part, and saying to Jesus, 'Jesus, what wilt thou have me to do.'"[20] At Sherman Institute, school officials believed that the objective of creating a Christian world went beyond conversion at the school. According to school and religious leaders, the "world" primarily meant other Indian people who lived on the reservation, so Sherman Institute trained Indian pupils in

Christianity to conquer their fellow Indians for Christ. School officials wanted Hopis to return to the reservation as mechanics, plumbers, and good house wives, and they eagerly desired Hopis to leave the school as Protestant missionaries.[21]

Don Talayesva evidenced this Christian-world objective in a sermon he delivered at Sherman Institute for the Young Men's Christian Association (YMCA). When Don and two other Hopi pupils, Adolph Hoye and Harry McClain, attended the gatherings, the association leaders expected them to rise from their seats and bear witness for Jesus Christ. During his three-year stay at Sherman Institute, Don wrote a short sermon that he willingly recited when called upon to give a Christian testimony. The sermon he wrote and memorized provides a telling commentary in how officials used Christianity at the school:

> Well, my partners, I am asked to speak a few words for Jesus. I am glad that I came to Sherman and learned to read and cipher. Now I discover that Jesus was a good writer. So I am thankful that Uncle Sam taught me to read in order that I may understand the Scriptures and take my steps along God's road. When I get a clear understanding of the Gospel I shall return home and preach it to my people in darkness. I will teach them all about Jesus Christ, the Heavenly Father, and the Holy Ghost.[22]

Don beseeched his friends to "pray to God" for enlightenment and told them that once God had opened their minds with his truth, they would be "ready for Jesus to come." Don ended his message by telling the group of YMCA boys that he did not "want any of [his] friends to be thrown into the lake of hell fire, where there is suffering and sorrow forever."[23]

Don's sermon was exactly what school officials and religious leaders wanted to hear from one of their Indian pupils. His appreciation for the education that he received at Sherman Institute, and the connection he saw between learning to read and the ability to understand Scripture, surely won him favor in the eyes of the YMCA leaders and the school's administration. What is perhaps most significant in Don's sermon is his apparent eagerness to return home and preach the Gospel to the Hopi people. In light of Don's sermon, one may be tempted to conclude that Don experienced Christian conversion. But Don's profession of faith did not make him a genuine convert. In fact, when Don returned home, he became a Sun Chief, or head religious leader of the Sun Clan, and participated in Hopi ceremonies.

Don Talayesva was not the only Hopi who migrated back to the reservation with a stronger commitment to Hopi religion and culture. In September 1924, J. H. McClintock, a reporter for the *Los Angeles Times*, noted that in spite of many years of Christian efforts to end the Hopi Snake Dance at Orayvi, many of the "Snake Dance priests" were "young men who [had] been given a reasonable degree of education in the Riverside and Phoenix schools and [had] returned to re-enter the tribal life as they had left it."[24] To the disappointment of Christian missionaries who ministered to the people on the reservation, many Hopi students who experienced a Christian education at Sherman Institute eventually returned home as leaders of various Hopi religious societies.

Hopis who resumed their religious culture once they returned to the reservation often had participated in the school's YMCA or the Young Women's Christian Association (YWCA). At the Indian school in Riverside, the two Christian organizations held weekly Bible studies and met regularly on campus for Christian fellowship. Pastors from local churches or important men from the greater Riverside area often gave inspirational talks to the boys in the YMCA. In March 1907, the Honorable C. E. Rumsey, noted as "one of Southern California's prominent and busy men," led the YMCA Bible study. Some of the students at the school observed that Rumsey "wields a strong influence for good, and Sherman appreciates his efforts."[25] At times the YMCA called on medical professionals such as Doctor William W. Roblee to address medical and religious issues. In May 1907, Roblee spoke to a group of forty-six Indian students, some of them Hopi, on health concerns that related to boys under the age of fourteen.[26]

The girls in the YWCA had a growing Bible study on campus as well. At the same time Roblee spoke to the boys on health issues, Alice Marmon and Mrs. Hall, wife of Superintendent Harwood Hall, facilitated a talk on "Covetousness or [P]etty Jealousy" to the YWCA girls. Those in attendance noted that the meeting was "very helpful," and commented how Mrs. Hall never failed "to enthuse and help the girls."[27] The practical effect of religion on the student's school life was a common theme in Christian messages at Sherman Institute. In April 1907, several YWCA girls, along with their leader Sadie Asquabe, spoke on "Our School Work and Our Religion" and "Weekday Practice of Sunday Preaching." In "Our School Work and Religion," the message emphasized that a "girl's religion, if genuine, will show in her daily deportment as well as in her industrial and class work."[28]

Because Hopi girls attended the YWCA meetings, religious leaders and school instructors expected Hopi pupils to conduct their work as unto the Lord to evidence the sincerity of their Christian conversion. Similar to policies followed at the Phoenix school, officials at Sherman Institute wanted students to practice the Christian faith. Historian Robert Trennert Jr. noted that officials at the school encouraged the YWCA and other Christian "activities because they supposedly instilled a spirit of Christian charity."[29] Officials at Sherman Institute likewise desired Hopi girls to attend the YWCA to show kindness and love to their fellow schoolmates. In 1918, while a student at Sherman Institute, Louise Talas [Talasitiwa], a Hopi pupil from the village of Moencopi, was baptized at the Presbyterian Christian Union.[30] Louise's profession of faith reflected her commitment to Christianity, which in turn affected her Christian involvement at the school. In November 1920, Louise led a YWCA Bible study and delivered a message titled "How I Should Treat the Bible." Those who attended the meeting commented that Louise's subject matter "was very interesting."[31]

At off-reservation Indian boarding schools, Indian students participated in Christian activities for various reasons. Although school officials at Sherman Institute encouraged students to join Christian organizations, the amount of student involvement largely depended on the individual pupil. Some students found the social environment appealing, often because their friends attended the Christian meetings. Both the YMCA and YWCA gatherings included food, music, and movie entertainment, all of which encouraged Indian pupil involvement. In November 1920, the YMCA boys showed a movie called *The Secret Garden* in the school's auditorium. Movie events were popular among Indian pupils at the school and provided the students with an opportunity to raise money for the YMCA.[32] In addition to the social and entertainment reasons for Hopi involvement, some Hopis possessed a genuine interest in the Christian faith and eagerly joined the school's religious organizations. Others Hopis, such as Roscoe Polewytewa, not only participated in the YMCA but held leadership roles as well. In November 1915, nearly sixty members in attendance for a YMCA gathering at Sherman Institute appointed Roscoe to lead the Devotional Committee for the upcoming year. Roscoe's appointment to the committee likely encouraged further Hopi involvement in the association.[33]

Alongside the YMCA and YWCA, Hopis participated in additional Christian events at the school. On rare occasion, officials permitted students to marry each other at the school (students ranged as old as their thirties between 1906 and 1929). In September 1907, two Hopi pupils from Orayvi, Arthur Sehauma and Delle Konawysia, took part in a so-called proper Protestant wedding that Mr. D. L. Macquarrie, pastor of the Arlington Presbyterian Church, officiated on campus. Considered a civil, as opposed to an Indian, marriage, the wedding was "believed to be the first occasion in which a bride and groom of the primitive Hopi tribe [had] been married according to the customs of the white people."[34]

In addition to several Hopi pupils, the Orayvi chief, Tawaquaptewa, was also an "interested spectator" of the event.[35] Tawaquaptewa could have protested the Christian marriage between the two Hopis, but instead he attended the ceremony and joined the others in wishing the young couple a happy and fulfilling life together. Unfortunately, the relationship that flourished at Sherman Institute came to an end eleven years later. In May 1918, Leo Crane, Superintendent of the Moqui Reservation, wrote Conser and informed him that the circumstances between Delle and Arthur had "become quite complicated." Eager to clear up a "very unsatisfactory condition among the Oraibi" people, Crane requested the exact date of Delle's and Arthur's marriage so that Arthur could officially file for a petition of divorce.[36] Don

Talayesva once remarked that the "American marriage is too easy to make and too hard to break. It is difficult and expensive to get married the Hopi way, but if a man finds he has made a mistake it is easy to escape."[37] Apparently, Delle and Arthur had made a mistake and were discovering how difficult and complicated it was to end an "American marriage."

Whereas some Hopis celebrated marriage according to the Christian custom, other Hopis at Sherman Institute participated in Christian ceremonies at their deaths. At many Indian schools and reservations in North America, diseases such as pneumonia, whooping cough, and tuberculosis affected Indian pupils. For those students who died at the Indian school in Riverside, Superintendent Hall allotted a small piece of land for the school's cemetery. Located near the Sherman Ranch, the cemetery served both Catholic and Protestant students, and indeed any Indian student who needed burial. In November 1908, Hopi pupil Adam Nakhaha died of "heart failure caused by pneumonia." Within hours of his death, Adam's classmates buried him in the school's cemetery where school officials administered a Christian funeral.[38] In April 1919, Amos Lomakatohya, a Hopi pupil from Orayvi, died of pulmonary tuberculosis. At the insistence of Amos' family, health officials buried Amos at the school's cemetery.[39]

Students and school officials often talked about tuberculosis at Sherman Institute. In November 1920, Superintendent Frank M. Conser addressed the subject in a Sunday chapel service held in the school's auditorium. The majority of Conser's talk centered on the Phoenix Sanatorium in Arizona, where government officials routinely sent Indian pupils infected with tuberculosis.[40] School officials often used the weekly chapel service to promote subjects such as Indian health or Indian compliance. In June

1909 Conser told a group of Hopi pupils to encourage their parents at Orayvi to take the U.S. government's allotment for them, "in order that they might get good land."[41] Conser's use of the Christian chapel service as a tool to enforce and encourage government policy is evident throughout his tenure at Sherman Institute from 1909 to 1931.[42]

Along with his use of the chapel for agendas deemed important by the U.S. government, Conser incorporated the chapel building in the celebration of Christian holidays. At Christmas, school officials decorated the campus and adapted chapel services to reflect messages that centered on baby Jesus and the virgin birth. Christmas was both an exciting and confusing time for Hopi students. In their children's book *Climbing Sun*, Marjorie Thayer and Elizabeth Emanuel note that prior to Hubert Honanie's first Christmas at Sherman in the late 1920s, the school's superintendent, Conser mandated that students attend church the Sunday before Christmas day. While Hubert sat in the chapel service, he listened carefully to what the minister said about the birth of Jesus, but he did not see why this baby was so important. Hubert concluded that Christmas held little significance. Although he liked having the day off from school and enjoyed eating the traditional Christmas food of turkey and cranberries, he would have "preferred stewed rabbit or mutton and corn" prepared according to Hopi custom.[43]

By the 1930s the tradition of Christmas had become very popular among Hopi children on the reservation. In *The Hopi Indians of Old Oraibi*, anthropologist Mischa Titiev noted that several children had taken part in Christmas programs at places such as Sherman Institute and the Phoenix Indian School, and that several of their parents enjoyed giving them presents on Christmas. Titiev observed that in December 1933, Hopi women walked to Kykotsmovi at the foot of Third Mesa to purchase Christmas presents for the Orayvi children. Afraid that the children would be disappointed if they did not receive gifts, the women purchased enough presents for each child in the village.[44] Although the Christmas tradition continues with many Hopis today, Hopis incorporate their culture into the holiday as well. Hopi artists demonstrate this through their art, and some Hopis, particularly those who belong to church congregations on the reservation, sing Christmas carols in the Hopi language.

At Sherman Institute, officials also taught Hopi women to be submissive housewives and encouraged them to be quiet and gentle in spirit, which reflected teachings expressed in the Christian Bible.[45] The submissive-housewife mentality fit well with Anglo-American culture at the time, but it went against the complex system of the Hopi matriarchal society. Edmund Nequatewa recalled that in the Hopi creation story some of the husbands told their wives that it was a "joy to cheat and steal another man's wife." In response, the Hopi women refused to be near their husbands and forced them out of the house. Without a place to stay, the Hopi men retreated to their kivas where they waited until they had enough courage to return to their wives. One by one, the husbands approached their homes, and as they did, they found all of their belongings piled outside the door.[46] Although the women eventually allowed their husbands to return, the Hopi creation story demonstrates the power and influence of women in Hopi society. At the Indian school in Riverside, Ranch instructors encouraged Hopi girls to abandon their tribal understanding of womanhood and instead become good Christian farm wives who would one day live faithful Christian lives on the Hopi Reservation.[47]

Clearly, school officials never intended Christianity to remain at the school once Hopis returned to the reservation. Along with their new industrial skills and familiarity with English, Hopi students were expected to share Christ with their families, who officials believed remained in spiritual darkness. Those who returned home and shared the Gospel did so with a mixture of fear, anxiety, and a genuine eagerness to see their families come to know Jesus. Effie Sachowengsie, a Hopi pupil from Orayvi who attended Sherman Institute from 1906 to 1909, considered it her calling to witness to her family and Hopi community after her school days in Riverside. Known at the school for her ability to bake, Effie noted on a 1911 Record of Graduates and Returned Students form that the focus of "her life" was Jesus Christ. She was "so happy in Him" that she had been involved in the Lord's "work every day" since she left Sherman Institute.[48] In a letter to an unknown individual, Effie wrote that she was "still laboring for the Lord" and commented that the "harvest is [plentiful], but the worker[s] are few."[49]

Shortly after Effie returned home in 1909, she worked as a cook at the Mission to the Navajo and Other Indian Tribes station at Tolchaco in north central Arizona near the town of Leupp. In May 1911, while working in Tolchaco, Effie received an invitation from Conser to attend the school's annual commencement ceremony. When Effie responded to Conser's letter, she informed the superintendent that she would not be able to attend the commencement since the "Lord's work" was in "great need" of her at Tolchaco.[50] Although likely disappointed about Effie's absence, Conser surely understood and valued the Christian work she was involved with on the reservation.[51]

Some Hopis who attended Indian schools wanted to return home as Christians but feared that their families would not be pleased with their commitment to Christ. Abigail Johnson, a

Baptist Missionary to Hopis in the 1920s, noted that a Hopi girl from the Phoenix Indian School wrote a relative on the Hopi Reservation and stated: "I want very much to come home this summer, but I am a Christian, and if I do, I know they will not let me go to church."[52] Johnson explains that the girl wanted to attend church on the reservation, but she was afraid of the ridicule she would receive from her uncles and other family members if they knew she had become a Christian. Instead of enduring the disappointment of her family, the young girl went to California where she worked for a summer. While living in California, she fell ill with tuberculosis and as her health condition worsened, she returned to the reservation to be close to her family.

The Baptist missionaries on the reservation sadly observed that when the Hopi girl regained her strength, she eventually married and lived her life according to the Hopi way.[53] Although it is uncertain why the Hopi girl abandoned her Christian faith, missionaries and religious leaders at boarding schools often feared that Christian students would revert back to their tribal ways once they returned to the reservation. In her examination of the Chilocco Indian School in Oklahoma, K. Tsianina Lomawaima observed that a major reason the U.S. government created off-reservation boarding schools was to separate Indian pupils from their familiar culture. Lomawaima noted that "attempts to teach children English, Christianity, and the moral superiority of a clean life of honest labor were constantly undermined by the so-called bad influences of family and tribe."[54] The Hopi influences on the reservation may have caused the young girl to reconsider her decision to follow Jesus, which would explain her desire to live life in a way that "pleased her people."[55]

Hopis at Sherman Institute had similar experiences as Hopis

who attended the Phoenix Indian School. In the 1920s, Johnson observed that she received a letter from a Hopi pupil at Sherman Institute who was terrified at the thought of returning to his village of Moencopi as a Christian. The boy noted that if he told his father that he converted to Christianity, he would be upset and disappointed with him. When the boy eventually confessed to his family about his commitment to Christ, the boy's father said: "I have seventy sheep for you, and they are yours if you come up here and live in the village, help me with my work, and help us with the Hopi ceremonies; but if you do not do that, I will not give the sheep to you." Certain of his decision to follow Jesus, the boy refused to deny Jesus for his father's inheritance, which may have caused division in his family for years to come.[56]

When Hopi pupils went to Sherman Institute, they encountered students from many different cultures. They also came across school officials, teachers, matrons, and ministers who encouraged them to replace their Hopi religious beliefs with teachings found in the Christian Bible. Their migration to the "land of the oranges," and their further exposure to Christianity, had various layers of meaning for the Hopi people. At the Indian school in Riverside, Hopis attended Christian services and events without the presence of their parents. When Hopis migrated back to their ancestral lands in northeastern Arizona, their decision to continue to embrace or to reject a Christian worldview became difficult and complicated. Hopi students soon realized that being "workers together with God" on the reservation was not an easy task. In her account of a Hopi woman's friendship with a white woman from New England during the 1920s and 1930s, historian and autobiographer Carolyn O'Bagy Davis noted that government officials referred to Hopi Christians as "Agency Indians," and gave incentives to Hopi converts with clothes, shelter, employment, and food.[57] However, so-called traditional Hopis despised those who returned to their villages as Christians, and they blamed Christianity for the erosion of the Hopi way of life.[58] This was only one of many difficult situations Hopis faced when they returned to the Hopi mesas.

7. Returning to Hopi

In the ancient Hopi migrations, the clans traveled beyond the mesas and migrated in the four cardinal directions. The clans did not stay away forever, but eventually returned to their ancestral lands. Hopi clans had experienced a different life beyond the Hopi mesas, and when they returned home they brought with them new skills, new ways of thinking, and altered perspectives on life. The tradition of Hopi migration continued as the Hopi pupils returned to their mesas from Sherman Institute. Although the majority of the Hopi students physically traveled back to the reservation after they had completed their term at the school, others became homesick while at school and came home in their thoughts and prayers. At certain times in the year, Hopi pupils thought longingly about the dances that were taking place at their villages. While the students could not join their families or village communities, they remembered how the fringes of the Hopi belts swayed as the Katsinas danced, and the smell and taste of food that their mothers, grandmothers, sisters, and aunties prepared.

Acoma writer and poet Simon J. Ortiz notes that Indian pupils who went to boarding schools were "necessary to the integrity" and "wholeness" of their families, clans, and people.[1] When Indian students attended U.S. government schools, the ceremonial and social life on their reservations continued on, and many of these students felt "rootless" and disconnected from their communities. In an interview with Hopi archivist Stewart B. Koyiyumptewa, Harry Nutumya from Orayvi recalled that when he left for Sherman Institute in 1971, the corn and other vegetables had just become ready to harvest. "That was kind of a little hard from the beginning," noted Nutumya. "We knew that now they're going to be roasting corn," and "we're going to miss out on that."[2] In some circumstances, students longed for home to such a degree that they ran away. Similar to other Indian pupils who attended off-reservation boarding schools in the early twentieth century, some Hopis became ill at school with tuberculosis, whooping cough, or pneumonia and tragically came home in a coffin.

Government officials did not intend for Hopi pupils to remain at off-reservation Indian boarding schools indefinitely. Schools such as Sherman Institute trained students in industrial vocations, and officials routinely encouraged Hopis to take their knowledge and skills to their reservation and village communities. In addition to encouraging Hopis to bring new skills and trades to their people, superintendents and teachers wanted the pupils to return home as "new Indians" who would influence their people in American ways and not "relapse into barbarianism" as some officials feared.[3] Hopis typically attended Sherman Institute for a period of one to three years, and Superintendent Hall kept students at the school until their term expired. Beginning in 1909, however, school officials extended standard school terms, which caused students to remain at Sherman Institute for longer periods of time. Only in certain circumstances did Hall permit the students to leave for home early. For example, Hall let students who lived "within a reasonable distance . . . visit their homes during" summer vacations, but he required parents to pay for their child's travel expenses. Hall's under-standing of "reasonable distance" was Southern California and did not include Indian reservations in Arizona or New Mexico.[4] Consequently, Hopi pupils at Sherman Institute rarely returned home during their schooling to visit their parents or other family members. Bessie Humetewa from Bacavi, a student at Sherman Institute in the 1920s, remained at the school for eight years before she went home to see her family.[5] Marsah Balenquah remained at Sherman Institute from 1920 to 1934; when she returned to the reservation after fourteen years away, she was unable to speak Hopi.[6]

Many Indian pupils lost the ability to speak their indigenous languages during their time at U.S. government-run schools. As David Wallace Adams observes: "For some schools, all of the object lessons, the copying over of sentences, and recitations, and the letter writing paid off to the point that some students began to lose touch with their Native tongue."[7] School policies that required students to communicate only in English had a detrimental effect on American Indian cultures. Some Hopis returned to the Hopi mesas as nonspeakers of Hopi, but many eventually reacquired their use of the language. Students came home to families who spoke Hopi and practiced Hopi ways. Consequently, it did not take long for most Hopis who attended off-reservation Indian boarding schools to communicate once again in their indigenous language. Although Marsah Balenquah was unable to speak Hopi when she returned from Sherman Institute in 1934, she reacclimated to life on the reservation and was able to speak fluent Hopi within a month.

School officials established the policy that prevented student visits home for several reasons. Most importantly, school ad-ministrators believed that students who frequently went home would return to the life and ways of their people. They feared that this frequent exposure to their communities would undermine the assimilation process taking place at Sherman Institute. School officials such as Hall and Conser desired that the Indian pupils would be convinced of the superiority of Anglo-American culture before they traveled back to their reservations. They also feared that students would not want to return to school after spending time at home. Additionally, the school could not easily absorb the cost of student travel expenses, which was aggravated when students visited home and failed to return to school. Even when school officials granted students permission to visit their families at their own expense, students or their parents could not afford the cost of transportation. In his work on the Rapid City Indian School in South Dakota, Scott Riney observes that "bringing students home for summer vacations, the only time during the year they could leave the school, proved costly, and again the burden fell on the families."[8] The policy that retained students at school resulted in student alienation from Native communities. Consequently, at the completion of their schooling, Indian pupils found the transition from boarding school to the reservation more difficult. In her examination of the Chemawa Indian Boarding School in Oregon, Sonciray Bonnell noted that the change from school to home "was not always an easy or pleasant one. The students who spent many years away from their homes learning foreign cultural values and life styles suffered severe transition problems upon returning home."[9] For the returned Hopi student, one of the areas that proved difficult was obtaining work.

In the early twentieth century Indian education focused on training pupils in vocational skills that qualified them to secure work once they returned home. When Hopi students returned to the reservation, they found employment in a number of occupations, including nursing, farming, cooking, and housekeeping, while others sought employment in seasonal or temporary jobs.[10] Although many Hopis became specialists in vocational skills, "some of the vocational skills learned at school were simply irrelevant to reservation life" or required working with materials not available on the reservation.[11] Girls learned to do laundry in large washing machines and driers, only to return to the reservation where electricity did not exist. Agriculture students learned farming methods that employed the latest technology of the day for use in Southern California, which included tractors, balers, and large combines. When they came home, they had to revert to their Hopi methods of raising crops with digging sticks, shovels, and hoes. Lack of modern equipment frustrated some students who had to readjust to reservation life. Their experience at Sherman Institute taught them about certain comforts that made work easier, and to go back to the old way of life proved to be a disheartening challenge. In his account of missionary involvement among Navajo and Pueblo pupils at off-reservation Indian boarding schools, John Dolfin observed that while it may have seemed "useless" to "teach the Indian youth these various branches of domestic science," and then "send them back to the desert and Reservation, where the facilities of Sherman Institute are unknown and undreamed of," officials at the school did encourage the pupils to conduct each industrial project as they would at home.[12]

At Sherman Institute, school officials taught the students to make and repair wagons, blacksmith, and work as carpenters. School officials attempted to provide Hopi students with training that would facilitate success when they returned home, but instruction was based on tools and techniques readily available in the white man's world but not on Indian reservations. In December 1913, Victor Sakiestewa, a pupil trained in wagon repairing, informed Superintendent Conser that since he returned home from Sherman Institute, he was working and "enjoying life" on the reservation. While occasionally busy "cutting [fire]wood" and gathering hay for the Oraibi Day School, Victor spent the majority of his time repairing wagons for Hopi and non-Hopi people in Northern Arizona. Although Victor had a "few tools to work" with, he told Conser that he needed to earn "some more money" to secure the tools that he needed.[13] Once at home, Victor and other Hopis became aggravated by a lack of adequate supplies on the reservation.

Whereas some Hopis came home to work in shop trades, others returned to the reservation as farmers. In April 1911 Hopi pupil Jackson Sohoema from the village of Moencopi told school officials that since he came home to Moencopi, he had been tending to his "garden" and "farming" his "own land" in Tuba City, Arizona. As well as farming, Jackson earned money "hauling 100 lbs" of "freight from Flagstaff" to Moencopi. Jackson noted that "all of the Hopis" enjoyed their time at a recent "dance," and that when he did not have to work in the fields, he and other Hopis from Moencopi traveled to Flagstaff, Arizona, to see a "band concert" and "play basketball."[14]

Some of the Hopis secured temporary work, but others found it difficult to find employment or simply chose not to work. In 1911, Dora Koyahonin reported to Conser that since leaving Sherman Institute in 1911, she had gone home for three months and then moved to Phoenix where she remained unemployed for a year. Dora eventually found work as a house servant for a white family in Phoenix. Earning twenty dollars a month, Dora used her job to reach a level of financial independence and proudly noted to Conser that she had sixty dollars saved in her account at the Valley Bank of Arizona.[15] Although school officials may have looked unfavorably on Dora's year of unemployment, her willingness to move to Phoenix and work as a domestic servant pleased administrators and teachers at Sherman Institute. Dora had made herself useful, a primary goal that school officials had for their students at Sherman Institute. School officials had long realized the unique challenges that Indian pupils faced when they lived in, or in close proximity to, their village communities. Fearful that pupils would revert to their old Indian ways after they returned home, school officials preferred that female former students quickly secure work in the homes of white families to continue their exposure to white culture. In this regard, the domestic work performed by returned Hopi pupils became an extension of the school's Outing Program.

When officials received correspondence from pupils such as Jackson and Dora, they routinely conveyed the news to students at the school. Since teachers and administrators trained Indian students for employment once they returned home, news of alumni who obtained work became a special feature in the *Sherman Bulletin*. In April 1927, the school's newspaper reported that during a recent visit to the school by David Haskell, a Hopi pupil who graduated from Sherman Institute in 1912, David told the students that he had "been employed [with] the Santa Fe" Railroad "for a number of years at Winslow, Arizona." He worked in "various capacities" with a hundred "Indian boys," and that all seemed to be "happy and making good wages."[16] David's story likely encouraged the Hopi pupils at the school and filled the students with pride in knowing that one of their own had succeeded to such a degree.

Several students who returned to the reservation after leaving

Sherman Institute had positive experiences when they arrived home. They adeptly put their training into practice, and many felt they had contributed to their communities. However, certain students found the readjustment into Hopi society much more arduous. These students sought ways to find a life away from their homes, and some pupils believed that more schooling would provide an escape from the challenging conditions on the reservation. Some students even wanted to go on to college. Although off-reservation Indian boarding schools provided a greater depth of training than reservation day schools, the academic rigor of places like Sherman Institute was often substandard, and it did not prepare students to enter or excel at the best colleges of the day. Cherokee activist and leader Ruth Muskrat Bronson lamented that one of the brightest students at Sherman Institute was unable to pass his "entrance exams" to prestigious colleges on the east coast. When Bronson took her concerns to Superintendent Donald H. Biery in 1933, Biery "discounted the eastern schools" as being too focused on subjects such as geometry, Latin, and other "foreign languages" that had "little" practical use in "everyday life."[17]

In the early twentieth century, many Hopi students who came home from Sherman Institute attempted to reenroll at one of several off-reservation Indian boarding schools. Some former students earnestly desired to return to school to gain a mastery of English or to further their vocational training. Other students wanted to go back because the manner of living off the reservation appealed to them. Once students experienced a Western lifestyle away from home, which included modern conveniences such as electricity and plumbing, some did not want to settle back into the traditional customs of their people. In July 1914, Victor Sakiestewa informed Superintendent Conser that he forgot most of his vocational training and thought that a third term at Sherman Institute would allow him to regain those skills that he lost.[18] Although he never again enrolled at the school, Victor was convinced that he needed further instruction and even tried to enroll at the Carlisle Indian Industrial School in 1916.[19] When his efforts to join Carlisle failed, Victor found employment as an engineer at the Greenville Indian Boarding School in Greenville, California.[20] In a letter to Conser dated November 26, 1917, Victor commented that he was "certainly thankful for what" he had "learned while at Sherman," and requested that Conser send his gratitude to all of his former "teachers and instructors for what they had taught" him.[21] Victor's previous training at Sherman Institute proved valuable in securing work at the Indian school in Greenville as well as later, when he ran a plumbing business in Tuba City, Arizona.

Victor was not the only Hopi student who sought to further his education beyond the mesas. In June 1924, former Sherman Institute student Grant Jenkins from Moencopi wanted to attend Haskell Institute and told Conser that he desired to "have as much education" as possible.[22] Grant's letter to Conser is a revealing example of one argument Hopis made for returning to school: by drawing attention to his poor grammar as evidence of his "need" for more schooling, Grant strengthened his case for readmittance to an off-reservation boarding school. After he wrote Conser, Grant received word that he was admitted to Haskell Institute. However, a year following his enrollment at Haskell, Grant's academic performance declined. In July 1925, G. E. Peters, assistant superintendent at Haskell Institute, informed Conser that Grant and another boy named Charles Good Luck ran away from school after learning they failed their junior year. Concerned about the welfare of both students, Peters asked

Conser to keep him informed if the pupils made their way back to the Indian School in Riverside.[23]

Two years after he ran away from Haskell, Grant contacted Conser and asked if he could return to Sherman Institute. Admitting that he often thought about how foolish he was for not completing his education at Sherman, Grant begged Conser to permit him to return to school so he could gain more knowledge. Sure that the U.S. government would allow him "another chance" at school, Grant informed Conser that he ran away from Haskell because there were so many differences between the two schools.[24] But Conser refused to admit runaways from other Indian schools, and told Grant that Sherman Institute had reached its student capacity for the year.[25] Grant's desire to return to Sherman Institute to "learn more" may have appeared to Conser to lack sincerity. Grant had demonstrated an unwillingness to complete his education at Haskell, and Conser believed that if he allowed Grant to return, the Hopi pupil would continue his pattern of running away.

At reservation day schools and off-reservation Indian boarding schools officials often faced the problem of student runaways.[26] K. Tsianina Lomawaima observed that "desertion rates" at the Chilocco Indian boarding school in Oklahoma, "were highest in the first months of the school year, when returning students and new enrollees were most homesick."[27] The same trend took place at Sherman Institute. Unlike the California Indians, who ran away more frequently, the Hopi pupils accounted for a small percent of the overall occurrences of runaways. The Hopi Reservation was located over four hundred miles from Riverside, and the impracticality of returning home dissuaded Hopi students from deserting. But this did not prevent all Hopi and non-Hopis from running away to their reservation homes in Arizona. In an executive dispatch to the *Los Angeles Times* in October 1921, a reporter noted that three Navajo pupils, "each about 15 years old," ran away from Sherman Institute and walked the "line from the Santa Fe Railroad to Flagstaff." Once at Flagstaff, the Navajo students traveled in a northeast direction and arrived at their homes in Keams Canyon, which was about six hundred miles from Sherman Institute.[28] Some pupils who ran away from the school did so in rebellion against school policies. Other pupils left when parents or siblings persistently wrote letters and asked Superintendent Conser to release the students from the school. Marsah Balenquah remembered that in the 1920s and 1930s, the Hopi girls rarely ran away, but "the boys would run away, and they would get a whipping a lot."[29]

When Tawaquaptewa attended Sherman Institute with his Hopi followers between 1906 and 1909, none of the Hopi students ran away, which bears testimony to the positive influence Tawaquaptewa had on the Hopi students. Hopi students never wavered in respect toward their kikmongwi. They looked to him for guidance and would not disrespect his presence or role as an elder by deserting the school. When Tawaquaptewa left the school in 1909, he took with him a major source of Hopi accountability. In the absence of Tawaquaptewa's authority, the Hopi students' commitment to the school lessened, and some of the Hopi boys ran away from Sherman Institute. The majority of the Hopi runaways, or "deserters" as school officials called them,[30] returned home for two main reasons. Some Hopis received letters from parents or other family members that relayed messages of illness, which caused the student to feel that he or she must go home. Other Hopi children received cruel treatment at the school and decided to take what few possessions they had and leave. Furthermore, Brenda Child noted that "students who missed their families, and who could not afford the expense of train travel, or those who simply wanted to avoid the bureaucratic details of gaining formal permission to go home, often just skipped the premises."[31]

Hopi pupil Walter Lewis from Moencopi was one of the students who "skipped the premises" at Sherman Institute. In 1914, Lewis ran away from the school for the second time. When Walter wrote Conser less than a year later and asked his permission to return to Sherman Institute, Conser informed Walter that he would be happy to have him "return" as long as he agreed to accept the consequences that he and other school officials believed that he deserved.[32] Although Conser did not elaborate on the details of Walter's punishment, it may have included extended work hours, or a demotion in Walter's grade level. When Indian pupils were charged of committing serious violations, such as running away, at Haskell Institute during the early 1890s, school officials determined the pupil's innocence or guilt by staging an elaborate "trial by court-martial."[33] However, by the 1910s, off-reservation Indian boarding schools functioned less like a branch of the U.S. military. In 1915, former Hopi student Helen Sekaquaptewa recalled that school officials at the Phoenix Indian School punished runaway girls by making them clean "yards" or cut "grass with scissors," while the boys had their heads shaved and were made to wear a girl's dress and carry a sign around school that read "I ran away."[34] These reprimands were neither progressive nor productive, but authorities used such techniques to humiliate Indian pupils and to dissuade other pupils from committing the same infraction.

When pupils fled Sherman Institute, they often left behind money in their student accounts. Although most "deserters" knew they would not see their savings again, the runaways that faced poor living conditions on the reservation would have ben-efited from that money. A few months after he ran away from Sherman, Walter requested that Conser send him the money in his school account. The superintendent noted that he could not agree to Walter's wish, and that he would keep the money until he determined to let Walter have it.[35] By withholding the money, school officials maintained control and authority over students who were otherwise outside of their jurisdiction. School officials also used these situations to teach runaways life lessons. For example, in Conser's letter to Walter, the superintendent firmly admonished Walter by saying that he "should understand" that he could not "always have [his] own way about everything" and that he would "appreciate this more" as time went on.[36]

Hopi runaways accounted for only a small percentage of re-turned Hopi students; Hopis more frequently returned home as a result of sickness, or even death. In the early twentieth century, many Indian pupils at off-reservation boarding schools suffered from poor living and sanitary conditions, which resulted in student illness and fatalities. Although Sherman Institute had health problems, overall, the school had fewer problems than other Indian schools. Historian and author of the first book on Sherman Institute, Jean A. Keller, observed that the "relatively good health of Sherman Institute students" resulted "from a number of factors" including the school's location and the ac-tions of superintendents Harwood Hall and Frank Conser, who placed a "premium on student health."[37] At the Indian School in Riverside, officials provided students with relatively clean living quarters, an opportunity to bathe once a week, a clean bed of their own, and three meals a day.[38]

During the first half of the twentieth century, living condi-tions on the Hopi Reservation did not mirror those that Hopi pupils experienced at Sherman Institute.[39] Disease and illness increased on reservations in the first decades of the twentieth century, particularly among infants and small children. A high percentage of Hopis who attended Sherman Institute between 1906 and 1929 came to the school sick. School officials often recorded the Hopi pupils' illness on an entrance examination form or on the school's enrollment roster. Health officials at Sherman Institute particularly watched for diseases that new students may have unknowingly brought to the school. Physicians who examined the incoming Hopis often mentioned on the pupils' medical form that the students had had a cough for several months, which might indicate tuberculosis.[40] Several Hopi students arrived at the school with trachoma, a contagious eye disease that required students to have their eyelids scraped with metal tools to remove the crust buildup on the eyes.[41]

Although government policies required that superintendents of off-reservation Indian boarding schools send infected students home at the "first positive signs" of a disease, officials at Sherman Institute preferred that severely ill pupils remain at the school's hospital to ensure "adequate" medical care.[42] This policy may appear commendable, but it caused tensions between Indian parents and officials at the school. Many Hopi parents had little familiarity with health policies or the medicines administered by the school's health officials. Consequently, some parents and village leaders looked suspiciously at the non-Hopi remedies. Oftentimes Hopi parents wanted their sick children to return home to be treated by a Hopi medicine man instead of a white physician.[43]

In addition to Hopi parents, siblings on the reservation occasionally wrote Superintendent Conser and voiced their concerns about the health of their brother or sister at the school. In June 1913, Keller Seedkoema, a former Hopi student at Sherman Institute, wrote Conser and begged him to allow his brother, Asa Lathiyo-Clifton, to return home. According to Keller, his brother wrote and told him that he was sick "in his chest of scarlet fever," and that his sickness resulted when he ate meat and ran at the school. Keller told Conser that he knew of Hopis who contracted the same illness at Chilocco Indian School in Oklahoma, and when they returned home they worsened and died. Fearful that the same thing would happen to his brother, Keller told Conser that he did not want Asa "to get worse like that," for Asa informed his brother that he "spit [up] blood when he" coughed. Convinced that the health facilities and remedies at Sherman Institute would not cure his brother, Keller demanded that Conser allow his brother to return home, where a Hopi medicine man would practice his medicine on him.[44] When Conser received Keller's cry for help, he informed Keller that he sent a school official to check on Asa's health. Asa reportedly told the official that he was "all right, was feeling good and working every day." Conser noted that Asa did not have "scarlet fever" as Keller had believed.[45]

Tuberculosis was the most common health reason that superintendents Hall and Conser sent Hopi pupils home. Jean A. Keller noted that for "almost one hundred years tuberculosis preyed upon Indian children in nonreservation boarding schools, resulting in higher morbidity and mortality rates than any other single disease."[46] In 1905, the superintendent in charge of the Moqui Reservation, Theodore G. Lemmon, reported that "tuberculosis in some form" was the "greatest cause of death among [Hopi] school children."[47] Some of these children became ill with tuberculosis at off-reservation schools, while others were infected at their village or at reservation day schools. In a letter to Horton H. Miller, superintendent of the Moqui Agency at Keams Canyon, Harwood Hall noted that on September 16, 1908, he sent "little Ray Seyumtewa home to Oraibi." Hall commented that Ray was the "son of Frank and Susie Seyumtewa," who also attended Sherman Institute with their son. According to Hall, a physician observed Ray on a number of occasions and claimed that one of Ray's lungs was "slightly infected" with tuberculosis.[48] News of Ray's medical condition provided Hall with enough reason to send Ray back to Orayvi. Although Ray lived a long and productive life on the reservation, other Hopi pupils from various schools returned home with tuberculosis and died. This unfortunate reality is echoed by field matron Miltona Keith, who reported that of "all the sad sights to be seen among the [Hopi] people the most pitiful cases are of those who have been returned from the boarding schools to die."[49]

David Wallace Adams observed that "parents resented boarding schools, both reservation and off-reservation, because they severed the most fundamental of all human ties: the parent-child bond."[50] Although school policy allowed and paid for Indian pupils to return home after their term expired, Superintendent Conser at times held Hopi pupils at the school against their wills, even if the students completed their school training. In September 1919, Quoyowyma, father of three Hopi boys at the school, wrote Conser a letter regarding his son, Albert Poleumptewa. Quoyowyma told Conser that although he wanted his children to receive as much education as possible, he still had to make a living for his family on the reservation and therefore needed his son's help. Unfortunately for Quoyowyma, Conser did not allow Albert to return home even though his term at the school had expired.[51]

At times Hopi family members pleaded with Superintendents Hall and Conser to allow their children to come home. In March 1924, Roger Honahnie, brother of Hopi pupil Rose Honahnie from Tuba City, Arizona, wrote Superintendent Conser and asked permission for his sister to return to the reservation. Roger told Conser that Rose had been enrolled at Sherman Institute for more than four years and that his father wanted her to come back to be with their family. At the time of the letter, Roger and his father lived with aunts, but the aunts did not provide adequate care for the ailing man. In Hopi culture, daughters often care for their elderly fathers. Rose's father, willing to pay her transportation cost, wanted Rose to return to the reservation to tend to his needs.[52] Roger's concerns fit with Hopi culture, but not with the Eurocentric mindset of superintendent Conser. In a letter to Conser dated April 1, 1924, Harvey K. Meyer, superintendent of the Western Navajo Agency in Tuba City, Arizona, commented that he "made inquiry about any necessity for Honahnie returning home" as "requested by her brother Roger," but that he found "no special reason why the request should be granted." Meyer suggested that Rose remain at Sherman Institute "until her period of enrollment [had] terminated" or if it was "shown conclusively that she should be allowed to return to her home."[53] Shortly after receiving Meyer's letter, Conser wrote Roger and told him that he thought it "advisable for Rose to remain" at the school, and did not "see the necessity of her going home."[54] Conser's decision surely disappointed Rose's father and likely contributed to even greater hardships for him on the reservation.

In November 1914, Earl Numkenu, brother of Hopi pupil Lewis Hoyeneptewa, wrote and asked Conser if he would allow Lewis to return home to help with their family business. Earl noted that he had a business to maintain in Tuba City, Arizona, and that no one but himself was there to run the store.[55] Conser suggested that Lewis stay until the school closed in the spring, and encouraged Earl to hire another man to run the store. In Conser's opinion, it was to Lewis' advantage if he remained at the school and received what education he could before he left for home and began working.[56] Superintendents of off-reservation boarding schools often believed that they knew what was best for the pupils under their care. The paternalistic attitude of school superintendents superseded the desires, concerns, and opinions of Indian parents and family members.

In the late 1920s, Lewis Meriam and others observed that uprooting a "child from his natural environment without making any effort to teach him how to adjust himself to a new environment, and then send[ing] him back to the old, especially with a people at a stage of civilization where the influence of family and home would normally be all-controlling, is to invite disaster."[57] Polingaysi Qoyawayma's stay at the Indian school in Riverside had a profound impact on her as a Hopi woman. When she returned to Orayvi in 1909, she struggled to live in the world of her Hopi parents. Polingaysi had changed at Sherman Institute, but her parents on the reservation had not. Although Polingaysi loved her family, "she did not relish the idea of going home to stay."[58] Prior to her attendance at school off the reservation, Polingaysi was familiar with one lifestyle and one way of living. The Hopi way lost its appeal for the young woman because she experienced the Western world in a way that would have been impossible had she remained on the reservation. At Sherman Institute, Polingaysi established many friendships and "learned the white man's way of living and liked it."[59]

Whether the Hopi pupils had a positive or negative experience at school, their time at Sherman Institute altered their opinion of life on the reservation. Within minutes after Polingaysi arrived at Orayvi, she scolded her parents for not having the commodities she learned to appreciate at school: "Why haven't you bought the white man's beds to sleep on? And a table? You should not be eating on the floor as the Old Ones did." Polingaysi reminded her parents that when she was a young girl, she "did not mind sleeping on the floor and eating from a single bowl in which everyone dipped." But she was "used to another way of living now," and did not plan on living as she once had. Polingaysi's words grieved her parents. Their grief intensified when she rejected all Hopi religious beliefs entirely and publicly professed Christianity before the Orayvi people. Christian missionaries at Orayvi encouraged Polingaysi to rid herself of Hopi religion and convinced her that taking part in the traditional katsina dances was "Devil worship."[60] Polingaysi's life had changed at the Indian school in Riverside. She had experienced a different way of living, and made new friends who had similar circumstances to face at home.

When Hopi pupils left Sherman Institute, many remembered the friends that they had made in Riverside. Oftentimes, Hopi pupils who returned home wrote to their friends at the school. School administrators and teachers also corresponded with the Hopi pupils on the reservation to convince them to return and finish their education, or to track their progress at home. In some cases, former students wrote the leadership at the school and asked for help. Former students kept in contact with people at Sherman Institute for different reasons, but the fact remained that the school made an indelible imprint on the lives of Hopi students, and several pupils desired to keep the ties to the school intact. One of these pupils was Don Talayesva.

Don Talayesva wrote in his autobiography that a year after he returned home in 1909, he walked with Tawaquaptewa to the post office and was surprised to see that five letters were waiting for him. As the two men started back to Orayvi, Don and Tawaquaptewa sat along the side of the road and read the letters. The first letter arrived from the school's principal, and the second one came from the school's head baker, both of whom urged Don to return to Sherman Institute to complete his education. The principal and baker promised Don a job at a bakery in Riverside if he returned to school. When Don informed Tawaquaptewa of what the head baker and principal had written, Tawaquaptewa told Don that he "hoped he had not made a mistake in taking" the Hopi pupils away from the education they were receiving at Sherman Institute.[61] Like many of the Hopi pupils who attended Sherman Institute, Don did not return to school, in spite of the offers presented by the principal and baker. Instead, Don reacclimated to reservation life and dedicated himself, along with Tawaquaptewa, to Hopi ways.

When Hopi pupils journeyed home from off-reservation Indian boarding schools, they left their school friends and established new relationships on the reservation that sometimes resulted in marriage. When Don received the letters from Hopis at Sherman Institute, he was engaged to marry a Hopi woman named Irene. The third letter Don received was from his clan sister Meggie who had gone to the school, and stated that when Mettie, Don's old girlfriend at Sherman Institute, "heard the news" of his impending "marriage, she cried all day, even though she had three lovers at school and had practically ruined herself in the eyes of the Whites." The fifth letter was from Mettie, who told Don that she was "heartbroken to hear" of his engagement to Irene. Crying herself to "sleep every night," Mettie told Don that she wanted to come home. She conveyed to Don that he was her "lover first" and that when she returned she would have him regardless of his wife or the village gossip. She further noted that Don would "never get away" from her. When Don finished reading the letters, he trashed Mettie's letter because Irene would not be happy if she discovered that Mettie had written him. Once Don saw Irene, he showed her the four remaining letters. After reading the letters, Irene asked Don if he had received one from Mettie. Don said that he had not, but Irene insisted that Mettie had written Don, because Meggie's letter had mentioned her. After a number of weeks of questioning Don about Mettie, Don finally told Irene the truth. News of Mettie's letter made Irene very upset, and Irene told Don to stop communicating with Mettie. Don eventually told his ex-lover to stop writing, but that he "still look[ed] forward to seeing her."[62]

Hopi students who returned to the reservation found themselves in other difficult and unfavorable situations. In September 1922 a woman from New Mexico wrote Superintendent Conser about a Hopi pupil who had recently attended the school.[63] She noted to Conser that she hardly knew "how to begin" her letter, but felt that bringing the situation to his attention would be the right thing to do. The woman recalled that in November 1920, a Hopi pupil who at the time was enrolled at Sherman Institute had molested her. The Hopi individual in question reportedly forced her down to the ground and "committed rape upon" her. Having "never in any way allowed a man to become familiar" with her, and being "absolutely a virgin," the woman was so stunned by the ordeal that she confided in no one about what happened. Six months later the woman discovered, to her "horror and despair," that she was pregnant.

Shortly thereafter, the woman located the Hopi pupil and

confronted him about his actions and her pregnancy, and he dropped "on his knees," and implored that she not "tell of his bastardly part in the affair." Along with showing remorse, the Hopi pupil agreed to financially help both mother and child if she kept the matter a secret. According to the woman, she believed that he would do the right thing, and even "fabricated a marriage" with another man and told others that her husband was absent. Ten days after the child was born, she returned to New Mexico and brought the baby with her to a friend's home. Still certain that the Hopi pupil would "keep his promise," the woman received no replies to her letters nor inquiries from the baby's father. In spite of sending a number of registered letters and acquiring hand-written receipts that proved the Hopi pupil received them, the woman never heard a response. Seeing that her efforts made no headway, the woman moved to Albuquerque, New Mexico, and hired a lawyer to handle her case.

The Hopi pupil also hired an attorney to represent him, but he did not attend the hearing or acknowledge that he knew the woman or received any of her letters. While the woman pursued her legal options, the baby had become sick and doctor bills began to pile up, which consequently placed the woman in a difficult financial situation. According to the woman, she had "given this Indian a year in which to prove himself" to be "even part of a man." By 1922, it became clear that even though she could have had him imprisoned for rape, all she really wanted was "support for the child—a child who was in every way forced upon" her. The woman wrote Conser to receive help in the matter. She hoped that the Superintendent had authority over the Hopi student, and asked him to exert his influence to make the former student honor his promise to help her financially.

Those students who committed illegal or questionable acts placed Conser and other school officials in difficult positions. When Conser replied to the woman's letter, he noted that while he regretted the situation, he did not have authority over the Hopi pupil since the student left the Indian school in Riverside to enroll at the Keams Canyon Boarding School in Arizona. Conser suggested that, although her accusations did not come with concrete evidence of the Hopi pupil's guilt, the woman contacted the pupil's reservation superintendent, R. E. L. Daniels, for assistance.[64] The incident demonstrates the role school officials had in the lives of former students, as people looked at school officials as mediators of all sorts of disputes when problems arose with students who once attended their schools.

When Hopis migrated back to the reservation, they told their friends and family members about their experience at Sherman. Several Hopis attended Sherman Institute because other family members went to the school. In October 1913, David Haskee, one of the school's Hopi alumni, wrote Superintendent Conser regarding his brother's eagerness to attend school. When David returned home from Sherman, he told his brother about the "beautiful" school in California. As a result of David's enthusiasm for the school, his brother wanted to attend Sherman Institute. David told Conser that his brother had requested that he write the superintendent about enrolling and asked if Conser would purchase a train ticket for his brother from Winslow, Arizona, to Riverside.[65] As with many other Sherman Institute alums, David's overall positive experience at the school directly motivated Hopi pupil attendance at the school, particularly with his immediate family. In May 1921, Hopi pupil Clarence Taptuka from Moencopi, a former student at the Indian school in Riverside and relative of Victor Sakiestewa, wrote Superintendent Conser and urged him to write the Hopi children on the reservation to encourage them to attend the school. Clarence noted that he spoke to the Hopi children at Moencopi and knew "for sure of two" Hopis that were interested. "I shall try and see," wrote Clarence, "if I can't get the whole sixth graders" at the Moencopi Day School "to go down" to Sherman Institute.[66] Some Hopis such as Clarence ventured beyond the mesas and enjoyed their experience at the school. Had Clarence detested his time at Sherman Institute, it would have been highly unlikely that he would have wanted the same fate to befall other members of his village community.

The trend of returned Hopi students who encouraged other Hopis to attend Sherman Institute continued throughout the twentieth century. Merle Polyestewa from Moencopi commented that while he could have gone to Tuba City High School in Tuba City, Arizona, in 1978 he chose to attend Sherman Institute because his three sisters went to the school.[67]

For more than a hundred years, the Indian school in Riverside has held special meaning for Hopi people and has played an important part in Hopi history. Although some Hopis at Sherman Institute struggled, found the rigid military approach to be a challenge, and on occasion experienced cruel and inhumane treatment, Hopis generally encouraged their family or village members to attend the school. Many Hopis used their boarding school experience to contribute back to their families and village communities. Bessie Humetewa stated, "We [Hopis] had a hard time learning when we went to Sherman, but we did it. It was tough, but I used what I learned and here I am."[68] Like so many Hopis before her, Bessie traveled far from home to enrich her life with different experiences, and she returned to the Hopi mesas with new knowledge and new skills. She and other Hopi students continued the pattern found in the ancient emergence and migration story, when the people traveled in the four cardinal directions and returned to their homes to face new lives and challenges, by traveling to Sherman Institute and returning to the Hopi mesas to share what they had learned.

Conclusion

Hopis have a long history of resisting and accommodating foreign powers. When the U.S. government demanded that Hopi children attend various day schools and the Keams Canyon School in the late nineteenth century, some Hopis resisted government officials with their actions and words, while others made strategic accommodations that allowed them to live in their villages, simultaneously practice their Hopi ways, and give their children an education beyond the Hopi mesas. Furthermore, when Indian agents and school superintendents sent Hopis to Sherman Institute in the early twentieth century, Hopis used their education and experiences there to contribute to their community once they returned home. Although the U.S. government created Sherman Institute to assimilate Hopis and other Indian pupils into mainstream white society, Hopis adapted to the formal education and used their cultural heritage to advance at the school.

In the early twentieth century, Hopi pupils excelled at Sherman Institute in part because their kikmongwi, Tawaquaptewa, often gathered his Hopi followers together and told them to do their very best. Tawaquaptewa's willingness to cooperate with school officials and learn academic subjects such as English became an example to the other Hopis at the school. As a result of Tawaquaptewa's position as a leader and elder, and the presence and leadership of his wife, Nasumgoens, and Frank Seumptewa and his wife, Susie, Hopis who attended Sherman Institute between 1906 and 1909 laid the foundation for Hopi advancement at the school for years to come.

In the years that followed 1909, Hopi pupils continued to demonstrate their culture within their boarding school experience. Hopi runners such as Philip Zeyouma, Guy Maktima, Harry Chaca, and Brian Gilbert all won marathons and races while students at the Indian school in Riverside. Since running has a central role in Hopi culture, it comes as no surprise that Hopis took their ability to run with them to Sherman Institute and were among the top runners at the school. Furthermore, while the Hopi boys made advancements in running, Hopi girls excelled in music organizations such as the Mandolin Club, or "Mosquito Band," as former Hopi pupil Bessie Humetewa called it.[1] She had played in the club in the 1920s, and she used her appreciation and knowledge of Hopi music to help her succeed in the music offered at the school. She was not alone, as other Hopi girls learned new instruments and songs at Sherman Institute, and they excelled in part because of their preparation in music while growing up on the Hopi mesas.[2]

For Hopi students such as Bessie Humetewa, Samuel Shingoitewa, and Marsah Balenquah, their experience at Sherman Institute had a tremendous impact on their lives. Often speaking about "dear ole Sherman" in positive terms, Hopis who attended Sherman Institute in the early twentieth century returned to the reservation with new skills, shared experiences, and different outlooks on life. For some Hopis, memories of Sherman Institute included the first time they ate an orange, experienced an earthquake, saw a motion picture, or visited the Pacific Ocean. Other Hopis remembered how homesick they were when they first arrived at the school, and how they just wanted to go home. But the majority of the Hopi pupils learned to adapt to their school and unfamiliar environment, and they established new friendships with other pupils and white teachers and families in the Riverside community, which allowed them to learn about the non-Native world and life beyond the mesas.

Prior to their attendance at Sherman Institute, most Hopi pupils interacted with other Hopis or Navajo people. When Hopis arrived at the school, they came into contact with people from many different communities and established relationships with non-Hopi pupils at the school. As students at the Indian school in Riverside, Hopis worked alongside other Indian pupils in the harness shop, at the Sherman Ranch, and in various occupations throughout the greater Riverside community. For some Hopis, coming into contact with so many different tribes required social adjustment as they began to realize that other students did not think or act in the same manner as Hopi people or as Hopi culture mandated. They learned of the great diversity among people, which included white teachers and school administrators. Hopis had lived a secluded life on the Hopi mesas of Arizona, and their schooling in California provided them with an opportunity to meet Indians from across the United States.

This increased level of Hopi interaction with other Native peoples began when Hopis attended Sherman Institute in 1902 and has continued to the present. Merle Polyestewa from Lower Moencopi recalled that when he first arrived at Sherman Institute in 1978, school officials assembled all of the students in the school gym to play basketball and other games. For Merle, this was the first time he was around such a variety of Indian people. Playing with a group of non-Hopi students, Merle kept calling out to his teammates in Hopi and became frustrated when they did not respond to his commands. When his sister, Natelle, also a student at Sherman Institute, saw how irritated he was getting at his teammates, she became exasperated with him and said, "You can't talk to them in Hopi; we are not the only ones here!" Laughing as he recalled this story, Merle noted that it did not take him long to realize that he was no longer going to school on the Hopi Reservation and that he had entered a new environment and way of life beyond the mesas.[3]

Leigh J. Kuwanwisiwma once remarked to me that the history of Hopi involvement at Sherman Institute is a "living history." Descendants of Hopis who attended Sherman Institute in the early twentieth century continue to tell their forebearers' stories about their experiences at the school as well as attend the school themselves. Furthermore, a small number of Hopis that came to Sherman Institute in the 1920s are still with us and sharing their stories today. Some of those interviewed for this book were asked if they remembered the Sherman Institute school song, "The Purple and Gold."[4] The majority of the former Hopi students, all in their late nineties, recalled singing the song throughout their time at the school. Samuel Shingoitewa even remembered the entire song word for word:

The Purple and Gold
Beneath Sierra's mountains high
With crested peaks of snow,
Here waves the Purple and the Gold
At the foot of Rubidoux
Whose cross on high against the sky
Our talisman shall be,
In hours of strife all through our lives
Will bring sweet thoughts of thee.

Oh Sherman, dear Sherman
We never shall forget;
The golden haze of student days
Which clings about us yet.
These happy days will soon be o'er,
But through our future years
The thoughts of you, so good, so true,
Will fill our hearts with cheer.[5]

Sherman Institute is one of several off-reservation Indian boarding schools that Hopis attended in the twentieth century. In the
early 1900s, government officials also sent Hopis to the Carlisle
Indian Industrial School, the Santa Fe Indian School, the Phoenix
Indian School, or the Albuquerque Indian School. Each of these
schools, and many others, has an important role in Hopi history.
A great deal of research has yet to be conducted by scholars on
Indian boarding school experiences, particularly studies that are
community specific and consider student experiences through
indigenous cultural frameworks. Unlike other histories that
primarily examine the Indian boarding school experience within
the context of U.S. government policy, studies that incorporate
both Indian education policies and indigenous culture provide
a more comprehensive and balanced approach to an important
era of American Indian history. Most importantly, community-
specific studies place American Indian cultures and histories at
the center of the boarding school narrative. They privilege the
society and past of Native people and better demonstrate the
ways American Indians navigated within their communities,
U.S. government policies, and other forces of colonialism.

The Hopi boarding school experience at Sherman Institute
does not mirror that of the Navajo, Apache, Zuni, or other Indians

at the same school. American Indian cultures and histories are distinct, and Indian students understood and experienced their time at boarding school in unique ways. The villages that Hopis came from greatly affected their experiences at Indian schools. The students were raised in tight-knit extended families where they gave common respect to community elders. At a young age, the students had been taught to be quiet and listen when elders spoke and to learn from the words spoken by the old ones and the actions of their teachers. The Hopi students had grown up in an agricultural society where their lives depended on the careful cultivation and nurturing of different colored corn, beans, squash, and melons. Water was sacred to them, and they prayed for rain and snow, the moisture that made their agriculture possible. The students were raised in a very religious society that valued the relationship of human beings to each other and their environment. The people celebrated and prayed through ritual and ceremony the entire year, giving thanks to unseen but known sources of power.

The Hopi students learned at a young age and through the oral tradition that their people were once great travelers, people that ventured out in all directions and put their marks upon the country from the Pacific to Central America and beyond. During this time in Hopi history, the people learned many lessons, which they remembered through songs, stories, and ceremonies. The Hopi students were part of a traveling, migrating tradition that took them to new places where they learned from their experiences and the people whom they met along the way. Still, the majority of the Hopis returned to their mesas of Northern Arizona, a place from which they could enjoy the sweet smell of burning wood, taste the crunch of roasted corn, and stand on the mesa tops and see their beautiful mountains with everything surrounded by a canopy of deep blue sky. In the spirit of tradition, Hopi students had left their villages to attend Sherman Institute and a host of other boarding schools. Some had embraced the adventure, but others had been reluctant participants. In either case, the students set out like the hero twins, Youth and Fireboy, and they faced the unknown with courage and skill. The "monsters" in life that Hopis came into contact with at Sherman Institute did not swallow them up. Instead, the Hopis conquered their fears and learned from their experiences.

Through good times and bad, the Hopi students had listened and learned. During their time at Sherman Institute, they grew and developed in new ways. They returned home with new ideas and memories of shared experiences, but they returned home Hopi. And as Hopis, they were obligated to live the best life for themselves, their families, and their people. Like the hero twins, they returned home to benefit their people and to enrich the Hopi world through their newly acquired skills and ways of thinking. Hopi students still attend Sherman Institute, now called Sherman Indian High School. They still learn and grow away from home. But they never forget their bond to the land and the people. In that way, they share a common heritage with the ancient Hopi travelers, the children who went off to Sherman Institute in the early 1900s, and the Hopi students of the future who will take the journey beyond the mesas to listen and learn about new and old ways that will benefit themselves, their families, and their village communities.

Appendix

A RETELLING OF JUS-WA-KEP-LA

A similar version of this story was originally published in the
Sherman Bulletin 11, no. 5 (January 31, 1912): 1.

At the ancient village of Orayvi in northeastern Arizona, a boy
named Jus-wa-kep-la lived with his father, mother, and two sisters. The boy had two eagles as pets, which he admired greatly.
One day his eagles became hungry, so he took his hunting stick
to find rabbits for his pets to eat. While he hunted for rabbits, the
boy's parents went to their field to gather corn, and his sisters
stayed at home and prepared dinner. As his sisters cooked the
meal, one of the eagles landed on the girl's shoulder, startling
her. In her anger, the sister picked up a broom and killed the
eagle by striking him on the top of his head. Shocked that she
had actually killed their bother's eagle, the girls quickly buried the body of the dead eagle, and made their way to another
family member's house to hide. When Jus-wa-kep-la returned
home from hunting, he saw that there was no one home and the
doors were locked. Not knowing where his sisters had placed
the keys, Jus-wa-kep-la looked through the window, and the
remaining pet eagle, who was inside, informed him that his
sister had buried the keys in a pile of ashes.

After Jus-wa-kep-la found the keys and entered the house, the
eagle said, "After you eat supper, we will go on a trip to a place
far from Oraibi. I will carry you there on my wings. Dress in
your dark blue suit so that you will blend in with the darkening

sky." The boy did as the eagle instructed, and upon leaving the house, he secured the door and put the key back under the pile of ashes. The eagle told Jus-wa-kep-la to climb on his back, lie flat, and align his body with the eagle's wings and tail. Jus-wa-kep-la obeyed, and they flew in the air, the boy having no idea where they were going. Soon, the two flew over a watermelon and corn field, and the eagle told Jus-wa-kep-la to sing one of the songs he had often sung in the past. As the boy began to sing, Jus-wa-kep-la's sisters heard him, and lifted their heads up toward the sky and witnessed the eagle taking their brother away into space.

The boy and the eagle flew in a circular spiral over the girls' heads, going further upward until all of the Hopis on the mesas leaned as far back as they could to gain sight of the boy and eagle as they disappeared into the distant, darkening sky. Witnessing their brother fly away into the heavens, the boy's sisters returned home saddened and with much guilt burdening them because of what they had done. Jus-wa-kep-la did not know where the eagle was taking him, and thought that he would end up in a world far beyond the mesas of his people. When the boy and the eagle eventually descended, the eagle flew to a tall butte from which there was no way to get down and told Jus-wa-kep-la to dismount. At this time, the eagle revealed that the other eagle had been killed at the hands of his sisters, and that Jus-wa-kep-la must suffer punishment because of the horrible misdeed of his family.

The eagle quickly flew off, leaving the boy alone without any food or water. Jus-wa-kep-la was sure he would die, and paced the top of the butte sobbing until a small bird alit on a bush next to him. The robin listened carefully to Jus-wa-kep-la's tale, and told the boy to lie on the ground with his eyes tightly shut, and not to open them until told to do so. Jus-wa-kep-la complied, and the robin gathered other birds together and they carried Jus-wa-kep-la to the ground. The bird then led the boy to the home of his grandmother, saying, "You must stay here until you are led to return home. You and your family are in danger because of your sister's act of anger." Not seeing any other choice, Jus-wa-kep-la remained at his grandmother's home for over a year, where he helped with chores and hunted daily, as he had always done.

One morning as he was hunting in the fields, a hawk swiftly scooped the boy up in his talons and carried him to Orayvi. Jus-wa-kep-la was startled, but soon realized that the hawk was in fact his uncle, transformed to look like a great bird of prey. The hawk delivered the boy to the door of his parents' home. Jus-wa-kep-la went inside and immediately saw that his entire family had been stricken by a terrible illness. Once Jus-wa-kep-la saw the condition of his sisters and parents, he realized that their suffering was punishment for when his sister killed the eagle in anger.

Notes

Abbreviations

ARCIA Annual Report of the Commissioner of Indian Affairs
ARDI Annual Report of the Department of the Interior
NARA National Archives and Records Administration
NEA National Education Association
RG Record Group
SSCF Sherman Student Case Files
YMCA Young Men's Christian Association
YWCA Young Women's Christian Association

Introduction

1. Leigh J. Kuwanwisiwma interview, March 21, 2006, Bacavi AZ, Hopi Reservation (hereafter cited as Kuwanwisiwma interview, March 21, 2006). In this interview, Kuwanwisiwma noted that the "fourth way of life" has often been described as the "fourth world" in popular American culture. However, the Hopi people consider this present world to be the "fourth way of life" for Hopis and for all humanity.

2. The Hopi emergence and migration stories are complicated and full of many more details than I have provided in these first two paragraphs. Each clan has their version of these stories, and they differ in emphasis from village to village. One important figure in these stories, whom I do not discuss in detail, is Ma'saw (Maasau), the Great Spirit and "Creator and leader" of Hopi ancestral lands. For more information on Ma'saw and the Hopi emergence and migrations stories from Hopi perspectives, see Alfred Hermequaftewa, *The Hopi Way of Life is the Way of Peace*, transcription of interview recorded by Thomas B. Noble (Indianapolis: Merideth Guillet, 1970), 1–9, and Nequatewa, *Truth of a Hopi*, 1–15. Also,

for an anthropological examination of Hopi migrations, see Lyons, *Ancestral Hopi Migrations*.

3. Anthropologist Wesley Bernardini of the University of Redlands once observed that to "gain entrance to Qöötasptuvela," an ancient Hopi settlement, the "Sand and Water Clans demonstrated their power to produce crops from sand dunes, and the Tobacco and affiliated Rabbit Clan contributed tobacco plants to gain entrance to Awat'ovi." Bernardini, *Hopi Oral Tradition*, 35.

4. Nequatewa, *Truth of a Hopi*, 28.

5. These are only a few of the states to which Hopis traveled to attend off-reservation Indian boarding schools.

6. Lummis, *Bullying the Moqui*, 44.

7. Coleman, *American Indian Children at School*, 29.

8. Kuwanwiswma interview, March 21, 2006. For additional information on the Hopi delegation to Washington, see Levy, *Orayvi Revisited*, 91.

9. "Tawaquaptewa," also spelled "Tewaquaptewa," Tewaquaptiwa," or "Tiwakwaptiwa," means Sun Down Rising in English. He was of the Bear clan from Orayvi. He was born in the early 1870s and died at Orayvi in 1960.

10. "Tewaquaptewa," April 20, 1909, NARA, RG–75, SSCF, Box 355.

11. In the early 1900s, most Hopi parents were not able to sign their Hopi names in English.

12. *Los Angles Times*, "Newsy Happenings South of the Tehachepi," December 27, 1908, I11.

13. *Sherman Bulletin*, May 11, 1923, 2, Sherman Indian Museum, Riverside, California.

14. I have written more about this in "Hopi Education Did Not Begin at Government Schools." For a comparative study, see Mann, *Cheyenne-Arapaho Education, 1871–1982*.

15. Hough, *The Hopi Indians*, 69.

16. See also Ramson Lomatewama, "More Words of Wisdom," in *Silent Winds: Poetry of One Hopi* (Cortez: La Plata Color Printing, 1983).

17. The military language reflects that off-reservation Indian boarding schools functioned like military forts or posts. Students dressed in uniforms, marched in formation to and from the school buildings, participated in roll calls, and the boys were given stripes to place on their uniforms to demonstrate their rank.

18. This story was conveyed to the author in a conversation with Samuel Shingoitewa's daughter Gayle Honanie in October 2003.

19. Samuel Shingoitewa interview, Upper Moencopi AZ, Hopi Reservation, July 8, 2004. Hereafter cited as Shingoitewa interview, July 8, 2004.

20. Hopitutskwa, or Hopi ancestral lands, extends well beyond the boundaries of the present day Hopi Reservation. See Richland, *Arguing with Tradition*, 28, 29.

21. In *Education for Extinction*, historian David Wallace Adams provides a comprehensive look at the U.S. government's policy of Indian boarding schools, but it is not intended to be a case study of a single tribe's school experience. Jean Keller's *Empty Beds*, a fascinating account of Indian student health at Sherman Institute from 1902 to 1922, briefly mentions Hopi pupils as part of a larger narrative of Indian health. In her examination of the Chilocco Indian School in Oklahoma, K. Tsianina Lomawaima demonstrates the value of oral history in a project on Indian boarding schools. *They Called It Prairie Light* recognizes the importance of family connections and encompasses each of the Indian tribes in attendance. Although Lomawaima's work does not go into depth on one particular tribe, it nevertheless provided a path that informed this manuscript. In comparison to Lomawaima's contribution, Devon Mihesuah's *Cultivating the Rosebuds*, Brenda Child's *Boarding School Seasons*, and Clyde Ellis's *To Change Them Forever* are all tribal specific. However, they do not examine in detail the Pueblo peoples such as the Hopis of Arizona. Recent scholarship by Michael C. Coleman (*American Indians, the Irish, and Government Schooling*), Amelia V. Katanski (*Learning to Write "Indian"*), Jacqueline Fear-Segal (*White Man's Club*), Margaret Connell Szasz (*Education and the American Indian*), and Clifford E. Trafzer have added to the historiography on U.S. government Indian education policy and the Indian boarding school experience, but these studies are inclusive of many Native peoples and are not intended to be tribal specific. My work, on the contrary, seeks to bring these larger historical concerns to bear on the Hopi people in order to examine how Hopis managed, survived, resisted, and capitulated to the U.S. government's desires for educated, "civilized" Indian subjects.

22. Trafzer, Keller, and Sisquoc, *Boarding School Blues*, 28, 237.

23. Fear-Segal, *White Man's Club*, 23, 214.

1. Hopi Resistance

1. James, *Pages from Hopi History*, 33.

2. For more information on Coronado's expedition of the Southwest, see Flint and Flint, *The Coronado Expedition to Tierra Nueva*.

3. Spicer, *Cycles of Conquest*, 189. Thomas Donaldson notes that the Zunis called the Hopis of the largest pueblos "people of Usaya," and therefore the Spaniards referred to this region as the "province of Tusayan." Donaldson, *Extra Census Bulletin*, 19.

4. Donaldson, *Extra Census Bulletin*, 20.

5. Calloway, *One Vast Winter Count*, 135.

6. L. Bradford Prince, quoted in Donaldson, *Extra Census Bulletin*, 19.

7. Montgomery et al., *Franciscan Awatovi*, 75.

8. Silverberg, *The Pueblo Revolt*, 88.

9. Dutton, *American Indians of the Southwest*, 35.

10. Ruth DeEtte Simpson, *Southwest Museum Leaflets: The Hopi Indians* (Los Angeles: Southwest Museum, 1961), 9.

11. Lomayumtewa C. Ishii, "Voices from Our Ancestors," 49. In 2001, Ishii became the first Hopi to receive a PhD in history at Northern Arizona University. He is a faculty member in the applied indigenous studies and history departments at Northern Arizona University.

12. Donaldson, *Extra Census Bulletin*, 22.

13. Donaldson, *Extra Census Bulletin*, 23.

14. Donaldson, *Extra Census Bulletin*, 23.

15. Miller, "The Limits of Schooling by Imposition," 43.

16. Peterson, "The Hopis and the Mormons," 189. For a detailed discussion of Mormons and the Hopis, see Clemmer, *Roads in the Sky*, 38–46. For more on the Deseret Alphabet, see http://www.deseretalphabet.com/.

17. Government officials and Christian missionaries often referred to the Hopi people as "Moqui Indians." Many Hopis consider the term "Moqui" (the "dead ones") to be derogatory. The *New York Times* noted: "The name of the Moqui Indian Agency in Arizona was changed today to the Hopi Indian Agency, by special order of Commissioner Burke of the Indian Office of the Department of the Interior. In the Indian language the word Moqui means 'The Dead Ones,' and was applied to the Hopi Indians by enemies to express contempt and derision. The Indian Office, not knowing the true significance of the word, used it as a name for the Indian agency. Indians of the Moqui Reservation resented being

referred to as 'the dead ones,' and a protest was made to the Government. Hopi means 'People of Peace.'" "Hopi Indians Get Rid of Title, 'Dead Ones,'" *New York Times*, May 10, 1923, 1.

18. Truax, ARCIA, (Washington DC: Government Printing Office, 1875), 212.

19. Mateer, ARCIA, 1878, 8.

20. Mateer, ARCIA, 1878, 9.

21. Mateer, ARCIA, 1878, 9.

22. Whiteley, *Deliberate Acts*, 42.

23. "The Five Moqui Chiefs," *Washington Post*, June 28, 1890, 8.

24. For more on the Hopi visit to Washington, see Whiteley, *Deliberate Acts*, 75, and Levy, *Orayvi Revisited*, 91.

25. "The Five Moqui Chiefs," *Washington Post*, June 28, 1890, 8.

26. Kuwanwisiwma interview, March 21, 2006.

27. Kuwanwisiwma, "'Let Us Not Be Afraid,'" 13.

28. Loftin, *Religion and Hopi Life*, 73.

29. Loftin, *Religion and Hopi Life*, 73.

30. Kabotie, *Fred Kabotie*, 1.

31. Whiteley, *Deliberate Acts*, 74.

32. "The Education of the Indians," *Los Angeles Times*, November 21, 1889, 4.

33. Miller, "The Limits of Schooling by Imposition," 84.

34. Donaldson, *Extra Census Bulletin*, 56. Commissioner Morgan's predecessor, John H. Oberly, also believed that education would save the "Indian race." In his annual report in 1888, Commissioner Oberly said: "The Indian is commencing the fact that he must become civilized; must, as he expressed it, 'learn the white man's way or perish from the face of the earth.'" Cited in "Aiding the Indians," *Los Angeles Times*, January 14, 1889, 5.

35. Fontana, "Historical Foundations," 36.

36. Jacobs, *White Mother to a Dark Race*, 159.

37. *Chicago Daily Tribune*, "Moqui Indians Threaten the Whites," June 26, 1891, 1.

38. Many Navajos also fiercely disagreed with the U.S. government's policy of Indian education. Government officials feared that thirty thousand Hopi and Navajo men would band together and create an uprising against the U.S. government. See "Another Indian Uprising Imminent,"

Chicago Daily Tribune, June 24, 1891, 1. In 1891 the issue of allotment added to the tension on the Hopi Reservation. In his 1893 census on the Hopi Indians, Thomas Donaldson states: "Much of the trouble arose from the fact that a scheme of allotment was about being applied to them, and they could not understand why United States surveyors should come to their farms and lands and proceed to survey them under orders of the department without their first having it fully explained to them; they could not comprehend why they should be disposed of land owned and occupied for homes by their ancestors and themselves for nearly 350 years, and perhaps thousands of years. In fact, being citizens of the United States, they could not understand why they should not be treated as other citizens and their property respected." Donaldson, *Extra Census Bulletin*, 37.

39. "The Indian Troubles," *Los Angeles Times*, June 27, 1891, 2.

40. Mischa Titiev writes about a Hopi medicine man in his examination of Orayvi. See Titiev, *The Hopi Indians of Old Oraibi*, 21, 22.

41. "The Moquis Subdued," *Los Angeles Times*, July 5, 1891, 1.

42. "The Moquis Subdued," *Los Angeles Times*, July 5, 1891, 1.

43. The *Chicago Daily Tribune* reported that Corbin had Navajos join him so they would be intimidated by the U.S. government's display of power among the Hopis. Corbin wanted the Navajos to stop resisting the U.S. government's plan to educate Navajo children and to learn a lesson from the situation at Orayvi. "Terrified the Indians," *Chicago Daily Tribune*, July 5, 1891, 10.

44. "The Moquis Subdued," *Los Angeles Times*, July 5, 1891, 1.

45. "Collegiate Indians," *Chicago Daily Tribune*, July 20, 1884, 4.

46. "The Indian School May be Emptied," *New York Times*, October 6, 1891, 3.

47. Jacobs, "A Battle for the Children," 41.

48. Donaldson, *Extra Census Bulletin*, 39.

49. E. H. Plummer to Commissioner Thomas J. Morgan, January 8, 1894, "1893 to 1894 FD 20," Navajo Agency Fort Defiance, Arizona, Letters Sent 1881–1927, NARA, RG–75.

50. During this time, the U.S. government was only able to send a small number of Hopis to off-reservation Indian boarding schools, including Haskell Institute in Lawrence, Kansas. See "Winning Their Way," *Chicago Daily Tribune*, August 14, 1892, 25.

51. "Rules for Indian Schools with Course of Study, List of Textbooks, and Civil Service Rules," (Washington DC: Government Printing Office, 1892), 7.

52. Unless otherwise noted, quotes in the following account of the Hopis' confrontation with government troops, arrest, and deportation to Alcatraz come from George H. Guy, "Mastering the Moquis," *Los Angeles Times*, January 27, 1895, 17.

53. Guy, "Mastering the Moquis," 17. In his critical examination of the ways American Indians were portrayed in the press from 1820 to 1890, John M. Coward notes: "The cultural and territorial conflicts between whites and Indians were often complicated, building on years of mutual mistrust and fear concerning land, trade, and other issues. But in the papers, these critical conflicts as well as stories of cooperation and mutual respect, were often obscured by reports of violence, stories rich in drama and easily understandable to journalists and readers alike. This emphasis on violence ensured that a major theme of Indian news would be inflammatory and consciously anti-Indian, the press solving the 'Indian problem' by advocating and justifying white revenge and genocide." Coward, *The Newspaper Indian*, 5–6.

54. Relying on Henser's account, Guy noted that the kiva was "about thirty feet wide and nine feet high" with walls "covered with weird and grotesque designs and drawings of snakes and other animals in gaudy colors." Guy, "Mastering the Moquis," 17.

55. James, *Pages from Hopi History*, 115, 116; Odier, *The Rock*, 227. Former historian for the Hopi Cultural Preservation Office Wendy Holliday has written a brief history on Hopis whom government officials sent to Alcatraz. See Wendy Holliday, "Hopi History: The Story of the Alcatraz Prisoners, Part 1," at *www.nps.gov/archive/alcatraz/tours/hopi/hopi-h1.htm*, and "Hopi History: The Story of the Alcatraz Prisoners, Part 2," at *www.nps.gov/archive/alcatraz/tours/hopi/hopi-h2.htm*.

56. Williams, ARCIA, 1896, 118, 119.

57. Hertzog, ARCIA, 1896, 359.

58. Collins, ARCIA, 1897, 361.

59. Collins, ARCIA, 1897, 361.

60. Guy, "Mastering the Moquis," 17.

61. Clemmer, *Roads in the Sky*, 108.

62. "A Faulty Educational System," *New York Times*, October 16, 1892, 4.

63. James, *Pages from Hopi History*, 113.

64. C. W. Goodman, ARCIA, 1893, 998.

65. Goodman, ARCIA, 1893, 998.

66. Collins ARCIA, 1896, 363.

67. Collins, ARCIA, 1896, 363.

68. See Qoyawayma, *No Turning Back*.

69. Lummis, *Bullying the Moqui*, 101.

70. Burton, "Report of School at Keams Canyon, Ariz.," in *Annual Reports of the Department of the Interior for the Fiscal Year Ending in June 30th 1900, Indian Affairs: Report of the Commissioner and Appendices*, 475, quoted in Whitely, *Deliberate Acts*, 91.

71. Charles E. Burton to the Commissioner of Indian Affairs, September 15, 1900, Keams Canyon Letterbooks, Hopi Indian Agency, Keams Canyon AZ, quoted in Whitely, *Deliberate Acts*, 91.

72. Whiteley, *Deliberate Acts*, 91, 92.

73. Nequatewa, *Born a Chief*, 155–56.

74. Nequatewa, *Born a Chief*, 159–60.

75. Lummis, *Bullying the Moqui*, 42–43.

76. Kolp affidavit, quoted in Lummis, *Bullying the Moqui*, 44.

77. Kolp affidavit, quoted in Lummis, *Bullying the Moqui*, 44.

78. Kolp affidavit, quoted in Lummis, *Bullying the Moqui*, 44.

79. Kolp affidavit, quoted in Lummis, *Bullying the Moqui*, 44–45.

80. Miller, *The Limits of Schooling by Imposition*, 86. Compare similar ways Navajo and Apache parents hid their children in Jacobs, *White Mother to a Dark Race*, 156, 157.

81. Government agents frequently mentioned in their official correspondence that Hopis often did not wear shoes outside when snow was present. Some of the barefoot Hopis had attended Indian boarding schools. In a letter dated January 16, 1906, Superintendent Murphy wrote Commissioner Francis E. Leupp and observed that the "women and children" of Moencopi "never wear shoes when there is snow on the ground; they do this not from necessity but from choice." Murphy noted: "I vested this village on the 2nd of this month; there was about six inches of snow on the ground and the thermometer registered several degrees below freezing, but women and children were walking about, barefoot, as unconcerned as they would be in July; at one place I saw about a dozen women and girls, and a number of nude children,

standing in the snow; the women were cleaning rabbits, and were chatting and laughing as gaily as any group of white women could, under the most favorable circumstances; many of the girls in this group were returned students, from boarding schools and had shoes and stockings in their houses, but preferred to go barefoot, as stated." Superintendent Matthew M. Murphy to Commissioner Francis E. Leupp, January 16, 1906, "Letter Book, Honorable Commissioner of Indian Affairs, January 1, 1905 to January 16, 1906," NARA, RG–75, TC-65, Western Navajo Reservation AZ, Box 5.

82. Lummis, *Bullying the Moqui*, 45.

83. See Hagen, *Six Friends of the Indian*, 54–56, 75, 76, 120–38, 190.

84. Lummis, *Bullying the Moqui*, 60.

85. "Not a Moqui Civilizer," *Los Angeles Times*, June 23, 1903, 2.

86. Lummis, *Bullying the Moqui*, 52.

87. "Charges against Indian Agent," *Washington Post*, June 23, 1903, SPII.

88. James, *Pages from Hopi History*, 129.

89. "Charges against Burton," *Los Angeles Times*, October 25, 1903, 2.

90. "Will Try to Stop Snake Dance," *New York Times*, November 8, 1904, 6.

91. "No Indian Troubles Expected," *Chicago Daily Tribune*, June 25, 1891, 3.

2. Policies and Assimilation

1. Trafzer, *As Long as the Grass Shall Grow*, 289.

2. Ladies Union Mission School Association, *Among the Pimas*, 94.

3. Bessie Humetewa interview, July 8, 2004, Bacavi AZ, Hopi Reservation (hereafter cited as Humetewa interview, July 8, 2004).

4. Adams, *Education for Extinction*, 97.

5. Fear-Segal, "Nineteenth-Century Indian Education," 339.

6. Hoxie, *A Final Promise*, 115.

7. Hoxie, *A Final Promise*, 117.

8. Hoxie, *A Final Promise*, 144.

9. Collins, introduction to *Assimilation's Agent*, by Chalcraft, xi.

10. Collins, introduction to *Assimilation's Agent*, by Chalcraft, xi.

11. Linton, *Acculturation in Seven American Indian Tribes*, 463, 464.

12. Pratt and Utley, *Battlefield and Classroom*, xiv.

13. Pratt and Utley, *Battlefield and Classroom*, xiv.

14. "The Indian Problem," *New York Times*, March 7, 1866, 8. See also "The Negro and Indian," *Washington Post*, December 19, 1879, 1. For a comprehensive and comparative account on black education in the United States, see James D. Anderson, *The Education of Blacks in the South, 1860–1935* (Chapel Hill: University of North Carolina Press, 1988).

15. The House Committee Report is quoted in Alice C. Fletcher, *Indian Education and Civilization*, Senate Exec. Doc. no. 95, 48th Cong., 2nd sess., 1888, serial 2542, 162–63, quoted in Adams, *Education for Extinction*, 6.

16. Kampmeier, "Report of Teacher of Polacca Day School, June 30, 1902," ARDI, (Washington DC: Government Printing Office, 1902), 155.

17. Ellis, *To Change Them Forever*, 23.

18. Kampmeier, "Report of Teacher of Polacca Day School, June 30, 1902," ARDI, 155.

19. "The Indian Problem," *New York Times*, March 7, 1866, 8.

20. Lomawaima, "Estelle Reel, Superintendent of Indian Schools, 1898–1910," 5–31.

21. "Tells of Indians," *Los Angles Times*, July 9, 1907, II6.

22. "Tells of Indians," *Los Angles Times*, July 9, 1907, II6.

23. On April 1, 1908, a reporter for the *Washington Post* noted that Leupp gave a lecture to the Anthropological Society at the Cosmos Club in Washington DC on March 31, 1908. Leupp's talk was titled "Some Sidelights on Indian Administration." The reporter wrote: "Mr. Leupp said that the government went to work in educating the Indian at the wrong end. They established large boarding schools, many of them a long distance from the homes of the Indians, and tried to educate them in literary subjects instead of establishing day schools on the reservation and keeping the pupils at home. He said that the government had seen its mistake, and had established these day schools, and that it had a better effect on the Indians. The boarding schools had too many frills, and the Indian was apt to become sick, as he was not used to this mode of living. Mr. Leupp declared that the chief aid and end was to show the white man his duty to the Indian, and that the former had to educate the latter in industrial rather than literary pursuits." "Tells Needs of Indians," *Washington Post*, April 1, 1908, 9.

24. Keller, *Empty Beds*, 1.

25. "Perris Protest," *Los Angeles Times*, January 28, 1898, 15.

26. "The Indian School," *Los Angeles Times*, October 11, 1899, 3.

27. "The Indian School Job," *Los Angeles Times*, April 3, 1900, 18.

28. "Perris School Gets a Setback," *Los Angeles Times*, November 12, 1900, 17.

29. William E. Curtis, "Sherman School Uplifts Indians," *Los Angeles Times*, May 30, 1911, 113 (originally published in the *Chicago Record Herald*); *Sherman Bulletin*, September 18, 1925, 1.

30. *Sherman Bulletin*, September 18, 1925, 1.

31. Marsah Balenquah interview, March 28, 2006, Bacavi AZ, Hopi Reservation, (hereafter cited as Balenquah interview, March 28, 2006).

32. Balenquah interview, March 28, 2006.

33. Harwood Hall, "Report of the School at Riverside," ARCIA, 1905, 416.

34. "Sherman Institute Record of Student Enrollment," The Sherman Indian Museum, Riverside CA, 120–80.

35. *Sherman Bulletin*, September 18, 1925, 1.

36. "Hayes Mortgage Is Foreclosed: Sherman Institute Full," *Los Angeles Times*, September 23, 1904, A8.

37. "Hayes Mortgage Is Foreclosed: Sherman Institute Full," *Los Angeles Times*, September 23, 1904, A8.

38. "Mokis at Last in School," *Los Angeles Times*, November 30, 1906, 117.

39. Reyhner and Eder, *American Indian Education*, 168–70.

40. Adams, *Education for Extinction*, 139.

41. Katanski, *Learning to Write "Indian,"* 35.

42. Donaldson, *Extra Census Bulletin*, 9. Although Hopis had been granted U.S. citizenship, because they were Indians, they did not have full citizenship. For instance, Hopis were not able to partake of the rights established under the Bill of Rights until 1924. See James, *Pages from Hopi History*, 191.

43. Hall, "Report of Riverside and Perris Schools, California, August 15, 1902," ARDI, 450.

44. "Educating the Indians," *Washington Post*, June 28, 1903, M8 (originally published in the *Kansas City Times*).

45. *Riverside Daily Enterprise*, June 21, 1907, 8, 9.

46. Tom Holm, *The Great Confusion in Indian Affairs*, 8. Holm notes that the "conferees were completely taken by the idea of assimilating the Indian population in the American body politic. They believed wholeheartedly that Indians should become thoroughly Americanized Christians in a cultural sense and fully indoctrinated in the competitive and individualized model that was, to them, the American way of life. By learning English, as well as to read and write, Native Americans would be better able to compete with their white neighbors" (8).

47. Valentine, "Indians as Workers," 31–32.

48. *Sherman Bulletin*, October 2, 1907, 1.

49. Victor Sakiestewa to Frank M. Conser, July 28, 1914, "Sakiestewa, Victor," NARA, RG–75, SSCF, Box 315.

50. *Sherman Bulletin*, October 2, 1907, 1.

51. *Sherman Bulletin*, September 25, 1907, 1.

52. Vučković, *Voices from Haskell*, 100.

53. *Sherman Bulletin*, September 25, 1907, 1.

54. *Sherman Bulletin*, October 2, 1907, 1.

55. Harwood Hall to Peter P. Hilliard, August 1907, Sherman Institute, Records of the Superintendent, Letters Sent, 1902–1948, NARA, RG–75, Box 58.

56. "Sherman Institute Booklet," 1908, Sherman Indian Museum, Riverside CA.

57. Hall, "Report of Riverside and Perris Schools, California, August 15, 1902," ARDI, 450.

58. Hall, "Report of Riverside and Perris Schools, California, August 15, 1902," ARDI, 41.

59. "Graduates Cook, Saw, Hammer," *Los Angeles Times*, June 5, 1908, II9.

60. Acoma poet and writer Simon J. Ortiz once remarked that being good at something at U.S. government schools was important for Indian pupils. He notes: "And even if you were Indian, or if you were black, Hispanic, or even if you were a minority, then the goodness became an asset. I mean, that kind of, not goodness in behavior, but if you were a good athlete, if you were a good student, that became the agent that you could demonstrate and show your qualities." Lucero, "Simon J. Ortiz," 139.

61. Shingoitewa interview, July 8, 2004.

62. Short, "Outing Program at Sherman Institute," 36. This master's thesis remains the most comprehensive examination of the Outing Program at Sherman Institute. For additional information on the Outing Program at other off-reservation Indian boarding schools, see Reyhner and Eder, *American Indian Education*, 139, 144, 145, 147, 153, 155, 164.

63. Adams, "Beyond Bleakness: The Brighter Side of Indian Boarding Schools," 47.

64. R. N. Ross to Orrington Jewett, October 22, 1917, "Sachamenema, Myra," NARA, SSCF, RG–75, Box 315. In this letter, Ross informed Jewett that she had recently purchased Myra a middy (blouse) for $1.25, a hair ribbon for 40 cents, a skirt to go with the middy for $3.00, shoes to wear at church for $3.00, and a pair of stockings for 60 cents, all of which Ross was planning on deducting from Myra's monthly salary of $4.00.

65. Szasz, *Indian Education in the American Colonies*, 54.

66. Trennert, *The Phoenix Indian School*, 72.

67. Frank Conser to Mr. H. J. Rose, July 1, 1909, "Tuvayyumtewa, Jennie," NARA, RG–75, SSCF, Box 368.

68. McKenzie, *The Indian in Relation to the White Population of the United States*, 58.

69. Leupp, *The Indian and His Problem*, 122, 123.

3. The Orayvi Split

1. The purpose of this chapter is not to explain the Orayvi Split in its entirety; rather I have set out to demonstrate the educational consequences of the Split. In addition to several Hopi accounts provided in Polingaysi Qoyawayma's *No Turning Back* (1977) and Helen Sekaquaptewa's *Me and Mine* (1969), Peter M. Whiteley gives a thorough examination of the Orayvi Split in *Deliberate Acts* (1988) and *The Orayvi Split: A Hopi Transformation* (2008).

2. Just prior to the Orayvi Split, Tawaquaptewa sent messengers to Moencopi, a satellite village of Orayvi, and asked the leaders at Moencopi to send men to help him with the situation at Orayvi. See James, *Pages from Hopi History*, 135.

3. Lee Wayne Lomayestewa interview, March 23, 2006, Shungopavi AZ, Hopi Reservation.

4. Kuwanwisiwma interview, March 21, 2006.

5. Kuwanwisiwma interview, March 21, 2006.

6. Tanner, "Fred Kabotie Hopi Indian Artist," 25. The English translation of this Hopi name is: "It happens again and again like the sunrise." See DeHuff, *Taytay's Tales*, v.

7. Tanner, "Fred Kabotie Hopi Indian Artist," 25.

8. In Hopi society, the people believe that divisions have both negative and positive consequences. This perspective is foreign to some people outside Hopi society who view tensions in only harmful terms.

9. Hayzlett, ARCIA, 1899, 159.

10. Geertz, *The Invention of Prophecy*, 127.

11. Hayzlett, ARCIA, 1899, 159.

12. Trennert, *White Man's Medicine*, 93.

13. Hayzlett, ARCIA, 1899, 159.

14. Hayzlett, ARCIA, 1899, 159.

15. Hayzlett, ARCIA, 1899, 159.

16. Whiteley, *Deliberate Acts*, 90.

17. Nequatewa, *Born a Chief*, 107–9.

18. Nequatewa, *Born a Chief*, 107–9.

19. Nequatewa, *Born a Chief*, 107–9.

20. Yava, *Big Falling Snow*, 13.

21. Sekaquaptewa, *Me and Mine*, 65.

22. Levy, *Orayvi Revisited*, 161.

23. In his examination of Hopi prophecies, Armin W. Geertz notes that by 1906 the situation at Orayvi was quickly deteriorating and both factions realized that the problem would soon reach a climax: "By this time Oraibians were resigning themselves to their fate. The town was already divided politically and religiously, and it was only a matter of time before the combined forces on the reservation would clash . . . Drought and harvest failures plagued the Hopis and, in the fateful year of 1906, the springs were failing. The Navajos were encroaching right up to the villages, the school program was being enforced, and the factional leaders were provoking each other more and more." Geertz, *The Invention of Prophecy*, 128.

24. Clemmer, *Roads in the Sky*, 109.

25. Clemmer, *Roads in the Sky*, 109.

26. Qoyawayma, *No Turning Back*, 39.

27. Miller, "The Limits of Schooling by Imposition," 104.

28. Ethel Sakiestewa Gilbert interview, Upper Moencopi AZ, Hopi Reservation, August 13, 2003 (hereafter cited as Sakiestewa Gilbert interview, August 13, 2003).

29. Leupp, ARCIA, 1906, 121.

30. Leupp, ARCIA, 1906, 121, 122.

31. Leupp, ARCIA, 1906, 122.

32. "Commissioner Leupp among the Indians," *Washington Post*, August 15, 1906, 12.

33. Paul L. Russell and Lillian K. Russell, "A 1911 Genesis of the Hopi Indians by Yukeoma A Hostile Hopi Chieftain, also The Establishment of the First Navajo and Hopi Indian Reservation and Schools in 1868," Cline Library Special Collections, Northern Arizona University, 1–40. A similar account has been published in Whiteley, *The Orayvi Split*, 1113–20.

34. Russell and Russell, "A 1911 Genesis of the Hopi Indians," 7.

35. Russell and Russell, "A 1911 Genesis of the Hopi Indians," 7.

36. Russell and Russell, "A 1911 Genesis of the Hopi Indians," 8.

37. Russell and Russell, "A 1911 Genesis of the Hopi Indians," 8.

38. "Perry arrested 101 'Hostile' men, sending eleven younger men to Carlisle Indian School in Pennsylvania, and sentencing seventeen to one year hard labor in Keams Canyon. Two were released when they signed agreements acknowledging the U.S. Government's authority. Police took the prisoners out daily in chain gangs of six to a chain and set them to work building a road from the canyon up the slope of the mesa, which eventually connected with the Holbrook road." Clemmer, *Roads in the Sky*, 111.

39. Russell and Russell, "A 1911 Genesis of the Hopi Indians," 9.

40. Russell and Russell, "A 1911 Genesis of the Hopi Indians," 9.

41. Russell and Russell, "A 1911 Genesis of the Hopi Indians," 12.

42. Russell and Russell, "A 1911 Genesis of the Hopi Indians," 12.

43. Tawaquaptewa referred to Frank Seumptewa as his "lieutenant." Titiev, *The Hopi Indians of Old Oraibi*, 347.

44. Russell and Russell, "A 1911 Genesis of the Hopi Indians," 13.

45. Russell and Russell, "A 1911 Genesis of the Hopi Indians," 13.

46. Sekaquaptewa, *Me and Mine*, 80.

47. Whiteley, *The Orayvi Split*, 1017.

48. Russell and Russell, "A 1911 Genesis of the Hopi Indians," 13.

49. In a letter to Commissioner Leupp dated September 20, 1906, Superintendent Matthew Murphy noted that he "found the 'hostiles' about four miles north west of the village of Oraibi, encamped near a small spring; they had erected rude shelters of stone and brush, which gave them protection against cold, but would afford no protection against snow or rain; this camp numbers 102 families, comprising of 165 men; old men and old women were very much in evidence in this camp; it was reported that that one old man could not be found; I saw no marks of violence except on one old man who had lost most of his hair; these people received me as kindly as did the friendly people, and if I had not been told I could not have distinguished one faction from other, except that these people acknowledged their opposition to schools." Matthew Murphy to the Commissioner of Indian Affairs, September 20, 1906, National Archives, Washington DC, RG–75, "Oraiba Troubles," File 1, 3–5. A reproduction of this letter can be found in Whiteley, *The Orayvi Split*, 1017.

50. Russell and Russell, "A 1911 Genesis of the Hopi Indians," 13. Mischa Titiev noted that Tawaquaptewa's brother, Bert Fredericks, said government officials had instructed Youkeoma to relocate his band of resisters to the Little Colorado River, but that Youkeoma was afraid that his followers would refuse to go with him. Titiev, *The Hopi Indians of Old Oraibi*, 58. Jerrold E. Levy argues that the resisting and accommodating Hopi factions understood the line used in the pushing battle of the Orayvi Split to be the Colorado River. See Levy, *Orayvi Revisited*, 147.

51. Theodore G. Lemmon to the Commissioner of Indian Affairs, September 9, 1906, National Archives, Washington DC, RG–75, "Oraiba Troubles," File 1, 6–7, quoted in Whiteley, *Deliberate Acts*, 110.

52. Murphy to Commissioner of Indian Affairs, September 20, 1906, quoted in Whiteley, *Deliberate Acts*, 110, 111.

53. Murphy to Commissioner of Indian Affairs, September 20, 1906, quoted in Whiteley, *Deliberate Acts*, 110, 111.

54. Sekaquaptewa, *Me and Mine*, 91. In a letter to President Roosevelt dated September 29, 1906, Commissioner Leupp recommended that "especial pains be taken to make the Indians understand that the Government had reached the limit of its patience with the old way of handling all these matters among the Indians, and that hereafter the Indians will conduct themselves reasonably like white men or be

treated as white people treat those of their own number who are forever quarreling or fighting among themselves." Whiteley, *Deliberate Acts*, 297.

55. Nequatewa, *Truth of a Hopi*, 58–59.

56. Nequatewa, *Truth of a Hopi*, 59.

57. Nequatewa, *Truth of a Hopi*, 59.

58. Whiteley, *Deliberate Acts*, 113.

59. Whiteley, *Deliberate Acts*, 113.

60. Whiteley, *Deliberate Acts*, 113.

61. Agreement Signed by Hostiles Returning to Oraibi, National Archives, Washington DC, RG–75, "Oraiba Troubles," File 3, quoted in Whiteley, *Deliberate Acts*, 307–8.

62. Sekaquaptewa, *Me and Mine*, 87.

63. Sekaquaptewa, *Me and Mine*, 87.

64. Sekaquaptewa, *Me and Mine*, 87.

65. Kuwanwisiwma interview, March 21, 2006; Hafford, "Along the Way," 2.

66. Whiteley, *Deliberate Acts*, 296.

67. James, *Pages from Hopi History*, 138, 139.

68. Peter Whiteley notes that the "Oraibi situation was being deliberated, then, in the highest echelons of government; as well as Roosevelt, the secretaries of war and interior were both personally involved in putting Leupp's program into effect." Whiteley, *Deliberate Acts*, 111. Whiteley also reproduces a letter that Leupp wrote to President Roosevelt on September 29, 1906, that outlines Leupp's plan to deal with Tawaquaptewa, Youkeoma, Orayvi as a whole, and the enrollment of Hopi children at U.S. government schools (295–97).

69. Sekaquaptewa, *Me and Mine*, 13, 14.

70. "A Sexagenarian at School," *New York Times*, August 22, 1888, 4.

71. "A Sexagenarian at School," *New York Times*, August 22, 1888, 4.

4. Elder in Residence

1. Qoyawayma, *No Turning Back*, 56.

2. Initially twenty-two Hopis from Oraibi Day School left with Tawaquaptewa and his family to Sherman Institute on November 15, 1906, and the remaining students from Orayvi made the trip to Riverside a few days later. Reuben Perry to Commissioner Leupp, November 17, 1906, cited in Whiteley, *The Orayvi Split*, 1046.

3. "Mokis at Last In School," *Los Angeles Times*, November 30, 1906, II7.

4. *Sherman Bulletin*, January 13, 1909, 1.

5. *Sherman Bulletin*, November 27, 1907, 4.

6. Qoyawayma, *No Turning Back*, 51.

7. "Report of the Superintendent of Indian Schools, September 25, 1906," ARCIA, 407.

8. "Report of the Superintendent of Indian Schools, September 25, 1906," ARDI, 407.

9. "Report of the Superintendent of Indian Schools, September 25, 1906," ARDI, 411.

10. "Report of the Commissioner of Indian Affairs—Disturbances Among the Hopi, 1906," ARDI, 118–25.

11. *Sherman Bulletin*, November 11, 1908, 2.

12. *Sherman Bulletin*, March 27, 1907, 2.

13. *Sherman Bulletin*, March 13, 1907, 4.

14. Deloria, "Knowing and Understanding," 45.

15. *Sherman Bulletin*, March 13, 1907, 4.

16. Harwood Hall to Francis E. Leupp, February 4, 1907, Sherman Institute, Records of the Superintendent, Letters Sent, NARA, RG–75, Box 58.

17. *Sherman Bulletin*, April 24, 1907, 3.

18. *Sherman Bulletin*, April 24, 1907, 3.

19. *Sherman Bulletin*, March 6, 1907, 1.

20. *Sherman Bulletin*, May 16, 1907, 2.

21. Hall to Leupp, February 4, 1907.

22. Hall to Leupp, February 4, 1907.

23. James, *Pages from Hopi History*, 173.

24. Curtis, *The Indian's Book*, 480.

25. Curtis, *The Indian's Book*, 475.

26. Superintendent of Indian Schools Estelle Reel also displayed the works of Indian pupils at the annual National Education Association conferences and at venues in the Washington DC area. For example, in July 1900, Reel brought an Indian exhibit from the NEA Convention in Charleston, South Carolina, to the Old Post Office Building in Washington DC. Reel collected all sorts of pieces for the exhibit. Every piece, which included examples of domestic and industrial work, was made by pupils at off-reservation Indian boarding schools throughout the United States. "Bright Little Indians," *Washington Post*, July 19, 1900, 9.

27. *Sherman Bulletin*, June 26, 1907, 3.

28. Harwood Hall to Estelle Reel, May 11, 1907, Records of the Superintendent, Letters Sent, 1902–1948, NARA, RG–75, Box 58.

29. *Sherman Bulletin*, May 16, 1907, 2.

30. In the 1930s, Tawaquaptewa prohibited people from taking pictures of Orayvi without his permission. See Titiev, *The Hopi Indians of Old Oraibi*, 4, 5.

31. For example, at Upper Moencopi, signs located at each entrance of the village read: "WELCOME TO MOENKOPI VILLAGE, TO ALL VISITORS, YOU ARE WELCOME TO RESPECTFULLY VISIT OUR VILLAGE AND OBSERVE OUR CEREMONIES = ABSOLUTELY NOT PERMITTED = 1. NO SOUND RECORDINGS, 2. NO SKETCHING, 3. NO PHOTOGRAPHY OF ANY KIND, 4. NO REMOVAL OF ANY OBJECTS, 5. NO VIDEO TAKING."

32. *Sherman Bulletin*, May 29, 1907, 4.

33. *Sherman Bulletin*, March 3, 1909, 2.

34. Harwood Hall to Francis E. Leupp, October 9, 1908, Records of the Superintendent, Letters and Telegrams from the Commissioner, June 1903–December 1904, NARA, RG–75, Box 43.

35. Hall to Leupp, October 9, 1908.

36. *Sherman Bulletin*, February 19, 1908, 3.

37. Victor Sakiestewa to Frank Conser, "Sakiestewa, Victor," December 24, 1913, NARA, RG–75, SSCF, Box 315.

38. Troutman, *Indian Blues*, 121.

39. Sakiestewa Gilbert interview, August 13, 2003.

40. Keller, *Empty Beds*, 34.

41. Keller, *Empty Beds*, 34.

42. *Sherman Bulletin*, February 19, 1908, 2.

43. "Killed in a Game of Football," *Los Angeles Times*, December 1, 1907, 19.

44. *Sherman Bulletin*, December 4, 1907, 3.

45. "Report of Superintendent of Riverside School (Sherman Institute), September 1, 1906," ARDI, 208.

46. *Sherman Bulletin*, March 6, 1907, 4.

47. *Sherman Bulletin*, March 6, 1907, 4.

48. *Sherman Bulletin*, April 16, 1909, 3.

49. *Sherman Bulletin*, January 22, 1908, 2.

50. *Sherman Bulletin*, November 20, 1907, 2.

51. "Sherman Institute Booklet, 1908," Sherman Indian Museum, Riverside CA.

52. Harwood Hall to Miltona M. Keith, November 27, 1906, Sherman Institute, Records of the Superintendent, Letters Sent, 1902–1948, NARA, RG–75, Box 58.

53. *Sherman Bulletin*, March 6, 1907, 2.

54. *Sherman Bulletin*, June 12, 1907, 3.

55. Harwood Hall to Horton H. Miller, August 2, 1907 Sherman Institute, Records of the Superintendent, Letters Sent, 1902–1948, NARA, RG–75, Box 58.

56. *Sherman Bulletin*, October 28, 1908, 1.

57. After the students wrote a letter their teachers would check for spelling, structural, and grammatical mistakes. Upon the teacher's approval, the corrected letter would be sent to the child's family. Whether the family was able to read the letter is another consideration entirely.

58. *Sherman Bulletin*, April 10, 1907, 3.

59. *Sherman Bulletin*, February 5, 1908, 4.

60. Peter Stauffer also participated in the "roundups" at Orayvi. See chapter 1.

61. *Sherman Bulletin*, December 11, 1907, 4.

62. *Sherman Bulletin*, December 11, 1907, 4.

63. Harwood Hall to Miltona M. Keith, November 26, 1906, Sherman Institute, Records of the Superintendent, Letters Sent, 1902–1948, NARA, RG–75, Box 58.

64. Harwood Hall to Horton H. Miller, November 20, 1906, Sherman Institute, Records of the Superintendent, Letters Sent, 1902–1948, NARA, RG–75, Box 58.

65. "Tewaquaptewa," April 20, 1909, NARA, RG–75, SSCF, Box 355.

66. Tawaquaptewa to Mootuma, May 27, 1907, Sherman Institute, Records of the Superintendent, Letters Sent, 1902–1948, NARA, RG–75, Box 58.

67. Harwood Hall to Tewaquaptewa, July 30, 1907, Sherman Institute, Records of the Superintendent, Letters Sent, 1902–1948, NARA, RG–75, Box 58.

68. Hall to Tewaquaptewa, July 30, 1907.

69. Spicer, *Cycles of Conquest*, 203.

70. Waters, *Book of the Hopi*, 361.

71. Indian Law Resource Center, *Report to the Hopi Kikmongwis and Other Traditional Leaders*, 19.

72. Francis E. Leupp to Frank Conser, "Tewaquaptewa," June 7, 1909, NARA, RG–75, SSCF, Box 355.

73. Frank Conser to Francis E. Leupp, "Tewaquaptewa," June 15, 1909, NARA, RG–75, SSCF, Box 355.

74. Conser to Leupp, June 15, 1909.

75. Although Tawaquaptewa briefly worked as a U.S. government policeman when he returned home to the reservation (*Sherman Bulletin*, December 14, 1909, 3), his compliant attitude toward government officials eventually ceased altogether.

76. Titiev, *The Hopi Indians of Old Oraibi*, 26.

77. James, *Pages from Hopi History*, 142.

78. *Sherman Bulletin*, January 13, 1909, 3.

79. Conser to Leupp, June 15, 1909.

80. *Sherman Bulletin*, June 16, 1909, 4.

81. *Sherman Bulletin*, June 2, 1909, 2.

82. Victor Sakiestewa to Frank Conser, "Sakiestewa, Victor," November 15, 1910, NARA, RG–75, SSCF, Box 315.

83. In 1908 the *Sherman Bulletin* reported that Leupp estimated that it cost the U.S. government $250.00 per year to educate Indians at off-reservation boarding schools. *Sherman Bulletin*, January 29, 1908, 1.

84. David Haskee to Frank Conser, "Haskee, David," October 2, 1913, NARA, RG–75, SSCF, Box 142.

5. Taking Hopi Knowledge to School

1. See Warrior, *The People and the Word*, 119–26; and Mann, *Cheyenne-Arapaho Education*, 15. Acoma writer and poet Simon Ortiz makes a distinction between the terms "education" and "knowledge" in relation to Indian students who attended boarding schools. Ortiz interprets the word "education" to be industrial skills that Indian pupils learned at schools. In this way, "education," according to Ortiz, is closely associated with the terms "assimilation" and "acculturation." My use of the term "education" is similar to Ortiz' understanding of indigenous "knowledge," which comes from one's tribal community. See Lucero, "Simon J. Ortiz," 141, 142.

2. For additional information on the cultural aspects of Hopi education from a Hopi perspective, see Nicholas, "Hopi Education."

3. Sekaquaptewa, *Me and Mine*, 64.

4. Miller, *Shingwauk's Vision*, 15.

5. Szasz, *Indian Education in the American Colonies*, 7.

6. Williams, "Tribal Education of the Hopi Indian Child," 35.

7. Adams, *Education for Extinction*, 108.

8. Leo Crane to Frank M. Conser, "Sakiestewa, Victor," August 31, 1918, NARA, RG–75, SSCF, Box 315.

9. Qoyawayma, *No Turning Back*, 28, 29.

10. Often in the *Sherman Bulletin* school officials provided only the student's name and not the student's tribal affiliation. Knowing the many different Hopi surnames became critical in differentiating between Hopi and non-Hopi students in the *Bulletin* and other documents.

11. *Sherman Bulletin*, June 4, 1909, 1.

12. See Malotki, *Hopi Tales*, xv.

13. Secakuku, *Hopi Kachina Tradition*, 10.

14. *Sherman Bulletin*, January 31, 1912, 1.

15. Courlander, *People of the Short Blue Corn*, 46–55.

16. Mullett, *Spider Woman Stories*, 127–31.

17. Based on the retelling in *Sherman Bulletin*, January 31, 1912, 3.

18. Trafzer, Keller, and Sisquoc, *Boarding School Blues*, xii. See also 2, 3, 4.

19. Balenquah interview, March 28, 2006.

20. Frank M. Conser to Superintendent Western Navaho School, "Pahsah, Bennie," August 16, 1910, NARA, RG–75, SSCF, Box 277.

21. J. B. Frey for Frank Tewanimptewa to Frank M. Conser, "Pahsah, Bennie," September 7, 1910, NARA, RG–75, SSCF, Box 277.

22. Frank M. Conser to C. R. Jefferis, "Pahsah, Bennie," December 6, 1911, NARA, RG–75, SSCF, Box 277.

23. Tsuamana to Frank M. Conser, "Pahsah, Bennie," July 3, 1912, NARA, RG–75, SSCF, Box 277.

24. "Record of Pupil in School," "Pahsah, Bennie," November 9, 1909, NARA, RG–75, SSCF, Box 277.

25. When Bennie returned to the reservation in 1912, he had a difficult time adjusting to life with one arm. In her July 3, 1912, letter to Frank Conser, Tsuamana told the superintendent that it was difficult for her son to work, his good arm often became tired, and other Hopi children

teased and made fun of Bennie's condition. See Tsuamana to Conser, July 3, 1912.

26. Curtis, The Indians' Book, xxviii.

27. Hough, The Hopi Indians, 105.

28. Lomatewama, Songs to the Corn, 18.

29. Qoyawayma, No Turning Back, 60, 61.

30. Qoyawayma, No Turning Back, 61.

31. Kuwanwisiwma interview, March 21, 2006.

32. Kathy Helm, "Something in the Wind: Former Hopi Chairman Talks About His Bout With Cancer," Gallup (NM) Independent, November 9, 2007, http://www.gallupindependent.com/2007/november/110907kh_smthngnthewnd.html.

33. For additional information on sports at Indian schools, see Bloom, To Show What an Indian Can Do.

34. Sherman Bulletin, November 6, 1907, 2.

35. Gilbert, "The Cultural Value of the Sports and Games," 99.

36. Sherman Bulletin, November 27, 1907, 3.

37. Bloom, To Show What an Indian Can Do, 1.

38. For fascinating accounts of Indian runners, including Hopi runners, see Peter Nabokov, Indian Running: Native American History & Tradition (Santa Fe: Ancient City Press, 1981), and Joseph B. Oxendine, American Indian Sports Heritage (Lincoln: University of Nebraska Press, 1988), 67–90.

39. Yava, Big Falling Snow, 13.

40. I have written at length about Hopi long-distance runners at Sherman Institute in "Hopi Footraces and American Marathons."

41. Sherman Bulletin, December 19, 1922, 3.

42. Quoted in Sherman Bulletin, December 19, 1922, 3.

43. James, The Indians of the Painted Desert Region, 90. On December 26, 1908, James gave a lecture on the Hopi Indians at the Glenwood Hotel in Riverside. Kikmongwi Tawaquaptewa and eight Hopi boys from Sherman Institute were present to hear this talk. See "Newsy Happenings South of Tehachepi," Los Angeles Times, December 27, 1908, I11.

44. "Corn is the most abundant crop produced by Hopi farmers; it is the food that has sustained the people for more than a millennium. Using dry farming techniques, Hopis grow many varieties of corn, and it is preserved and cooked in an amazing variety of dishes. Seasonal and

religious activities are all related to planting, growing, and preserving corn. The complex religious ceremonies of the Hopi are focused on the end result of bringing rain for corn and other substance crops to grow. From the perfect ear of 'mother corn' placed next to a Hopi infant, to the ritual grinding of corn in puberty and wedding rituals, for the corn-meal that is blessed for use in ceremonies, corn figures prominently in Hopi life passages and ceremonies." Koyiyumptewa, Davis, and the Hopi Cultural Preservation Office, *The Hopi People*, 7.

45. Quoted in *Sherman Bulletin*, June 26, 1907, 3.

46. The author wishes to acknowledge Stewart B. Koyiyumptewa, archivist for the Hopi Tribe, for pointing this out to him.

47. Talayesva, *Sun Chief*, 51.

48. Hopi boys also did well in the industrial examinations at the school. Those who demonstrated the highest achievement at the primary level included John Posyesva (Carpenting—First Grade, 100%), Herbert Homesvytewa (Shoemaking—First Grade, 95%), Fritz Navakuku (Steam Cooking—Ranch, 95%), and Keller Seedkoema (Baking—First Grade, 90%). *Sherman Bulletin*, May 1, 1907, 2.

6. Learning to Preach

1. Porter's speech was printed in full in *Sherman Bulletin*, June 02, 1915, 5.

2. Government officials routinely emphasized the importance of hard work among Indian people. At the Lake Mohonk Conference in 1908, Robert G. Valentine remarked: "In every Indian there is a workman if you can only get at him. This is testified to by the examples from twenty-seven kinds of work on which Indians are engaged within the Indian Service and from the forty different kinds of work on which they are engaged outside of the service on equal terms with white men. This is a good argument against the old idea that all Indians could and should become farmers." Valentine, "Indians as Workers," 32, 33.

3. Compare Rathbun, "Hail Mary."

4. Trafzer, *As Long as the Grass Shall Grow*, 289.

5. Cobb, *Listening to Our Grandmothers' Stories*, 49, 50.

6. Adams, *Education for Extinction*, 23.

7. Prucha, *The Churches and the Indian Schools*, 133, 134.

8. Francis E. Leupp to B. B. Custer, September 21, 1905, Sherman

Institute, Records of the Superintendent, Letters and Telegrams from the Commissioner, NARA, RG–75, Box 55. Leupp's opinion resembled an observation made in the 1928 Meriam Report that "under the American system of complete separation of church and state," the U.S. government's involvement in education in religious affairs must remain unbiased. Meriam, et. al, *The Problem of Indian Administration*, 818.

9. Leupp to Custer, September 21, 1905.

10. Leupp to Custer, September 21, 1905.

11. Humetewa interview, July 08, 2004.

12. James, *Pages from Hopi History*, 55.

13. The Mennonites ministered among various Indian nations throughout the United States. For a comparative case study, see Raylene Hinz-Penner, *Searching for Sacred Ground: The Journey of Chief Lawrence Hart, Mennonite* (Telford PA: Cascadia, 2007).

14. James, *Pages from Hopi History*, 148.

15. Whiteley, *Rethinking Hopi Ethnography*, 145.

16. Qoyawayma, *No Turning Back*, 14.

17. Qoyawayma, *No Turning Back*, 60, 61.

18. Talayesva, *Sun Chief*, 41.

19. Talayesva, *Sun Chief*, 41.

20. *Sherman Bulletin*, May 5, 1909, 3.

21. *Sherman Bulletin*, May 5, 1909, 3.

22. Talayesva, *Sun Chief*, 116–117.

23. Talayesva, *Sun Chief*, 117.

24. J. H. McClintock, "Decay Hits Oldest Town," *Los Angeles Times*, September 14, 1924, B9.

25. *Sherman Bulletin*, March 6, 1907, 2.

26. *Sherman Bulletin*, April 24, 1907, 4. Additional information on William W. Roblee can be found in Keller's *Empty Beds*, 84–89.

27. *Sherman Bulletin*, April 10, 1907, 3.

28. *Sherman Bulletin*, May 1, 1907, 3.

29. Trennert, *The Phoenix Indian School*, 50.

30. "Louise Talas [Talaswitiwa]," date unknown, NARA, RG–75, SSCF, Box 351.

31. *Sherman Bulletin*, November 05, 1920, 3.

32. *Sherman Bulletin*, November 05, 1920, 2.

33. *Sherman Bulletin*, November 17, 1915, 3.

34. "Hopi Bride Wears Dress," *Los Angles Times*, September 20, 1907, III11. For another example of Hopi students who married each other at Sherman Institute, see Titiev, *Hopi Indians of Old Oraibi*, 9.

35. "Hopi Bride Wears Dress," *Los Angles Times*, September 20, 1907, III11.

36. Leo Crane to Frank Conser, "Konawysia, Della," May 8, 1918, NARA, RG–75, SSCF, Box 193.

37. Talayesva, *Sun Chief*, 276.

38. Harwood Hall to Horton H. Miller, November 20, 1906, Sherman Institute, Records of the Superintendent, Letters Sent 1902–1948, NARA, RG–75, Box 59.

39. Frank Conser to the Commissioner of Indian Affairs, "Lomakatchia, Amos," May 27, 1919, NARA, RG–75, SSCF, Box 212.

40. *Sherman Bulletin*, November 5, 1920, 3.

41. Frank Conser to Francis E. Leupp, "Tewaquaptewa," June 15, 1909, NARA, RG–75, SSCF, Box 355.

42. *The Los Angeles Times*, November 8, 1931, C13.

43. Thayer and Emanuel, *Climbing Sun*, 60. For another example of a Hopi student at Sherman Institute who missed traditional Hopi food, see Titiev, *The Hopi Indians of Old Oraibi*, 16.

44. Titiev, *The Hopi Indians of Old Oraibi*, 174.

45. See Ephesians 5:21–22 and 1 Peter 3:1–4.

46. Nequatewa, *Truth of a Hopi*, 2.

47. "Sherman Institute Booklet," 1908.

48. Effie Sachowengsie, "Sachowengsie, Effie," Record of Graduates and Returned Students, March 25, 1911, NARA, RG–75, SSCF, Box 315.

49. "Effie Sachowengsie," date unknown, NARA, RG–75, SSCF, Box 315.

50. Effie Sachowengsie to Superintendent Conser, date unknown, NARA, RG–75, SSCF, Box 315.

51. In April 1915, another former Hopi pupil of Sherman Institute, Otto Talasvama [Lomavitu] from Orayvi, wrote Superintendent Conser and told him that he was involved in "evangelistic work" as a Mennonite missionary in Orayvi, and that the "harvest (spiritual harvest)" was "plenteous" among his people. Otto Talasvama to Frank Conser, "Talasvama, Otto," April 19, 1915, NARA, RG–75, SSCF, Box 351. For more on Otto's missionary role on the Hopi Reservation, see Geertz, *The Invention of Prophecy*, 21–23.

52. Johnson, *Beyond the Black Buttes*, 151.

53. Johnson, *Beyond the Black Buttes*, 151.

54. Lomawaima, *They Called It Prairie Light*, 3.

55. In 1914, Leupp commented that the YMCA and YWCA were "important" features of "missionary work among the pupils in the various government schools and among" students who returned to the reservation. Students who came home "from schools such as Carlisle and Hampton to the comparative isolation and limitations of tribal life, [were] not only subject to temptations incident to both heredity and environment," but great "differences in the changes and modes of life." In Leupp's opinion, the two organizations acted as a godsend to Indian students who needed "friendly sympathy" upon their return home from school. According to Leupp, the religious organizations had proven "to be greatly helpful" in "ministering to those who" would likely go on to influence "their tribes." Leupp, *In Red Man's Land*, 156.

56. Johnson, *Beyond the Black Buttes*, 155, 156.

57. Davis, *Hopi Summer*, 57.

58. Don Talayesva recalled that after he returned from Sherman Institute in 1909, he despised Christian missionaries and blamed Christians for the erosion of Hopi culture: "I had avoided the missionaries, unless I could get something from them, and paid no attention to their Sabbath, and their sermons. I resented the way they meddled in our private affairs, encouraged strife among us, destroyed our Hopi way of life, and brought on draughts and disease . . . When disease and droughts came and when our crops were bad, we blamed the Whites—especially the missionaries—and cussed them to their backs." Talayesva, *Sun Chief*, 299.

7. Returning to Hopi

1. Lucero, "Simon J. Ortiz," 133.

2. Harry Nutumya, interview by Stewart B. Koyiyumptewa, July 7, 2004, interview 61-1, Hopi History Project, Hopi Cultural Preservation Office and Cline Library Special Collections, Northern Arizona University. Transcript accessed at: http://www.nau.edu/library/speccoll/images/text/txt/30660.htm

3. ARCIA, 1905, 40.

4. Harwood Hall to Peter P. Hilliard, August 1907, NARA, RG–75, SSCF, Box 58.

5. Humetewa interview, July 8, 2004.

6. Balenquah interview, March 28, 2006.

7. Adams, *Education for Extinction*, 142.

8. Riney, *The Rapid City Indian School*, 219.

9. Bonnell, "Chemawa Indian Boarding School," 25.

10. Sakiestewa Gilbert interview, August 13, 2003.

11. Coleman, *American Indians, the Irish, and Government Schooling*, 258.

12. Dolfin, *Bringing the Gospel in Hogan and Pueblo*, 347.

13. Victor Sakiestewa to Frank Conser, December 24, 1913, "Sakiestewa, Victor," NARA, RG–75, SSCF, Box 315.

14. Record of Graduates and Returned Students, "Soheoma, Jackson," April 1, 1911, NARA, RG–75, SSCF, Box 340.

15. Dora Koyahonin to Frank Conser, April 12, 1911, "Koyahonin, Dora," NARA, RG–75, SSCF, Box 193.

16. *Sherman Bulletin*, April 29, 1927, 2.

17. Harvey, "Cherokee and American," 92, 93.

18. Victor Sakiestewa to Frank Conser, July 28, 1914, "Sakiestewa, Victor," NARA, RG–75, SSCF, Box 315.

19. Victor H. Sakiestewa to F.M. Conser, October 28, 1916, "Sakiestewa, Victor," NARA, RG–75, SSCF, Box 315.

20. "In Indian Valley a small school was opened at Greenville by female settlers and the Women's National Indian Association in 1888. The self-proclaimed mission of the women was to Christianize the small native population by providing education and a haven free from persecution by Whites. The school struggled under economic hardship and began receiving partial government support in 1894 before bequeathing full control to the Bureau of Indian Affairs (BIA) in 1899. The BIA transformed the Greenville Indian School into a non-reservation boarding school the following year, and it served as a temporary, if involuntary, home for Indian students from all over California until it burned down in 1920." Ben Poff, "The Maudi of Indian Valley, California: A Short History," 3. http://www.sierraserviceproject.org/SiteInformation_files/indianvalley.history.pdf, (accessed April 16, 2009).

21. Sakiestewa to Conser, November 26, 1917.

22. Grant Jenkins to Frank Conser, August 30, 1924, "Jenkins, Grant," NARA, RG–75, SSCF, Box 172.

23. G. E. Peters to Frank Conser, August 17, 1925, "Jenkins, Grant," NARA, RG–75, SSCF, Box 172.

24. Grant Jenkins to Frank Conser, September 3, 1927, "Jenkins, Grant," NARA, RG–75, SSCF, Box 172.

25. F. M. Conser to Grant Jenkins, September 7, 1927, "Jenkins, Grant," NARA, RG–75, SSCF, Box 172.

26. In the 1880s and 1890s, school officials often took drastic and cruel measures to prevent students from running away. In February 1891, a *Los Angeles Times* reporter noted that Fannie B. Shannon, an employee at an Indian school on the Pine Ridge Agency in South Dakota once remarked that the "Indian children were treated in such fashion in the school that they were sure to run away at the first opportunity. To guard against this, their coats were taken away and an order was issued to stop the rations of the parents of runaways. Little boys of seven years were made to split wood all day in bitter cold weather, clad only in cotton clothing, and when they came in at night there was no place where they could sit down in a warm room." "Indians and the Indian Bureau," *Los Angeles Times*, February 7, 1891, 4.

27. Lomawaima, *They Called It Prairie Light*, 121.

28. "Red Boys Don't Like White Man's School," *Los Angeles Times*, October 2, 1921, 13.

29. Balenquah interview, March 28, 2006.

30. School officials at most Indian boarding schools called the student runaways "deserters." Child, *Boarding School Seasons*, 7.

31. Child, *Boarding School Seasons*, 89.

32. Frank Conser to Walter Lewis, July 7, 1914, "Lewis, Walter," NARA, RG–75, SSCF, Box 12.

33. "Winning Their Way," *Chicago Daily Tribune*, August 14, 1892, 25.

34. Sekaquaptewa, *Me and Mine*, 137.

35. Conser to Lewis, July 7, 1914.

36. Conser to Lewis, July 7, 1914.

37. Keller, *Empty Beds*, 9.

38. Keller noted that although students at Sherman ate consistent meals throughout the day, "little thought was given to food's nutritive value, taste, or freshness. Incorporation of traditional native foods into the student's diet never received consideration, since it would have been antithetical to the assimilationist focus of the schools." Keller, *Empty Beds*, 53.

39. For a case study, see Davis, *Hopi Summer*.

40. School officials included a health inspection form in the student's school application.

41. Two Hopi students who suffered from trachoma were Mabel Yoy-wetewa and Bessie Humetewa. When I interviewed Bessie at her home in Bacavi, she was completely blind. She began losing her eyesight in the 1970s. She was known in her community for her ability to make beautiful quilts, but as she became older, her eyesight worsened and it was difficult for her to quilt. She blamed her loss of sight on the crude ways health officials treated her trachoma while a student at Sherman Institute. "Yoywetewa, Mabel," Physicians Certificate, June 31, 1916, NARA, RG–75, SSCF, Box 402; Humetewa interview, July 8, 2004.

42. ARCIA, 1905, 37.

43. Keller Seedkoema to Frank Conser, June 4, 1913, "Lathiyo-Clifton, Asa," NARA, RG–75, SSCF, Box 200.

44. Seedkoema to Conser, June 4, 1913.

45. Frank Conser to Keller Seedkoema, June 13, 1913, "Lathiyo-Clifton, Asa," NARA, RG–75, SSCF, Box 200.

46. Keller, *Empty Beds*, 151.

47. "Report of Superintendent in Charge of Moqui," June 30, 1905, ARDI, 165.

48. Harwood Hall to Horton H. Miller, September 1908, "Seumptewa, Ray," NARA, RG–75, SSCF, Box 328.

49. "Report of Field Matron at Oraibi, 1904," ARDI, 140.

50. Adams, *Education for Extinction*, 215.

51. Quoyowyma to Frank Conser, "Cooyawyma, Alfred," September 14, 1919, NARA, SSCF, Box 76, RG–75.

52. Roger Honahnie to Frank Conser, March 8, 1924, "Honahnie, Rose," NARA, RG–75, SSCF, Box 154.

53. Harvey Meyer to Frank Conser, April 1, 1924, "Honahnie, Rose," NARA, RG–75, SSCF, Box 154.

54. Frank Conser to Roger Honahnie, April 4, 1924, "Honahnie, Rose," NARA, RG–75, SSCF, Box 154.

55. Earl Numkenu to Frank Conser, November 24, 1914, "Hoy-eneptewa, Lewis," NARA, RG–75, SSCF, Box 159.

56. Frank Conser to Earl Numkenu, November 30, 1914, "Hoy-eneptewa, Lewis," NARA, RG–75, SSCF, Box 159.

57. Meriam, *The Problem of Indian Administration*, 406–7.

58. Qoyawayma, *No Turning Back*, 67.

59. Qoyawayma, *No Turning Back*, 67.

60. Qoyawayma, *No Turning Back*, 69. Historian Katherine C. Turner notes, if "Yukeoma gave way to the government and sent the Hopi children to the white man's school, then they would grow up in the white man's way—there was no help for it. And when they came back to the adobe dwellings of their fathers, they would start using the scant water for washing their bodies, when every thimbleful was needed by the melons and the corn; they would refuse to sit on the dirt floor as their parents had done for generations—wanting fancy white men's chairs and tables. They would not wish to work in the beans and melons, nor dry the peaches; they would instead go flying off for a fortnight to the white man's railroad or the white man's orchards to earn some quick money." Turner, *Red Men Calling on the Great White Father*, 195.

61. Talayesva, *Sun Chief*, 219.

62. Talayesva, *Sun Chief*, 219–20.

63. The following account is based on Zsido to Frank Conser, September 10, 1922, "S, J," NARA, RG–75, SSCF, Box 324.

64. Frank Conser to Zsido, "S, J," September 20, 1922, NARA, RG–75, SSCF, Box 324.

65. David Haskee to F. M. Conser, October 2, 1913, "Haskee, David," NARA, RG–75, SSCF, Box 142.

66. Clarence Taptuka to Supt. F. M. Conser, "Taptuaka, Clarence," May 15, 1921, Tuba City, Arizona, NARA, RG–75 SSCF, Box 353.

67. Merle Polyestewa interview, October 9, 2004, Sherman Indian Museum, Riverside CA (hereafter cited as Polyestewa interview, October 9, 2004).

68. Humetewa interview, July 8, 2004.

8. Conclusion

1. Bessie Humetewa noted that the students at Sherman Institute called the group the "Mosquito Band" because when all of the girls played at the same time, it sounded like a swarm of mosquitos. Humetewa interview, July 8, 2004.

2. Humetewa interview, July 8, 2004.

3. Polyestewa interview, October 9, 2004.

4. The school song was officially adopted in 1906. Sherman Indian Museum, Riverside CA, *http://www.shermanindianmuseum.org/history3.htm* (accessed July 20, 2009).

5. Shingoitewa interview, July 8, 2004.

Bibliography

Archives

A. K. Smiley Public Library Special Collections. Redlands CA.

Cline Library Special Collections. Northern Arizona University.

Colorado Plateau Digital Archives. Northern Arizona University.

Costo Collection. Tomás Rivera Library, University of California, Riverside.

Hopi Cultural Preservation Office Collections. The Hopi Tribe, Kykotsmovi AZ.

Sherman Indian Museum. Sherman Indian High School, Riverside CA.

Sherman Institute Records. Record Group 75. National Archives and Records Administration, Pacific Region, Laguna Niguel CA.

University of Illinois Archives. University of Illinois at Urbana-Champaign.

Published Sources

Aberle, David Friend. *The Psychological Analysis of a Hopi Life-History.* Berkeley: University of California Press, 1951.

Adams, David Wallace. "Beyond Bleakness: The Brighter Side of Indian Boarding Schools," in Trafzer, Keller, and Sisquoc, *Boarding School Blues*, 35–64.

———. *Education for Extinction: American Indians and the Boarding School Experience, 1875–1926.* Lawrence: University Press of Kansas, 1995.

Adams, E. Charles. *Homol'ovi: An Ancient Hopi Settlement Cluster.* Tucson: University of Arizona Press, 2002.

Annual Report of the Commissioner of Indian Affairs. Washington DC: Government Printing Office, 1882–1929.

Archuleta, Margaret L., Brenda Child, and K. Tsianina Lomawaima, eds. *Away from Home: American Indian Boarding School Experiences.* Phoenix: Heard Museum, 2000.

Bakken, Gordon M., and Alexandra Kindell, eds. *Encyclopedia of Immigration and Migration in the American West.* Vol. 2. Thousand Oaks CA: Sage Publications, 2006.

Bataille, Gretchen M., and Kathleen Mullen Sands. *American Indian Women: Telling Their Lives.* Lincoln: University of Nebraska Press, 1984.

Beaglehole, Ernest. *Notes on Hopi Economic Life.* New York: AMS Press, 1937.

Benedek, Emily. *The Wind Won't Know Me: A History of the Navajo-Hopi Land Dispute.* Norman: University of Oklahoma Press, 1999.

Bernardini, Wesley. *Hopi Oral Tradition and the Archaeology of Identity.* Tucson: University of Arizona Press, 2005.

Bloom, John. *To Show What an Indian Can Do: Sports at Native American Boarding Schools.* Minneapolis: University of Minnesota Press, 2000.

Boissiere, Robert. *Meditations with the Hopi.* Santa Fe NM: Bear & Company, 1986.

Bonnell, Sonciray. "Chemawa Indian Boarding School: The First One Hundred Years." MA thesis, Dartmouth College, 1997.

Brandt, Richard B. *Hopi Ethics: A Theoretical Analysis.* Chicago: University of Chicago Press, 1954.

Brill de Ramirez, Susan Berry, and Evelina Zuni Lucero. *Simon J. Ortiz: A Poetic Legacy of Indigenous Continuance.* Albuquerque: University of New Mexico Press, 2009.

Breunig, Robert Glass. "Hopi Perspectives on Formal Education." PhD diss., University of Kansas, 1973.

Burton, Henrietta K. *The Re-Establishment of the Indians in Their Pueblo Life Through the Revival of Their Traditional Crafts: A Study in Home Extension Education.* New York: Teachers College, Columbia University, Bureau of Publications, 1936.

Calloway, Collin G. *One Vast Winter Count: The Native American West before Lewis and Clark.* Lincoln: University of Nebraska Press, 2003.

Chalcraft, Edwin L. *Assimilation's Agent: My Life as a Superintendent in the Indian Boarding School System.* Edited by Gary C. Collins. Lincoln: University of Nebraska Press, 2004.

Child, Brenda J. *Boarding School Seasons: American Indian Families, 1900–1940.* Lincoln: University of Nebraska Press, 2000.

Clemmer, Richard O. *Roads in the Sky: The Hopi Indians in a Century of Change.* Boulder CO: Westview Press, 1995.

Cobb, Amanda J. *Listening to Our Grandmothers' Stories: The Bloomfield Academy for Chickasaw Females, 1852–1949*. Lincoln: University of Nebraska Press, 2000.

Coleman, Michael C. *American Indian Children at School*. Jackson: University Press of Mississippi, 1993.

————. *American Indians, the Irish, and Government Schooling*. Lincoln: University of Nebraska Press, 2007.

Courlander, Harold. *People of the Short Blue Corn: Tales and Legends of the Hopi Indians*. New York: Henry Holt, 1970.

Course of Study for the Indian Schools of the United States. Washington DC: Government Printing Office, 1901.

Course of Study for United States Indian Schools. Washington DC: Government Printing Office, 1922.

Coward, John M. *The Newspaper Indian: Native American Identity in the Press, 1820–90*. Urbana: University of Illinois Press, 1999.

Curtis, Natalie. *The Indians' Book: The Songs and Legends of the American Indians*. New York: Dover, 1968. First published 1907 by Paul Burlin.

Davis, Carolyn O'Bagy. *Hopi Quilting: Stitched Traditions from an Ancient Community*. Tucson: Sanpete Publication, 1997.

————. *Hopi Summer: Letters from Ethel to Maud*. Tucson: Rio Nuevo Publishers, 2007.

DeHuff, Elisabeth Willis. *Taytay's Tales: Collected and Retold*. Illustrated by Fred Kabotie and Polelonema. New York: Harcourt, Brace, 1922.

Deloria, Vine, Jr. "Knowing and Understanding." In *Power and Place: Indian Education in America*, ed. Vine Deloria Jr. and Daniel R. Wildcat, 41–46. Golden CO: Fulcrum, 2001.

Dennis, Wayne. *The Hopi Child*. New York: Arno Press, 1972. First published in 1940 as monograph no. 26, University of Virginia Institute for Research in the Social Sciences.

Dolfin, John. *Bringing The Gospel in Hogan and Pueblo (1921)*. Grand Rapids MI: Van Noord Book and Publishing Company, 1921.

Donaldson, Thomas. *Extra Census Bulletin: Moqui Pueblo Indians of Arizona and Pueblo Indians of New Mexico*. Washington DC: United States Printing Office, 1893.

Dozier, Edward P. *The Pueblo Indians of North America*. Long Grove IL: Waveland Press, 1983. First published in 1970 by Holt, Rinehart and Winston.

Dutton, Bertha P. *American Indians of the Southwest*. Albuquerque: University of New Mexico Press, 1983.

Ellis, Clyde. *To Change Them Forever: Indian Education at the Rainy Mountain Boarding School, 1893–1920*. Tulsa: University of Oklahoma Press, 1996.

Emanuel, Elizabeth, and Marjorie Thayer. *Climbing Sun: The Story of a Hopi Indian Boy*. New York: Dodd, Mead, 1980.

Fear-Segal, Jacqueline. "Nineteenth-Century Indian Education: Universalism Versus Evolutionism." *Journal of American Studies* 33, no. 2 (1999): 323–41.

————. *White Man's Club: Schools, Race, and the Struggle of Indian Acculturation*. Lincoln: University of Nebraska Press, 2009.

Flint, Richard, and Shirley Cushing Flint, eds. *The Coronado Expedition to Tierra Nueva: The 1540–1542 Route Across the Southwest*. Boulder: University Press of Colorado, 2004.

Fontana, Bernard L. "Historical Foundations." In *Indians of Arizona: A Contemporary Perspective*, ed. Thomas Weaver, 26–41. Tucson: University of Arizona Press, 1979.

Foster, Morris W. *Being Comanche: A Social History of an American Indian Community*. Tucson: University of Arizona Press, 1991.

Fynn, A. J. *The American Indian: As a Product of Environment, With Special Reference to the Pueblos*. Boston: Colonial Press, 1907.

Geertz, Armin W. *The Invention of Prophecy: Continuity and Meaning in Hopi Indian Religion*. Berkeley and Los Angeles: University of California Press, 1994.

Gilbert, Willard Nathan. "The Cultural Value of the Sports and Games of the Hopi Indians of Arizona and a Unit of Instruction Reflecting their Games and Activities." EdD diss., University of New Mexico, 1986.

Gilman, Benjamin Ives. "Hopi Songs." *Journal of American Ethnology and Archaeology* 5, 1908.

Goddard, Pliny Earle. *Indians of the Southwest*. New York: American Museum of Natural History, 1931.

Gonzales, Angela Ann. "American Indian Identity Matters: The Political Economy of Identity and Ethnic Group Boundaries," PhD diss., Harvard University, 2002.

Gonzales, Nathan Daniel. "'Visit Yesterday, Today': Ethno-tourism and Southern California, 1884–1955." PhD diss., University of California, Riverside, 2006.

Hafford, William. "Along the Way." *Arizona Highways*, October 1991.

Hagen, William Thomas. *Six Friends of the Indians*. Tulsa: University of Oklahoma Press, 2002.

Harvey, Gretchen G. "Cherokee and American: Ruth Muskrat Bronson, 1897–1982," PhD diss., Arizona State University, 1996.

Holm, Tom. *The Great Confusion in Indian Affairs: Native Americans & Whites in the Progressive Era*. Austin: University of Texas Press, 2005.

Hopi Dictionary: Hopìikwa Lavàyatutveni. Tucson: University of Arizona Press, 1998.

Hough, Walter. *The Hopi Indians*. Cedar Rapids IA: The Torch Press, 1913.

Hoxie, Frederick E. *A Final Promise: The Campaign to Assimilate the Indians, 1880–1920*. 1984. Reprint with a new introduction by the author. Lincoln: University of Nebraska Press: 2001.

Indian Education and Civilization: A Report Prepared in Answer to the Senate Resolution of February 23, 1885. Washington DC: Government Printing Office, 1888. Prepared by Alice C. Fletcher.

Indian Law and Resource Center. *Report to the Hopi Kikmongwis and Other Traditional Hopi Leaders on Docket 196 and the Continuing Threat to Hopi Land and Sovereignty*. Washington DC: Indian Law and Resource Center, 1979.

Ishii, Lomayumtewa C. "Voices from Our Ancestors: Hopi Resistance to Scientific Historicide." PhD diss., Northern Arizona University, 2001.

Jacobs, Margaret D. "A Battle for the Children: American Indian Child Removal in Arizona in the Era of Assimilation." *Journal of Arizona History* 45, no. 2 (Spring 2004): 31–62.

———. *White Mother to a Dark Race: Settler Colonialism, Maternalism, and the Removal of Indigenous Children in the American West and Australia, 1880–1940*. Lincoln: University of Nebraska Press, 2009.

James, George Wharton. *The Indians of the Painted Desert Region: Hopis, Navahoes, Wallapais, Havasupais*. Boston: Little, Brown, 1905.

James, Harry C. *Pages from Hopi History*. Tucson: University of Arizona Press, 1994.

Johnson, Abigail E. *Beyond the Black Buttes: True Stories of Hopiland*. Kansas City: Western Baptist Publishing, 1935.

Kabotie, Fred, as told to Bill Belknap. *Fred Kabotie: Hopi Indian Artist.* Flagstaff: Museum of Northern Arizona and Northland Press, 1977.

Katanski, Amelia V. *Learning to Write "Indian": The Boarding-School Experience and American Indian Literature.* Norman: University of Oklahoma Press, 2005.

Katchongva, Dan. *Hopi: A Message for All People.* Rooseveltown NY: White Roots of Peace/Akwesasne Notes, 1937.

Keller, Jean A. *Empty Beds: Indian Student Health at Sherman Institute, 1902–1922.* East Lansing: Michigan State University Press, 2002.

Koyiyumptewa, Stewart B., Carolyn O'Bagy Davis, and Hopi Cultural Preservation Office. *The Hopi People.* Images of America. Mount Pleasant SC: Arcadia Publishing, 2009.

Kuwanwisiwma, Leigh J. "Hopi Face a New Millennium: 'Let Us Not Be Afraid.'" In *Thirst for Survival*, ed. , 12–15. Overland Park KS: Hopi Tribe and Ascend Media, 2005.

Ladies Union Mission School Association. *Among the Pimas: Or the Mission to the Pima and Maricopa Indians.* Albany NY: Ladies Union Mission School Association, 1893.

Laird, W. David. *Hopi Bibliography.* Tucson: University of Arizona Press, 1977.

Leupp, Francis E. *The Indian and His Problem.* New York: C. Scribner's Sons, 1910.

———. *In Red Man's Land: A Study of the American Indian.* New York: Fleming H. Revell, 1914.

Levy, Jarrold E. *Orayvi Revisited: Social Stratification in an "Egalitarian" Society.* Santa Fe NM: School of American Research, 1992.

Linton, Ralph. *Acculturation in Seven American Indian Tribes.* New York: Appleton-Century, 1940.

Loftin, John D. *Religion and Hopi Life in the Twentieth Century.* Bloomington: Indiana University Press, 1991.

Lomatewama, Ramson. *Ascending the Reed.* Flagstaff AZ: Badger Claw Press, 1987.

———. *Songs to the Corn: A Hopi Poet Writes About Corn.* Illustrated by Jeffrey Chapman. Barrington IL: Rigby, 1979.

Lomatuway'ma, Michael, Lorena Lomatuway'ma, and Sidney Namingha Jr. *Hopi Ruin Legends: Kiqötutuwutsi.* Collected, translated, and edited by Ekkehart Malotki. Lincoln: University of Nebraska Press, 1993. Published for Northern Arizona University.

Lomawaima, K. Tsianina. "Estelle Reel, Superintendent of Indian
Schools, 1898–1910: Politics, Curriculum, and Land." *Journal of American Indian Education* 35 (Spring 1996): 5–31.

————. *They Called It Prairie Light: The Story of the Chilocco Indian School.*
Lincoln: University of Nebraska Press, 1994.

Lomawaima, K. Tsianina and Teresa L. McCarty. *To Remain an Indian:
Lessons in Democracy from a Century of Native American Education.* New
York: Teachers College Press, 2006.

Lucero, Evelina Zuni. "Simon J. Ortiz: In His Own Words." In *Simon J.
Ortiz: A Poetic Legacy of Indigenous Continuance,* ed. Susan Berry Brill de
Ramirez and Evelina Zuni Lucero, 125–67. Albuquerque: University of
New Mexico Press, 2009.

Lummis, Charles F. *Bullying the Moqui.* Prescott AZ: Prescott College
Press, 1968.

Lyons, Patrick D. *Ancestral Hopi Migrations.* Anthropological Papers of the
University of Arizona 68. Tucson: University of Arizona Press, 2003.

Malotki, Ekkehart. *Hopi Tales: A Bilingual Collection of Hopi Indian Stories.*
Flagstaff: Museum of Northern Arizona Press, 1978.

————. *Hopi Time: A Linguistic Analysis of the Temporal Concepts in the Hopi
Language.* New York: Mouton Publishers, 1983.

Mann, Henrietta. *Cheyenne-Arapaho Education, 1871–1982.* Boulder: University Press of Colorado, 1998.

Manual for Sherman Institute. Riverside CA: Institute Press, 1912.

McKenzie, Fayette Avery. "The Indian in Relation to the White Population of the United States." PhD diss., University of Pennsylvania,
1908.

McNickle, D'Arcy. *The Indian Tribes of the United States.* London: Oxford
University Press, 1962.

Means, Florence Crannell. *Sunlight on the Hopi Mesas.* Philadelphia:
Judson Press, 1960.

Medina, William Oscar. "Selling Indians at Sherman Institute, 1902–
1922." PhD diss., University of California, Riverside, 2007.

Meriam, Lewis, et. al. *The Problem of Indian Administration.* Baltimore:
Johns Hopkins Press, 1928.

Mihesuah, Devon A. *Cultivating the Rosebuds: The Education of Women at
the Cherokee Female Seminary, 1851–1909.* Urbana: University of Illinois
Press, 1993.

Miller, Donald Eugene. "The Limits of Schooling by Imposition: The Hopi Indians of Arizona." PhD diss., University of Tennessee, 1987.

Miller, J. R. *Shingwauk's Vision: A History of Native Residential Schools.* Toronto: University of Toronto Press, 2006.

Montgomery, Ross Gordon, et al. *Franciscan Awatovi.* Papers of the Peabody Museum of American Archaeology and Ethnology 36. Cambridge MA: Harvard University, 1949.

Mora, Joseph. *The Year of the Hopi: Paintings and Photographs by Joseph Mora, 1904–1906.* New York: Smithsonian Institution, 1979.

Mullett, G. M. *Spider Woman Stories: Legends of the Hopi Indians.* Tucson: University of Arizona Press, 1979.

Nagata, Shuichi. *Modern Transformations of Moenkopi Pueblo.* Urbana: University of Illinois Press, 1970.

Nequatewa, Edmund. *Truth of a Hopi: Stories Relating to the Origin, Myths, and Clan Histories of the Hopi.* Flagstaff AZ: Northland Publishing, 1994.

Nequatewa, Edmund, as told to Alfred F. Whiting. *Born a Chief: The Nineteenth Century Hopi Boyhood of Edmund Nequatewa.* Tucson: University of Arizona Press, 1993.

Nicholas, Sheilah Ernestine. "Hopi Education: A Look at the History, the Present, and the Future." MA thesis, University of Arizona, 1991.

Odier, Pierre. *The Rock: A History of Alcatraz, The Fort/The Prison.* Eagle Rock CA: L'Image Odier, 1982.

O'Kane, Walter Collins. *The Hopis: Portrait of a Desert People.* Norman: University of Oklahoma Press, 1953.

———. *Sun in the Sky.* Norman: University of Oklahoma Press, 1957.

Peterson, Charles S. "The Hopis and the Mormons, 1858–1873," *Utah Historical Quarterly* 39, no. 2 (1971): 179–94.

Powell, J. W. *The Hopi Villages: The Ancient Province of Tusayan.* Palmer Lake CO: Filter Press, 1972.

———. *Twenty-First Report of the Bureau of Ethnology to the Secretary of the Smithsonian Institution, 1899–1900.* Washington DC: Government Printing Office, 1903.

Pratt, Richard Henry, with Robert M. Utley, ed. *Battlefield and Classroom: Four Decades with the American Indian, 1867–1904.* New Haven CT: Yale University Press, 1964.

Proceedings of the Lake Mohonk Conference. Albany NY: Lake Mohonk Conference, 1907–1911.

Prucha, Francis Paul. *The Churches and the Indians Schools, 1888–1912*, Lincoln: University of Nebraska Press, 1979.

———. *Indian Policy in the United States*. Lincoln: University of Nebraska Press, 1981.

Qoyawayma, Polingaysi, as told to Vada F. Carlson. *No Turning Back: A Hopi Indian Woman's Struggle to Live in Two Worlds*. Albuquerque: University of New Mexico Press, 1964.

Rand, Jacki Thompson. *Kiowa Humanity and the Invasion of the State*. Lincoln: University of Nebraska Press, 2008.

Rathbun, Tanya L. "Hail Mary: The Catholic Experience at St. Boniface Indian School," in Trafzer, Keller, and Sisquoc, *Boarding School Blues*, 155–75.

Reyhner, Jon, and Jeanne Eder. *American Indian Education, A History*. Norman: University of Oklahoma Press, 2004.

Rhodes, Robert. *Hopi Music and Dance*. Tsaile AZ: Navajo Community College Press, 1977.

Richland, Justin B. *Arguing with Tradition: The Language of Law in Hopi Tribal Court*. Chicago: University of Chicago Press, 2008.

Riney, Scott. *The Rapid City Indian School, 1893–1933*. Norman: University of Oklahoma Press, 1999.

Rules for Indian Service Schools. Washington DC: Government Printing Office, 1913.

Ryan, Marah Ellis. *Flute of the Gods*. New York: Frederick A. Stokes, 1909.

Sakiestewa Gilbert, Matthew. "Christmas Experiences at Sherman Institute and Phoenix Indian School." *Hopi Tutuveni*, December 21, 2005, 6.

———. "Dark Days: American Presidents and Native Sovereignty, 1880–1930." In *American Indians/American Presidents: A History*, ed. Clifford E. Trafzer, 108–43. New York: Harper and Smithsonian Institution, 2009.

———. "Hopi Education Did Not Begin at Government Schools." *Hopi Tutuveni*, November 10, 2005, 9.

———. "'The Hopi Followers': Chief Tawaquaptewa and Hopi Student Advancement at Sherman Institute, 1906–1909." *Journal of American Indian Education* 44, no. 2 (Fall 2005) 1–23.

———. "Hopi Footraces and American Marathons, 1912–1930." *American Quarterly* 62, no. 1 (March 2010): 77–101.

————. "'I Learned to Preach Pretty Well, and to Cuss, Too': Hopi Acceptance and Rejection of Christianity at Sherman Institute, 1906–1928." In *Eating Fire, Tasting Blood: An Anthology of the American Indian Holocaust*, ed. MariJo Moore, 78–95. New York: Thunder's Mouth Press, 2006.

————. "Philip Zeyoma's Rightful Place among the Great Hopi Runners." *Hopi Tutuveni*, September 15, 2005, 12.

————. "Retelling Hopi Stories at Sherman Institute." *Hopi Tutuveni*, February 1, 2006, 4.

————. "The Sherman Project." MA thesis, University of California, Riverside, 2004.

Schaaf, Gregory. *Hopi Katsina: 1,600 Artist Biographies*. Santa Fe NM: CIAC Press, 2008.

Secakuku, Alph H. *Hopi Kachina Tradition: Following the Sun and Moon*. Flagstaff AZ: Northland Press and Heard Museum, 1995.

Sekaquaptewa, Helen, as told to Louise Udall. *Me and Mine: The Life Story of Helen Sekaquaptewa*. Tucson: University of Arizona Press, 1993.

Shaul, David Leedom. *Hopi Traditional Literature*. Albuquerque: University of New Mexico Press, 2002.

Short, Kelly M. "Outing Program at Sherman Institute." MA thesis, University of California, Riverside, 2004.

Silverberg, Robert. *The Pueblo Revolt*. Lincoln: University of Nebraska Press, 1994.

Spicer, Edward H. *Cycles of Conquest: The Impact of Spain, Mexico, and the United States on the Indians of the Southwest, 1533–1960*. Tucson: University of Arizona Press, 1976.

Stephen, Alexander M. *Hopi Journal of Alexander M. Stephen*. Ed. Elsie C. Parsons. 2 vols. New York: Columbia University Press, 1936.

Szasz, Margaret Connell. *Education and the American Indian: The Road to Self-Determination Since 1928*. 3rd ed. Albuquerque: University of New Mexico Press, 1999.

————. *Indian Education in the American Colonies, 1607–1783*. 1988. Reprint with a new introduction by the author. Lincoln: University of Nebraska Press, 2007.

Talayesva, Don. *Sun Chief: The Autobiography of a Hopi Indian*. Ed. Leo W. Simmons. New Haven CT: Yale University Press, 1970.

Tanner, Clara Lee. "Fred Kabotie Hopi Indian Artist." *Arizona Highways*, July 1951.

Thayer, Marjorie, and Elizabeth Emanuel. *Climbing Sun: The Story of a Hopi Indian Boy.* New York: Dodd, Mead, 1980.

Thompson, Laura, and Alice Joseph. *The Hopi Way.* Chicago: University of Chicago Press, 1945.

Titiev, Mischa. *The Hopi Indians of Old Oraibi; Change and Continuity.* Ann Arbor: University of Michigan Press, 1972.

————. *A Hopi Visit to the Afterworld.* Papers of Michigan Academy Of Science, Arts & Letters, 26 (1940) 495–504.

Trafzer, Clifford E. *As Long as the Grass Shall Grow and Rivers Flow: A History of Native Americans.* Fort Worth TX: Harcourt College Publishers, 2000.

Trafzer, Clifford E., Jean A. Keller, and Lorene Sisquoc, eds. *Boarding School Blues: Revisiting American Indian Educational Experiences.* Lincoln: University of Nebraska Press, 2006.

Trennert, Robert Jr. *Alternative to Extinction: Federal Indian Policy and the Beginnings of the Reservation System, 1846–51.* Philadelphia: Temple University Press, 1975.

————. "Educating Indian Girls at Nonreservation Boarding Schools, 1878–1920." *The Western Historical Quarterly* 13, no. 3 (July 1982): 271–90.

————. *The Phoenix Indian School: Forced Assimilation in Arizona, 1891–1935.* Norman: University of Oklahoma Press, 1988.

————. *White Man's Medicine: Government Doctors and the Navajo, 1863–1955.* Albuquerque: University of New Mexico Press, 1998.

Trotta, Cathy Ann. "Crossing Cultural Boundaries: Heinrich and Martha Moser Voth in the Hopi Pueblos, 1893–1906." PhD diss., Northern Arizona University, 1997.

Troutman, John W. *Indian Blues: American Indians and the Politics of Music, 1879–1934.* Norman: University of Oklahoma Press, 2009.

Turner, Katherine C. *Red Men Calling on the Great White Father.* Norman: University of Oklahoma Press, 1951.

Valentine, Robert G. "Indians as Workers." In *Report of the Twenty-Sixth Annual Meeting of the Lake Mohonk Conference of the Friends of the Indian and Other Dependent Peoples, 1908,* ed. Lillian D. Powers, 30–35. Albany NY: Brandow Printing Company, 1908.

Vučković, Myriam. *Voices from Haskell: Indian Students Between Two Worlds, 1884–1928. Lawrence: University Press of Kansas, 2008.*

Walsh, Barry. "Kikmongwi As Artist: The Katsina Dolls of Wilson Tawaquaptewa." *American Indian Art Magazine,* Winter 1998, 52–59.

Warrior, Robert Allen. *The People and the Word: Reading Native Nonfiction.* Minneapolis: University of Minnesota Press, 2005.

Waters, Frank. *Book of the Hopi: The First Revelation of the Hopi's Historical and Religious World-View of Life.* New York: Ballantine, 1963.

———. *Pumpkin Seed Point: Being Within the Hopi.* Athens: Ohio University Press, 1969.

Weaver, Thomas. *Indians of Arizona: A Contemporary Perspective.* Tucson: University of Arizona Press, 1979.

Whiteley, Peter M. *Bacavi: Journey to Reed Springs.* Flagstaff AZ: Northland Press, 1988.

———. *Deliberate Acts: Changing Hopi Culture Through the Oraibi Split.* Tucson: University of Arizona Press, 1988.

———. *The Orayvi Split: A Hopi Transformation. Part I: Structure and History. Part II: The Documentary Record.* Anthropological Papers of the American Museum of Natural History 87. New York: American Museum of Natural History, 2008.

———. *Rethinking Hopi Ethnography.* Washington DC: Smithsonian Institution Press, 1998.

Williams, James R. "Tribal Education of the Hopi Indian Child." MA Ed. thesis, Arizona State College, 1948.

Wright, Barton. *The Unchanging Hopi: An Artist Interpretation in Scratchboard Drawings and Text.* Flagstaff AZ: Northland Press, 1975.

Yava, Albert, and Harold Courlander. *Big Falling Snow: A Tewa-Hopi Indian's Life and Times and the History and Traditions of His People.* Albuquerque: University of New Mexico Press, 1978.

Index

52, 188n8; education based on, 95–113; effect of Christian missionaries on, 201n58; factionalism over, 62–64; games and sports in, 107–8; government officials' ignorance of, 29–30; government's attempts to break down, xx–xxii, 11–12, 29–30, 48, 68, 70, 79–80, 92–93; Heinrich Voth's knowledge of, 121; influence on Sherman Institute experience, 94, 163–65; maintenance at Sherman Institute, xxvi, 76–81, 108; music and storytelling in, 42; and resistance to forced attendance, 10; role of land in, xxviii–xxix, 110; and smallpox epidemic, 53; travel in, 137, 168; women's role in, 131; worry about loss of, 73, 155, 205n60; Youkeoma on, 59–60. *See also* acculturation; assimilation; Hopi Indians; Native cultures

Hopi Cultural Preservation Office (HCPO), ix, x

Hopi families, 87, 96, 159–60, 168, 194n57. *See also* Hopi clans

"The Hopi Followers" (Sakiestewa Gilbert), xi

Hopi girls: absence on reservation, 73; curriculum at Sherman Institute, 45; difficulty finding work, 141; lack of clothing, 182n81; musical talent of, 82, 164, 205n1; in outing program, 46–47; and riyànpi, 107; as runaways, xxvii, 147; at Sherman

Ranch, 84–85; traditional education of, 95, 96. *See also* Hopi children; Hopi Indians; Hopi pupils; Young Women's Christian Association (YWCA)

Hopi Hearing (1955), 66

Hopi Indian Agency, 178n17

Hopi Indians: attitudes toward white man, 5–7, 8, 103; factions of, xxii–xxiii, 7, 56, 188n23; history of resistance and accommodation, 163; lack of clothing, 25, 182n81; opposition to education policy, 9–12, 179n38; oral history of, xvii, 175n2; paternalistic attitude toward, 35, 154; protection of intellectual property, ix—xi; responsibilities to society of, 98; as U.S. government priority, 71–72. *See also* Hopi boys; Hopi clans; Hopi culture; Hopi girls; Hopi pupils

The Hopi Indians of Old Oraibi (Titiev), 130–31

Hopi judges, 65

Hopi language, xx, 98, 121, 131, 139, 165–66

Hopi medicine men, 9–10, 53, 105, 150, 151. *See also* deaths; health concerns; illness

Hopi names, 96–97, 188n6, 196n10

Hopi, Pierce, 82

Hopi prophecy, 7, 52, 188n23

Hopi pupils: adjustment to Sherman Institute, 82; attempts to reenroll in schools, 144–46;

Talashoenewa, Dennis, 82

Talasquaptewa (Hopi), 78, 91–92

Talas [Talasitiwa], Louise, 127

Talasvama [Lomavitu], Otto, 200n51

Talawaltewa, Archie, 82

Talayesva, Don: on agricultural work, 112; attitude toward Christianity, xxvii; boarding school experience of, xxxi; on Hopi Christian marriage, 128–29; on missionaries among Hopis, 122–23, 201n58; reacclimation to reservation life, 156; sermon of, 124–25; ties to Sherman Institute, 155–56

Taptuka, Clarence, 159–60

Tawamana, Louisa, 84–85

Tawaquaptewa, Kikmongwi (Hopi): biography of, 176n9; chieftainship of, 64–68; curriculum at Sherman Institute, 75; detention of family at Orayvi, 89–90; Eagle Dance of, 77–81; at George Wharton James's lecture, 197n43; at Hopi Christian wedding, 128; influence on runaways, 147; on land allotment, 91–92; on language, 74; leadership at Sherman Institute, 75–77, 92–93, 97, 163–64; letter written by, 88; music tradition of, 77–80; name change of, 97; in Orayvi Split, xxiii–xxiv, 51, 57–63, 66, 187n2; and Peter Stauffer, 89; on picture taking, 81, 193n30; progress as pupil at

Sherman Institute, 75; relationship with U.S. government, xxiv, 70, 89–90, 92, 195n75; return to Orayvi, 89–90, 93; role as elder, xxiv–xxv, 70, 92–93, 163–64; to Sherman Institute, 68–70, 71–72, 191n2, 191n68; succession of father as leader, 56; ties to Sherman Institute, 156. See also elders

teachers, 73–74

Tewanima, Louis, 67–68, 109

Tewanimptewa, Bennie Pahsah, 104–5, 196n25

Tewanimptewa, Loky, 109

Tewanimptewa, Tsuamana, 104–5, 196n25

Thayer, Marjorie, 130

They Call It Prairie Light (Lomawaima), 177n21

Third Mesa, xxii, 53, 63, 64. See also Hotevilla; Orayvi

Titiev, Mischa, 130–31, 190n50

To Change Them Forever (Ellis), 177n21

Tolchaco AZ, 132

Tonner, A. C., 37

Toreva, 38. See also Second Mesa

Toreva Day School, 39. See also day schools

Tovar, Don Pedro de, xix, 1–2

trachoma, 150, 204n41

Trafzer, Clifford E., xxx, 103, 177n21

Treaty of Guadalupe Hidalgo (1848), 40

Trennert, Robert A., Jr., 47, 53, 127

In the Indigenous Education series

Urban Indians in Phoenix Schools, 1940–2000
Stephen Kent Amerman

American Indians, the Irish, and Government Schooling
A Comparative Study
Michael C. Coleman

White Man's Club
Schools, Race, and the Struggle of Indian Acculturation
Jacqueline Fear-Segal

Education beyond the Mesas
Hopi Students at Sherman Institute, 1902–1929
Matthew Sakiestewa Gilbert

The Bearer of This Letter
Language Ideologies, Literacy Practices, and
the Fort Belknap Indian Community
Mindy J. Morgan

Indian Education in the American Colonies, 1607–1783
Margaret Connell Szasz

To order or obtain more information on
these or other University of Nebraska Press
titles, visit www.nebraskapress.unl.edu.